EDUCATING CHILDREN WITH LIFE-LIMITING CONDITIONS

Educating Children with Life-Limiting Conditions supports teachers who are working with children with life-limiting or life-threatening conditions in mainstream schools by providing them with the core knowledge and skills that underpin effective practice within a whole-school and cross-agency approach.

Mainstream schools now include increasing numbers of children with life-limiting or life-threatening conditions, and this accessible book is written by a team comprised of both education and health professionals, helping to bridge the gap between different services.

Recognising the complexity of individual cases, the authors communicate key principles relating to the importance of communication, multi-professional understanding and working and proactive planning for meeting the needs of any child with a life-limiting or life-threatening condition that can be applied to a range of situations.

Reflective activities and practical resources are provided and are also available to download. This book will be of interest to teachers in mainstream schools, as well as teachers, SENCOs and senior leaders in all school settings, school nurses, children's nurses and allied health professionals.

Dr Alison Ekins is Course Director of the National Award for SEN Coordination at Canterbury Christ Church University, UK.

Dr Sally Robinson is Principal Lecturer in Health Promotion and Public Health at Canterbury Christ Church University, UK.

Ian Durrant is Senior Lecturer at Canterbury Christ Church University, UK.

Kathryn Summers is Principal Lecturer in Children's Nursing at Canterbury Christ Church University, UK.

EDUCATING CHILDREN WITH LIFE-LIMITING CONDITIONS

A Practical Handbook for Teachers and School-based Staff

Alison Ekins, Sally Robinson, Ian Durrant and Kathryn Summers

Routledge
Taylor & Francis Group

LONDON AND NEW YORK

First published 2017
by Routledge
2 Park Square, Milton Park, Abingdon, Oxon OX14 4RN

and by Routledge
711 Third Avenue, New York, NY 10017

Routledge is an imprint of the Taylor & Francis Group, an informa business

British Library Cataloguing-in-Publication Data
A catalogue record for this book is available from the British Library

Library of Congress Cataloging-in-Publication Data
A catalog record for this book has been requested

ISBN: 978-1-138-67808-8 (hbk)
ISBN: 978-1-138-67809-5 (pbk)
ISBN: 978-1-315-55914-8 (ebk)

Typeset in Interstate
by Apex CoVantage, LLC

Visit the eResources: www.routledge.com/9781138678095

Printed and bound in Great Britain by
TJ International Ltd, Padstow, Cornwall

CONTENTS

ACKNOWLEDGEMENTS

We would like to thank the many people who have helped us both in our research and in making this book possible.

First, our thanks must go to colleagues at Canterbury Christ Church University, who have provided support so that we could complete and write up our original Teaching for Life research, and those who have provided us with advice and suggestions to enhance our own understandings of the practical implications of what we found out. In particular, we would like to thank Anna Playle for her very helpful contributions.

Most importantly, however, our thanks go to all the SENCOs and school staff, including the staff at St Nicholas Special School, who gave their time to share their valuable experiences with us. They, like us, were all motivated by a deep desire to do more and understand better how we can more effectively meet the needs of children with life-limiting or life-threatening conditions.

1 Teaching children with life-limiting or life-threatening conditions

Understanding the issues

In this chapter, we:

- Consider the current context for working with children with life-limiting or life-threatening conditions
- Define life-limiting or life-threatening conditions
- Examine the current policy context
- Explore what research tells us about the needs of teachers working with children with life-limiting or life-threatening conditions
- Introduce the Teaching for Life project
- Highlight key findings from the Teaching for Life project
- Outline the structure of the book

Introduction

This book is a practical resource to support teachers who are working with children with life-limiting or life-threatening conditions in mainstream schools. The book provides teachers with the core knowledge and skills that underpin effective practice within a whole-school, multi-professional approach. Recognising the complexity of individual cases, the book sets out to communicate key principles that can be applied to a range of situations. From the start, reflective activities and practical resources are provided to enable the busy practitioner to immediately engage with the concepts being discussed and plan how to implement effective strategies in practice.

Mainstream schools are currently supporting increasing numbers of children with life-limiting or life-threatening conditions. This has been reflected in recent government policy documents such as *Supporting the Medical Needs of Pupils in Schools* (DfE, 2014, 2015). Research shows that the needs of these children are not being well met: the symptoms of their condition and its treatment can interfere with a child's whole-school experience including their learning, their self-esteem and their relationships. Many children, siblings and parents feel under supported by schools who are unable to meet their complex medical, emotional and social needs effectively.

The Teaching for Life research project (Durrant et al., 2014) explored the needs of teachers in relation to working with children with life-limiting or life-threatening conditions. It identified what types of information, guidance and support teachers need when teaching children with life-limiting or life-threatening conditions. This book builds directly from this research, providing practical and useful information which addresses the issues identified by teachers in relation to understanding the key issues and principles for effective working that they need to consider. The book has been written by a multi-professional team comprising colleagues from across the education and health sectors.

Education colleagues

Dr Alison Ekins is a Senior Lecturer in the Directorate of Special Education and Inclusion and School of Teacher Education and Development. She is programme leader for the National Award in Special Educational Needs Coordination and supervises doctoral and PhD students specialising in SEN and inclusive education. In addition to her role in the University, Alison also works as Head of Foundation Learning and Director of SEN in a local academy trust and as a chair of governors for a local special school for pupils with complex, profound and multiple learning needs.

Ian Durrant is a Senior Lecturer in Education in the Directorate of Early Childhood Studies and School of Childhood and Education Sciences. He has taught extensively on SEN and inclusion courses, including the National Award in Special Educational Needs (SEN) Coordination and undergraduate SEN and inclusion courses. Ian is a chartered psychologist and has published research in a diverse range of areas including extended services in schools, the challenges of inclusive leadership for SENCOs (special educational needs coordinators), the development of citizenship education and an evaluation of the impact of developing teaching assistants to better work with children with SEN, commissioned by MENCAP. Ian has also acted as a consultant for a number of local authorities and third-sector organisations in the development of questionnaires, interviews and impact measures.

Health and public health colleagues

Dr Sally Robinson leads the public health team within the School of Public Health, Midwifery and Social Work. She has developed, led and taught a wide range of public health courses for undergraduates, public health and health care professionals and postgraduates, including running short courses for student teachers. She is a supervisor of PhDs and has completed local and international research in the field of children's health promotion. Sally is also a registered play therapist.

Kathryn Summers is a Principal Lecturer in the School of Nursing. She is a qualified children's nurse with extensive experience in caring for children and their families with acute and complex health care needs. She delivers high-quality education to children's nursing students, managing both child-specific and inter-professional modules across the undergraduate and post-graduate frameworks. She is a member of the Royal College of Nursing Steering Committee for the children and young people's professional issues forum. She proactively leads the Child Health Forum, which is a key Academic Practice Partnership group whose membership consists of educators, senior child health nurses from both the NHS (National Health Service) and PVI (private, voluntary and independent) sector across Medway and Kent.

As a group coming from different professional backgrounds, we came together because of a shared professional interest in and passion for finding ways to both meet the needs of vulnerable children and understand and address the needs of practitioners from diverse professional backgrounds working together. Individually through our professional careers and then again as a group through our collaborative work, we have experienced first-hand the barriers and difficulties in multi-professional work in relation to breaking down differences in terminology and approach in order to achieve shared, cross-disciplinary understanding leading to effective practice. We have learnt much from each other, and this shared understanding and learning has enabled us to both individually and collectively develop our expertise and understandings in this area.

The current context

There are increasing numbers of children living with serious health conditions who, but for recent medical advancements, may previously not have lived or may only have lived short-ened lives. Fortunately now children with a range of medical conditions, including cancer and cystic fibrosis, are much more likely to live into adulthood than at any time in the past (Gatta et al., 2005; Simmonds, 2013). Technical advances in medical care and targeted funding have also allowed children who would have been hospital or housebound to not only attend school but also access the full array of opportunities the modern school has to offer. As a result, we are now seeing many more children with life-limiting or life-threatening conditions being educated in mainstream schools. This, however, is a relatively new phenomenon and, as such, mainstream schools generally lack the knowledge and specialist skills to be able to understand and meet the complex needs that children with life-limiting or life-threatening conditions may have. This book therefore recognises that the need to provide a range of school and health care professionals with advice, guidance and strategies to enable them to provide children with life-limiting or life-threatening conditions with the highest quality of education has never been so important.

Understanding life-limiting or life-threatening conditions

For the purpose of this book life-limiting conditions are those from which there is no reasonable hope of cure and from which children or young people will die, and life-threatening conditions are those for which curative treatment may be possible but can fail. These include:

- Conditions in which medical treatment might fail (e.g. cancer, organ failure and HIV/AIDS);
- Conditions in which the child has long periods of intensive treatment and in which premature death is possible (e.g. cystic fibrosis, Duchenne muscular dystrophy);
- Progressive conditions for which there is no cure (e.g. Batten's disease, muscular dystrophy, cerebral palsy, mucopolysaccharidoses);
- Conditions in which children have a severe neurological disability which could lead to death (e.g. complex needs such as those following brain or spine injuries, severe cerebral palsy).

(based on Association for Children's Palliative Care, 2009)

Reflective activity

Before moving on, reflect on the definitions provided.

- How familiar are you with the different conditions identified?
- Are there any that you do not know about at all?
- How could you/would you start to find out about that condition?
- What information would you like to have about the conditions in order to be able to meet the needs of a child with that condition in your school/class?
- Do you currently have any children with any of the conditions listed in your school/class setting?
- How do you currently meet their needs?
- Is there anything more that you would like to know/do?

The current policy context

Whilst Chapter 2 will provide a more in-depth discussion about relevant policies relating to meeting the needs of children with life-limiting or life-threatening conditions in schools, it is important to understand from the outset the policy context and the implications of this for practice in schools. The need to meet the needs of children with a range of medical conditions, including those with life-limiting or life-threatening conditions, has recently become a statutory duty for all schools through the government document *Supporting Pupils at School with Medical Conditions* (DfE, 2014; 2015). This has heightened awareness of the school's duty to children with a medical condition, highlighting the rights of the child:

> Children and young people with medical conditions are entitled to a full education and have the same rights of admission to school as other children. This means that no child with a medical condition can be denied admission or prevented from taking up a place in school because arrangements for their medical condition have not been made.
>
> (DfE, 2015: 7)

Statutory guidance does, however, identify that the admission and attendance in schools of children with life-limiting or life-threatening conditions must be continually monitored in relation to the health of and risks for other pupils in the school. Thus,

> In line with their safeguarding duties, governing bodies should ensure that pupils' health is not put at unnecessary risk from, for example, infectious diseases. They therefore do not have to accept a child in school at times where it would be detrimental to the health of that child or others to do so.
>
> (DfE, 2015: 8)

The school's ability to effectively include and meet the needs of children with life-limiting or life-threatening conditions will be considered by OFSTED (Office for Standards in Education, Children's Services and Skills) and is included in the common inspection framework (OFSTED, 2015):

> Inspectors must consider how well a school meets the needs of the full range of pupils, including those with medical conditions. Key judgements will be informed by the progress and achievement of these children alongside those of pupils with special educational needs and disabilities, and also by pupils' spiritual, moral, social and cultural development.
>
> (DfE, 2015: 17)

In recent years, the focus for schools in meeting the particular needs of children with life-limiting or life-threatening conditions has therefore moved beyond a narrow focus just on attendance and progress/attainment (although these will still be scrutinised) but now also includes a focus on broader measures of the child's overall well-being. Within a challenging and ever-changing educational context in which accountability measures retain a relentless focus on ever-improving academic attainment and standards, and with changing relationships between schools, local authorities and wider professionals, ways to support all staff to have the confidence, knowledge and skills to be able to work effectively to meet the needs of children with life-limiting or life-threatening conditions therefore need to be developed. As a result, it is essential that all teachers are provided with not only information and signposting about what practical help is available but advice, guidance and templates about how to effectively manage any emotional, pedagogical and social challenges of working with children with complex medical needs.

Reflective activity

- How aware are you and other colleagues in your school about recent and relevant statutory legislation and guidance on meeting the needs of children with life-limiting or life-threatening conditions?
- How up to date is the information you have?
- How does your school ensure that processes and practices to meet the needs of children with life-limiting or life-threatening conditions are regularly reviewed in light of changing policy and statutory requirements?
- How is statutory guidance about medical needs reflected in school policies?
- And how do these policies inform practice on a day-to-day basis?

What does current research tell us about the needs of teachers working with children with life-limiting or life-threatening conditions?

Despite a clear need for supportive systems to ensure that all children are equipped with equitable and inclusive educational experiences that are of the very highest quality possible, recent research suggests a lack of any coherent systems for providing key information to teachers working in mainstream school settings. Research to date has demonstrated that the needs of children with life-limiting or life-threatening conditions are not well understood and are not being well met in schools. It shows that: the symptoms of the child's condition and treatment can interfere with a child's whole school experience including their learning, their self-esteem and their relationships. Many children and parents feel under-supported by schools and many teachers feel unsure of how to meet the needs of children with life-limiting or life-threatening conditions (Robinson and Summers, 2012). Some key points from the research show that:

- Children with life-limiting or life-threatening conditions often find it very difficult to meet the expectations of schools. This is due to a number of reasons, including:
  - o the effect of their symptoms such as tiredness, nausea or pain; ongoing treatment and its after-effects;
  - o missing out on key points of learning;
  - o having to cope with changes in their appearance and stigma related to that
  - o possible diminished self-confidence and social isolation; and
  - o living with a level of uncertainty about their future.

(Robinson and Summers, 2012)

- Parents and children indicate that teachers need to have a better understanding of children's medical conditions as well as their social, educational and emotional needs.

(Robinson and Summers, 2012)

- Teachers have an important role to play in facilitating peer contact, providing information to others, helping with reintegration into school after an absence and providing support for siblings.

(Robinson and Summers, 2012)

- More than a third of parents report that their child had been bullied or teased by peers due to their diagnosis or treatment.

(CLIC Sargent, 2012)

- Nearly half of parents report that their child had grown apart from friends.

(CLIC Sargent, 2012)

- Schools need to recognise that both the medical model, which focuses on the condition, and the social model, which focuses on the environment, have value. Ecological models, which recognise the real-life interplay of the home, school and health services, are therefore recommended by some authors.

(Robinson and Summers, 2012)

- Only 13% of 1,580 teachers across mainstream primary and secondary schools think that there is enough information, resources and guidance available to teachers to support a pupil with cancer in school.

(Pyle, 2013)

- One third of the parents in one study had not been consulted about how their child's diagnosis was to be communicated to teachers and children at their child's primary school.

(CLIC Sargent, 2012)

Despite the growing statutory focus on meeting the needs of children with life-limiting or life-threatening conditions, there remains a lack of information for mainstream teachers who may very suddenly find themselves needing to support a child and their family through a serious illness.

Introducing the Teaching for Life project

It was as a response to the growing numbers of children with life-limiting or life-threatening conditions attending mainstream schools and the lack of available, accessible and consistent information to support teachers that the Teaching for Life project (Durrant et al., 2014) was set up. This research project set out to investigate, through individual and group interviews and an online questionnaire, the needs of teachers working with children with life-limiting or life-threatening conditions with 38 mainstream teachers and 6 special school members of staff, and an online questionnaire was sent to all SENCOs who had attended the University's National Award for Special Educational Needs Coordinators (N = 90 returned, 16.4% response rate). Different individual and group interviews were set up for those who self-identified themselves as WITH experience of working with children with life-limiting or life-threatening conditions and those who identified themselves as WITHOUT experience. This provided data about actual experience as well as perceived fears.

Those WITH experience were asked to:

- share their experience of working with children with life-limiting or life-threatening conditions;
- consider whether it affected how they taught;
- consider whether they faced any challenges;
- identify useful resources they had accessed; and
- reflect on what they would require if they were to face this situation again.

Those WITHOUT experience were asked:

- how they would react to being told they had to work with a child with a life-limiting or life-threatening condition;
- what they would do to respond to this;

- what resources they would wish for; and
- how it might affect the wider life of the school.

The online questionnaire contained a mix of closed- and open-ended questions. It was designed to gain a better understanding of the scale of the issue in schools, including the types of conditions mainstream teachers were working with, sources of training and support currently on offer and the support and resources staff felt they needed.

The online questionnaire included the definition of life-limiting or life-threatening conditions provided at the beginning of the chapter and was structured into four different sections:

- Role in school
- Experience of working with children with a life-limiting or life-threatening condition
- Training and information sources
- Information about the school (type of school, location of school etc.)

Summary of key findings

The key findings are summarized in what follows and then discussed more fully through the various chapters of this book, where information is provided about the sources of support teachers felt they had needed or would need in order to do the best for both the children and the families personally affected, as well as the wider school community.

Key findings

- The most common life-limiting or life-threatening condition that teachers had come across in schools was cancer, followed by cerebral palsy, Duchenne muscular dystrophy and cystic fibrosis.
- There was wide variance across schools about who was responsible for keeping medical and care needs of pupils updated.
- About half the teachers in this study had provided medical care for a child.
- Many teachers were anxious and concerned that meeting a child's medical needs in school was very challenging, and some felt that they were failing children.
- Teachers wanted better and quicker access to information and support related to providing medical care and administering medicines in particular.
- The need for good multi-disciplinary working around the child was recognised, but a number of barriers were identified. These included teachers not always understanding which health care professionals could support them or how to contact them, delays in the school receiving medical information from health care professionals, health care professionals not being able to provide the right kind of information at the right time and difficulties in getting the right professionals together for a meeting.
- Parents were cited as a key source of information and guidance for teachers who want to understand the medical and non-medical needs of a child. However, parents' own emotional trauma made this vitally important communication extremely difficult.
- Teachers felt a strong professional responsibility to be informed and to try to find support for themselves and the child, but their inability to get sufficient information or support from the parents, health care professionals or the school meant that many turned to what they could find on the Internet.
- Teachers described themselves as floundering at the centre of an emotional web as they tried to balance the needs of the child with the condition, their parents, other pupils and their

parents, themselves and other staff, all within a school culture that could feel insecure and uncertain. Some spoke of the subject being 'taboo', with people not knowing whether they could or could not 'talk about it'.

- The need for support with the emotional strains that are associated with having a child with a life-limiting or life-threatening condition in school was highlighted.
- Teachers wanted certainty and clarity. They wanted to work within a clear framework that provides clarity about school processes and decision making, such as in the recording of pupil absences and pastoral support when a child has a life-limiting or life-threatening condition.
- Teachers wanted to be better equipped for communicating with others about serious illness, death and bereavement.
- Teachers wanted relevant educational resources that could provide a structure for their teaching and from which they could model what to say, what to do and how to be really supportive teachers in this difficult situation.
- Teachers wanted to understand more about how life-limiting or life-threatening conditions might affect children emotionally and behaviourally and strategies for dealing with the outcomes.
- Teachers felt that the experience of teachers who had worked with children with life-limiting or life-threatening conditions could be usefully shared with teachers for whom this is a new experience.

In summary, teachers were well aware of the medical, emotional and social needs of both the child with a life-limiting or life-threatening condition, the other children and those adults that surround the child. They also showed awareness of the importance of the culture of the school, as well as relevant physical attributes of the school which may impact the child, particularly in relation to accessibility and provision such as medical or rest rooms. The teachers wanted more information, guidance and support, particularly identifying their needs around emotional support for themselves and others within the school context. Finally, the importance of effective collaboration between teachers and inter-professional health care and social care agencies was highlighted.

Reflective activity

Using the list of key findings and the findings from other research presented earlier, consider these questions:

- Which key findings/issues particularly resonate with your experience of working with children with life-limiting or life-threatening conditions or resonate with your assumptions about working with children with these conditions?
- Do you have any systems or structures in place in your school already to alleviate any of those key issues?
- What else could you develop or enhance to ensure that the needs of children with life-limiting or life-threatening conditions and their families are effectively met?
- Are there any findings that surprised you?

The structure of this book

This book is intended as a handbook of practical tips and suggestions for understanding and implementing effective ways to work with children with life-limiting or life-threatening conditions as well as their families. Through its accessible approach, it will help de-mystify some of the terminology and health specific protocols, practices and processes. It will enable the mainstream teacher to achieve a fuller understanding of their role and responsibilities in meeting the needs of children with life-limiting or life-threatening conditions. To help the reader engage as fully and quickly as possible with key sections that are of importance to them, the book has been structured into five key sections:

Section 1 – Policy and practice (Chapters 1 and 2)

Section 1 sets out the current policy context and related statutory guidance as it pertains not only to children with life-limiting or life-threatening conditions and their families but to the rights and duties of the school community as a whole.

Section 2 – Knowledge and skills (Chapters 3–9)

Each of the chapters in Section 2 are clearly structured to cover four key aspects:

- *Introduction*: which makes direct links to the Teaching for Life research gathered and the challenges that were identified by teachers
- *Policy review*: brief information about any statutory requirements or guidance to guide the development of practices and policies in schools, in particular in relation to DfE (2015) *Supporting Pupils at School with Medical Conditions*
- *Practical considerations*: practical suggestions and discussion of key principles underpinning effective ways of working
- *Practical resources*: resources, templates or flow diagrams linked to the discussion in the chapter

The key themes covered in this section include:

- *Chapter 3*: definitions of common life-limiting or life-threatening conditions with information about associated medical treatments and their effects on the child
- *Chapter 4*: the most common types of medical care; guidance about the responsibilities of all; medical care plans; administering and storage of medication; legal liability
- *Chapter 5*: communicating effectively with the child and their family
- *Chapter 6*: working collaboratively and understanding the role and remit of a range of professionals; developing effective multi-professional communication strategies
- *Chapter 7*: communicating and sharing information with others; ethics and confidentiality
- *Chapter 8*: teaching and learning approaches to support day-to-day teaching
- *Chapter 9*: understanding and supporting emotional and behavioural changes

Section 3 – A whole-school approach (Chapters 10 and 11)

Again, the structure for the chapters in Section 2 is used to provide a consistent approach to the discussions in this section. The key themes covered in this section include:

- *Chapter 10*: whole-school policies: consultation and collaboration
- *Chapter 11*: whole school cultures; supporting the emotional needs of staff and adults in the school

Section 4 - Conclusions

At the heart of this book is the principle of learning from each other to improve and develop practice.

Section 4 focuses on ways in which we as a learning community can move forward, sharing information across professions and learning lessons from each other, in multi-disciplinary teams.

Section 5 - Additional resources

Section 5 provides additional practical resources in addition to those included in each chapter. It includes a glossary of terms, and references to useful web sites, addresses and sources of advice.

Concluding comments

This book is focused on the needs of school-age children with life-limiting or life-threatening conditions. It is not intended to address the additional needs of pre-school children and/or adults. Throughout the book, to simplify the terminology used, we have adopted the use of "child"/"children" to refer to any child or young person within a school setting. We have also used the term "parents" to include parents, carers and guardians, including carers of looked after children who also have life-limiting or life-threatening conditions.

2 Understanding and responding to the policy context

In this chapter, we:

- Identify key English educational and health policies relevant to working with children with life-limiting or life-threatening conditions
- Identify where to find key information within the policies

Introduction

Medical advancements have enabled more children with complex conditions to be born and survive than in the past. Although there are more sophisticated treatments for a wide range of conditions than ever before, 40,000 children and young people in the UK are living with a life-limiting or life-threatening condition (Fraser et al., 2011). Many of these children are accessing education not only in special schools but also in mainstream schools. Many of the anxieties raised by teachers who participated in the Teaching for Life research project (Durrant et al., 2014) were related to a lack of clarity about what they should, could and could not do and where to turn when finding themselves with responsibility for children with life-limiting or life-threatening conditions.

Key English policies

This chapter focuses on policies for England; the governments of Scotland, Wales and Northern Ireland have their own education and health policies. The Children and Families Act (2014) placed a legal duty on schools to support children with medical conditions. Subsequent policies have emerged to provide a clear framework within which multiple services, including education, can work together to ensure that the needs of children with life-limiting or life-threatening conditions and their families are met. These provide important guidance for teachers. This chapter cannot replace reading the policies fully, but it aims to help orientate teachers and enable them to find what they need more quickly.

The key policy documents include:

- **Integrated Personal Commissioning Emerging Framework (NHS England/LGA, 2016)**
  This is the grand plan for England. It is a framework to enable the integration of health, social and education services. It puts the child and family at the centre of their care. It sets out the expectation that services will provide child and family-centred support.
- **National Framework for Children and Young People's Continuing Care (DH, 2016)**
  This is the framework for all children who have complex medical needs and require additional or specialised health care support. The framework discusses their right to have an additional

budget to support their care. A sub-group of children with complex medical needs is those who have life-limiting or life-threatening conditions.

- **Special Educational Needs and Disability Code of Practice: 0 to 25 years (DfE/DH, 2015)**
  Some children who have complex medical needs and/or life-limiting or life-threatening conditions will also have special educational needs or disabilities. The SEN and Disability Code of Practice (DfE/DH, 2015) provides guidance for teachers in relation to how education, health and social care must work together to support pupils with complex needs.
- **Supporting Pupils at School with Medical Conditions (DfE, 2015)**
  This policy provides guidance to teachers about supporting all children with medical conditions at school, many of whom will have conditions which are not life-limiting or life-threatening.
- **Our Commitment to You for End of Life Care (DH, 2016)**
  This is a steer from government that education, health and social services need to provide child- and family-centred end-of-life support.

Integrated Personal Commissioning Emerging Framework

Integrated Personal Commissioning (IPC) is a grand plan for England which enables the joining up of health care funds, social care funds and education funds to provide personal health budgets for individuals who have significant needs. This includes children with complex needs, including learning disabilities and autism, long-term medical conditions and severe and enduring mental health problems. Children and families will be sent an estimate of the individual's personal health budget. They and the IPC team will discuss how to use the budget in order to create a bespoke package of services to best support the individual's needs. This process is called 'personalised care and support planning', and the agreed plan is the 'personalised care and support plan'. For those children who are eligible, this planning process is directly linked to that for Education, Health and Care Plans. This planning process must emphasise child-centredness and choice. The aim is that IPC will be available in every locality by 2020.

National Framework for Children and Young People's Continuing Care

Most children with life-limiting or life-threatening conditions will have continuing needs, which means that they need additional support over and above what is routinely provided by NHS health care services. Obtaining additional care comes from requesting a 'continuing care package'. This can be funded through Integrated Personal Commissioning, as outlined earlier. Children and families will be sent an estimated personal health budget, which is discussed ('personalised care and support planning'), and an agreed 'personalised care and support plan' is produced. For those children who are eligible, this planning process is directly synchronised to that for Education, Health and Care Plans. Both planning processes include:

- understanding the preferences of the child and their family.
- undertaking a holistic assessment of the child.
- reviewing reports and risk assessments from the professionals within the child's multi-disciplinary team.
- making a decision using the Decision Support Tool for Children and Young People. This comprises assessment of breathing, eating and drinking, mobility, continence and elimination, skin and tissue viability, communication, drug therapies and medicines, psychological and emotional needs, seizures and challenging behaviour.
- informing the child and their family.

- detailed arrangements for the 'continuing care package', including how the care is going to integrate with other provisions such as that for special educational needs and disability, who is to provide it and where.
- review the continuing care package 3 months after its inception and at least annually thereafter.
- planning for transition of care from the age of 14 years, to be ready to enter adult care at 18.

Special Educational Needs and Disability Code of Practice: 0 to 25 years

The Special Educational Needs (SEN) and Disability Code of Practice (DfE/DH, 2015) identifies the four key categories of need:

- Cognition and Learning
- Communication and Interaction
- Social, Emotional and Mental Health
- Physical/Sensory Needs

Whilst a medical need is not seen to be a specific special educational need, other than in the context of broad physical/sensory needs, the Code (DfE/DH, 2015) includes guidance about meeting the needs of children with complex needs and medical conditions. The school's governing body must ensure that arrangements are in place to support such pupils, and school leaders must consult health care and social care professionals, pupils and parents to make sure that the needs of these children are effectively supported. Practitioners now have a duty to support children through the SEN and Disability legislation from birth to 25 years rather than the previous 5 to 16 years of age.

Education, Health and Care Plans (EHCP)

The purpose of an Education, Health and Care Plan is

> to make special educational provision to meet the special educational needs of the child or young person, to secure the best possible outcomes for them across education, health and social care and, as they get older, prepare them for adulthood.
>
> (DfE/DH, 2015: 142)

An Education, Health and Care Plan is only provided following statutory assessment of the child's needs and is only given where there is high level evidence of need despite high levels of appropriate support and intervention that has already been put into place to meet the child's identified needs. The content of an Education, Health and Care Plan covers:

- 'The views, interests and aspirations of the child and his or her parents or the young person.
- The child or young person's special educational needs.
- The child or young person's health needs which are related to their SEN.
- The child or young person's social care needs which are related to their SEN or to a disability.
- The outcomes sought for the child or young person.
- The special educational provision required by the child or the young person.
- Any health provision reasonably required by the learning difficulties or disabilities which result in the child or young person having SEN. Where an individual healthcare plan is made for them, that plan should be included.
- Any social care provision which must be made for a child or young person under 18.

- Any other social care provision reasonably required by the learning difficulties or disabilities which result in a child or young person having SEN.
- The name and type of the school . . . or other institution attended by the child or young person.
- Where there is a personal budget, the details of how the personal budget will support particular outcomes.
- The advice and information gathered during the Education, Health and Care needs assessment.

In addition, where the child or young person is in or beyond Year 9, the Education, Health and Care Plan must include the provision required . . . to assist in preparation for adulthood and independent living.'

(DfE/DH, 2015: 161–162)

Personal budgets

Some children with an Education, Health and Care Plan are eligible for a personal budget which provides funding for additional education, health care and social care services. A personal budget for health services is called a personal health budget. Decisions about personal health budgets are the responsibility of the local National Health Service. Families whose children who are receiving a continuing care package have the 'right to have' a personal health budget including direct payment.

The Local Offer

Local authorities are required to publish a Local Offer which sets out the services that are available to meet the needs of children with SEN and disabilities within and outside of the local geographical area. This is more than a simple directory of existing services, and it must be collaborative (involve parents, children, schools, colleges and other services), accessible, comprehensive, up to date and transparent. The Code (DfE/DH, 2015) provides an extensive list of what the Local Offer must include, such as:

- special educational, health and social care provision for children with special educational needs or disabilities;
- an explanation of how to request an assessment for an Education, Health and Care Plan;
- other educational provision such as sports, arts or paired reading schemes;
- support for when children move between phases of education such as primary to secondary;
- childcare;
- leisure activities; and
- the local authority's accessibility strategy.

The Local Offer must include:

- '. . . services assisting relevant . . . schools . . . to support children and young people with medical conditions.
- arrangements for making those services which are available to all children and young people in the area of those with SEN or disabilities.'

(DfE/DH, 2015: 70)

It should also include:

- 'speech and language therapy and other therapies such as physiotherapy and occupational therapy and services relating to mental health (these must be treated as special educational provision where they educate or train a child or young person).
- wheelchair services and community equipment, children's community nursing, continence services.
- palliative and respite care and other provision for children with complex health needs.
- other services, such as emergency care provision and habilitation support.
- provision for children and young people's continuing care arrangements (including information on how these are aligned to the local process for developing Education, Health and Care Plans).
- support for young people when moving between healthcare services for children to healthcare services for adults.'

(DfE/DH, 2015: 71)

Transition to adulthood

The SEN and Disability Code of Practice (DfE/DH, 2015) includes information about supporting young people's educational, social and emotional needs as they transition to adulthood and to adult health services. In particular, it notes that:

- 'A child with significant health needs is usually under the care of a paediatrician.
- As an adult, they might be under the care of different consultants and teams.
- Health service and other professionals should work with the young person and, where appropriate, their family.
- They should gain a good understanding of the young person's individual needs, including their learning difficulties or disabilities, to co-ordinate healthcare around those needs and to ensure continuity and the best outcomes for the young person.
- This means working with the young person to develop a transition plan, which identifies who will take the lead in co-ordinating care and referrals to other services.
- The young person should know who is taking the lead and how to contact them.'

(DfE/DH, 2015: 136)

Children in alternative provision because of health needs

The SEN and Disability Code of Practice (DfE/DH, 2015) notes that local authorities, as well as schools, must have regard to the statutory guidance on alternative provisions for children who are unable to attend school because of health needs. In this, they identify that:

- '... children and young people who are in hospital or placed in other forms of alternative provision because of their health needs should have access to education that is on a par with that of mainstream provision, including appropriate support to meet the needs of those with SEN.
- The education they receive should be good quality and prevent them from slipping behind their peers.
- It should involve suitably qualified staff who can help pupils progress and enable them to successfully reintegrate back into school as soon as possible.
- This includes children and young people admitted to hospital under Section 2 of the Mental Health Act 2007.

- Where children or young people with health needs are returning to mainstream education then the local authority should work with them, their family, the current education provider and the new school or post-16 provider to produce a reintegration plan.
- This will help ensure that their educational, health and social care needs continue to be met.
- Where relevant, a reintegration plan should be linked to a child or young person's Education, Health and Care Plan or individual healthcare plan.
- Decisions about educational provision should not, however, unnecessarily disrupt a child or young person's education or treatment.'

(DfE/DH, 2015: 218-219)

Supporting pupils at school with medical conditions

Section 100 of the Children and Families Act 2014 places a duty on governing bodies of maintained schools, proprietors of academies and management committees of PRUs [Pupil Referral Units] to make arrangements for supporting pupils at their school with medical conditions.

(DfE, 2015: 3-4)

This guidance sets out to ensure that children with medical conditions are enabled to play a full and active role when they are at school, and like all children, they are supported to fulfil their academic potential and to remain as healthy as possible. The Department for Education (DfE) (2015) therefore states that:

- 'Pupils at school with medical conditions should be properly supported so that they have full access to education, including school trips and physical education.
- Governing bodies must ensure that arrangements are in place in schools to support pupils at school with medical conditions.
- Governing bodies should ensure that school leaders consult health and social care professionals, pupils and parents to ensure that the needs of children with medical conditions are properly understood and effectively supported.'

(DfE, 2015: 4)

Some children will have medical conditions which can be successfully treated, some may have medical conditions that are life-limiting or life-threatening, some may be disabled, according to the definition of the Equality Act (2010), some will have special educational needs, most will have a health care plan, some will have a continuing care package, some will have an Education, Health and Care Plan and some will have all of these. The school will need to work in partnership with multiple agencies as well as the family. Governing bodies are responsible for producing a school policy about appropriate staff training, support and ongoing review. The *Supporting Pupils at School with Medical Conditions* (DfE, 2015) guidance provides essential information to help schools to develop their practices and covers:

- the role of governing bodies, proprietors and management committees;
- developing the school's policy;
- procedures to be followed;
- roles and responsibilities;
- staff training and support;
- the child's role;

- managing medicines on school premises;
- record keeping;
- emergency procedures;
- day trips, residential visits and sporting activities;
- liability and indemnity; and
- complaints.

Where needed, school staff will work with the family and other professionals to develop a health care plan. When doing so, it will be important for the school to be aware that it is generally unacceptable to:

- 'prevent children from easily accessing their inhalers and medication and administering their medication when and where necessary;
- assume that every child with the same condition requires the same treatment;
- ignore the views of the child or their parents; or ignore medical evidence or opinion (although this may be challenged);
- send children with medical conditions home frequently for reasons associated with their medical condition or prevent them from staying for normal school activities, including lunch, unless this is specified in their individual healthcare plans;
- if the child becomes ill, send them to the school office or medical room unaccompanied or with someone unsuitable;
- penalise children for their attendance record if their absences are related to their medical condition, e.g. hospital appointments;
- prevent pupils from drinking, eating or taking toilet or other breaks whenever they need to in order to manage their medical condition effectively;
- require parents, or otherwise make them feel obliged, to attend school to administer medication or provide medical support to their child, including with toileting issues. No parent should have to give up working because the school is failing to support their child's medical needs; or
- prevent children from participating, or create unnecessary barriers to children participating in any aspect of school life, including school trips, e.g. by requiring parents to accompany the child.'

(DfE, 2015: 23)

The DfE (2015) highlights that school staff must take into account the needs of children with medical conditions for whom they have responsibility. They should receive sufficient and suitable training to achieve the necessary level of competency before they take on health-related responsibilities. They must know what to do and how to respond appropriately when a child needs help.

Our commitment to you for end of life care

This government 'commitment' to every person is

'. . . as you approach the end of life, you should be given the opportunity and support to:

- have honest discussions about your needs and preferences for your physical, mental and spiritual wellbeing, so that you can live well until you die;
- make informed choices about your care, supported by clear and accessible published information on quality and choice in end of life care; this includes listening to the voices of children and young people about their own needs in end of life care, and not just the voices of their carers, parents and families;

- develop and document a personalised care plan, based on what matters to you and your needs and preferences, including any advance decisions and your views about where you want to be cared for and where you want to die, and to review and revise this plan throughout the duration of your illness;
- share your personalised care plan with your care professionals, enabling them to take account of your wishes and choices in the care and support they provide, and be able to provide feedback to improve care;
- involve, to the extent that you wish, your family, carers and those important to you in discussions about, and the delivery of, your care, and to give them the opportunity to provide feedback about your care;
- know who to contact if you need help and advice at any time, helping to ensure that your personalised care is delivered in a seamless way.'

(DH, 2016: 10)

The government's commitment recognises that schools and teachers are often an important part of the network that surrounds a child who is on the journey of palliative, end-of-life care. Children with life-limiting or life-threatening conditions need to be enabled to live their lives as they and their families wish, enjoying independence. The commitment emphasises the importance of listening to children and young people, allowing them to express their needs and preferences, and to make informed choices. It also extends to the period of bereavement, in which teachers can play an important role in supporting parents and especially siblings.

The commitment includes an undertaking by the government to explore extending the model of Integrated Personal Commissioning (IPC) to end-of-life care. This may be an improved way of supporting children with complex needs by joining up the health care, social care and other services around the child for more personalised support.

Where to find key information within the policies

Concluding comments

Statutory guidance sets out what local authorities, schools and the NHS must do to comply with the law. Schools need to be especially aware of all the relevant statutory guidance that might apply to a pupil with a life-limiting or life-threatening condition. In particular, schools must pay attention to the key policies discussed in this chapter, including the SEN and Disability Code of Practice (DfE/DH, 2015) and *Supporting Pupils at School with Medical Conditions* (DfE, 2015).

3 Understanding life-limiting or life-threatening conditions

In this chapter, we:

- Define life-limiting or life-threatening conditions
- Consider different types of life-limiting or life-threatening conditions
- Discuss different treatments and treatment regimes
- Explain enteral feeding
- Identify different types of care that children with life-limiting or life-threatening conditions may access

Introduction

Thousands of children with life-limiting or life-threatening conditions are being taught in mainstream schools. The numbers are predicted to rise, and teachers therefore need to be equipped to support their needs. As a result of advances in medicine, many children are now surviving and living with serious health conditions who might have died in the past. Children with cancer and cystic fibrosis, for example, are now much more likely to live into adulthood and be engaged in education than previously (Gatta et al., 2005; Simmonds, 2013). It is therefore essential that teachers working in schools have some understanding of what life-limiting or life-threatening conditions are and how they impact children's lives at school. First, it is essential to have a clear understanding of what the terminology 'life-limiting or life-threatening' refers to. In the Teaching for Life research, we used the following definition from the Association for Children's Palliative Care (2009).

Life-limiting conditions are those for which there is no reasonable hope of cure and from which children or young will die, and life-threatening conditions are those for which curative treatment may be possible, but can fail. These include:

- Conditions where medical treatment might fail (e.g. cancer, organ failure and HIV/AIDS);
- Conditions where the child has long periods of intensive treatment and where premature death is possible (e.g. Cystic fibrosis, Duchenne muscular dystrophy);
- Progressive conditions for which there is no cure (e.g. Batten's disease, muscular dystrophy, cerebral palsy, mucopolysaccharidoses); and
- Conditions where children have a severe neurological disability which could lead to death (e.g. complex needs such as those following brain or spine injuries, severe cerebral palsy).

(based on Association for Children's Palliative Care, 2009)

In our research, the common life-limiting or life-threatening conditions that teachers came into contact with in schools included:

- cancer (leukaemia, brain tumour)
- cerebral palsy
- Duchenne muscular dystrophy
- cystic fibrosis
- heart condition
- epilepsy
- Alexander's diseases
- HIV
- spina bifida/hydrocephalus

These findings reflect national statistics that show that these are the most common types of life-limiting or life-limiting conditions currently found in schools. Whilst some teachers identified and had experience of a number of life-limiting or life-threatening conditions, others reported a range of other conditions which may 'threaten life' but which do not fall within the established definition of life-limiting or life-threatening conditions. These included asthma, allergies and types of complex special educational needs. This demonstrated that teachers need support to gain a clearer understanding about what is meant by the term 'life-limiting or life-threatening conditions'.

Teachers in the research generally and automatically assumed that a child with a life-limiting or life-threatening condition would only have a very short time to live, yet this is not necessarily the case. Many children with life-limiting or life-threatening conditions successfully complete their education in schools and transition into full and successful adult lives. It became clear, therefore, that teachers need more support to understand the needs of children who have life-limiting or life-threatening conditions to help ensure that they are supported to achieve the very best that they can in school.

Policy review

It is not expected that teachers in schools will automatically know and understand everything about complex life-limiting or life-threatening conditions. However, it is now expected that schools are much more aware of the needs of children with medical conditions and that they find ways to ensure that those children are fully supported to access and participate positively in school (DfE, 2015). *Supporting Pupils at School with Medical Conditions* (DfE, 2015) therefore identifies that:

- 'Governing bodies should ensure that school leaders consult health and social care professionals, pupils and parents to ensure that the needs of children with medical conditions are properly understood and effectively supported.'

(DfE, 2015: 4)

The Department for Education (2015) also provides direct advice on the role of school staff, indicating that:

- 'Any member of school staff may be asked to provide support to pupils with medical conditions, including the administering of medicines, although they cannot be required to do so.
- School staff should receive sufficient and suitable training and achieve the necessary competency before they take on responsibility to support children with medical conditions.

- Any member of school staff should know what to do and respond accordingly when they become aware that a pupil with a medical condition needs help.'

(DfE, 2015: 14)

- '[School staff] will need an understanding of the specific medical conditions they are being asked to deal with, their implications and preventative measures.'

(DfE, 2015: 18)

The discussions that follow will therefore support the educational practitioner to develop some awareness of and knowledge about some of the specific medical conditions they may encounter in their school. This general information will then need to be extended through further training specific to the needs of the individual concerned.

Practical considerations

School is very important to children with life-limiting or life-threatening conditions. It provides learning opportunities, contributes to the child's personal and social development and helps the child to have as normal a daily life as possible. Parents report that school can be a further source of support for them, providing a break during the day as well as other practical help for them (ACT, 2010).

Table 3.1 Four broad categories of life-limiting or life-threatening conditions (Together for Short Lives, 2013)

Category one	Life-threatening conditions for which curative treatment may be feasible but can fail	For example, cancer, irreversible organ failures of heart, liver, and kidney
Category two	Conditions in which premature death is inevitable, in which there may be long periods of intensive treatment aimed at prolonging life and allowing participation in normal activities	For example, cystic fibrosis
Category three	Progressive conditions without curative treatment options in which treatment is exclusively palliative and may commonly extend over many years	For example, Duchenne muscular dystrophy, Batten's disease
Category four	Irreversible but non-progressive conditions causing disability leading to susceptibility to health complications and likelihood of premature death	For example, severe cerebral palsy

Reflective activity

- Do you currently have or have you previously had any children with life-limiting or life-threatening conditions in your school?
- Which category of need do you think they would have been grouped into?
- Why?
- What could be the different educational implications at school for children in each of the different categories?
- What support does your school already put in place for children in each of the different categories?

Types of life-limiting or life-threatening conditions

> ## Reflective activity
>
> - What life-limiting or life-threatening conditions are you already aware of?
> - What do you know about these?
> - How might they impact the child within your school setting?

There are 49,000 children and young people aged 0 to 18 years of age in the United Kingdom who have been diagnosed with life-limiting or life-threatening conditions. Half of these have substantial palliative care needs (Fraser et al., 2011). However, many more children living with life-limiting or life-threatening conditions will be attending school. Cystic fibrosis used to be a fatal disorder in childhood; now most children reach adult life with projected survival into the early 40s. There is an increase in life expectancy for Duchenne muscular dystrophy with survival rates occurring into the early 30s. These examples illustrate that children with life-limiting or life-threatening conditions are living longer and, as a result, more are entering and remaining within mainstream education.

For teachers to deliver effective education for children with palliative care needs, it is important to understand the nature of the life-limiting or life-threatening conditions which affect the children in their care and the ways in which their palliative care needs are different. Whilst it is not possible to provide full details about every life-limiting or life-threatening condition, we provide some key details about the most common conditions.

Understanding care for children with life-limiting or life-threatening conditions

A number of different terms are used to describe the care provided or planned for children with life-limiting or life-threatening conditions, and it is helpful for school staff to have a general understanding about what each of these refers to.

The term 'palliative care' encompasses three phases of care:

- palliative care
- end-of-life care
- terminal care

Palliative care for children with life-limiting or life-threatening conditions is 'An active and total approach to care from the point of diagnosis or recognition of the child's life, death and beyond. It embraces the physical, emotional, social and spiritual elements and focuses on the enhancement of quality of life for the child, young person and support for the family' (Together for Short Lives, 2013: n.p.).

End-of-life care refers to the period when a child with advanced disease lives with the condition from which they will die (West Midlands Children and Young People's Palliative Care Toolkit, 2012).

Terminal care refers to care provided when a child is thought to be in the dying phase and usually refers to the last days or hours of life (West Midlands Children and Young People's Palliative Care Toolkit, 2012).

Childhood cancers

The prevalence of childhood cancers is increasing. Within the United Kingdom, almost 4,000 children are diagnosed with cancer every year. Childhood cancers are different from the cancers that affect teenagers and young adults. Malignant cancer cells can arise from any tissue in the body. They are classified according to tissues and cell type. By definition, the term 'cancer' only applies to malignant tumours. Nationally, childhood cancers make up 0.5% of all cancers. The following cancers are most common in childhood (Children's Cancer and Leukaemia Group, 2016).

Leukaemia (type of cancer of the white blood cells) 31% of all childhood cancers
Brain and spinal tumours 26%
Lymphomas (type of blood cancer such as non-Hodgkin's and Hodgkin's lymphoma) 10%
Soft-tissue sarcomas 7%
Neuroblastoma 6%
Bone tumours 4%

Children find that their lives alter following a diagnosis of cancer: 'Most children and young people will readjust well to school after being diagnosed, however cancer can bring physical, emotional and cognitive changes which may affect the child in school' (McCarthy et al., 1998 cited in Selwood, 2013: 14).

Leukaemia

Leukaemia is commonly defined as a cancer of the white blood cells. Acute lymphoblastic leukaemia (ALL) is a cancer of immature lymphocytes (lymphoblast's or blast cells). Lymphocytes are white blood cells that fight infection. ALL is the only form of leukaemia that is more common in children than adults, occurring in about 400 children in the UK each year. About 85% of cases of childhood leukaemia are ALL. White blood cells repair and reproduce themselves in an orderly and controlled manner, but in leukaemia the process gets out of control and the cells continue to develop but do not mature. These immature cells fill up the bone marrow and prevent it from making blood cells properly. As the leukaemia cells do not mature, they cannot do the work of normal white blood cells, leading to an increased risk of infection. As the bone marrow becomes overcrowded with immature white cells it cannot then make the right numbers and quality of red cells and platelets. As a result, symptoms such as anaemia and bruising will occur (Children's Cancer and Leukaemia Group, 2016). The child will present with symptoms such as bone/joint pain, fever, bruising, weight loss, weakness, headache and enlarged lymph nodes (glands).

A blood test usually shows low numbers of normal white blood cells and the presence of abnormal cells. A high white blood cell count indicates the immune response. A sample of bone marrow is then required to confirm the diagnosis, and a lumbar puncture is performed to see whether the spinal fluid contains any leukaemia cells. A chest x-ray is also performed, which will show if there are any enlarged glands in the chest.

Brain tumours

Reflective activity

- What do you know already about brain tumours?
- What impact might a brain tumour have on a child in school?
- When would a child with a brain tumour be able to attend school?
- What provision/support would they need?

Brain tumours, a cancer of the brain, are currently the second-most-common childhood malignancy in the United Kingdom. They are the most common cause of cancer-related death in childhood (about 100 deaths/year; Head Smart UK, 2013, cited in Paul et al., 2014). There are different types of brain tumours, and they are named after the type of cells that make up the brain. The first main type of brain tumour is 'glioma', which originates from the glia cells which support the brain. The second type of brain tumour is known as a 'medulloblastoma', which develops in the cerebellum at the back of the brain (Macmillan, 2013). The signs and symptoms associated with brain tumours are directly related to the location of the tumour in the brain. A headache is the most common presenting feature and can be seen in 60% of all children with brain tumours. Treatment can include surgery, radiotherapy or chemotherapy or a combination of all three depending on the type of tumour.

Cancer treatment centres

Children with cancer are treated in 20 principal treatment centres in the United Kingdom (Children's Cancer and Leukaemia Group, 2014).

Table 3.2 Principal treatment centres (Children's Cancer and Leukaemia Group, 2014)

Addenbrooks Hospital	Our Lady's Children's Hospital Crumlin
Alder Hey Children's Hospital Liverpool	Royal Aberdeen Children's Hospital
Barts and the London	Royal Belfast Hospital for Sick Children Northern Ireland
Birmingham Children's Hospital	Royal Hospital for Sick Children Edinburgh
Bristol Hospital for Sick Children	Royal Hospital for Sick Children Glasgow
Children's Hospital of Wales Cardiff	Royal Manchester Children's Hospital
East Midlands Integrated Service of Queen's Medical Centre and Leicester Royal Infirmary	Royal Marsden Hospital Sutton
Great Ormond Street Hospital Children's Hospital and University College London Hospital	Royal Victoria Hospital Newcastle-Upon-Tyne
John Radcliffe Hospital Oxford	Sheffield Children's Hospital
Leeds General Infirmary	Southampton General Hospital

Protocols

Children with cancer are assigned to a protocol depending on their diagnosis and prognosis. Protocols are an agreed medical regime for different malignant diseases that set out appropriate actions. Protocols are changed in response to clinical trials which look at the response rate and outcome for children following one drug (Children's Cancer and Leukaemia Group, 2016). The care for children with cancer is often shared with the local district general hospital and local health care professionals such as the general practitioner or community children's nurse.

Reflective activity

- What do you understand by the term 'shared care'?
- What are the benefits for the child and the family?
- What are the challenges?

If you have a child with life-limiting or life-threatening conditions currently:

- What shared care is the child accessing?
- Where is the child currently accessing shared care?
- How much shared care is taking place, and what treatment does this involve?
- Who are the key contacts for the child and family?

Medical treatment for cancer

The main treatments for cancer involve one or more of the following:

- surgery
- radiotherapy
- chemotherapy
- stem cell transplantation

Surgery

Surgery is almost inevitable for all children who are diagnosed with cancer. Once diagnosed, children often require surgery in the form of a biopsy or for the insertion of a central venous access device (CVAD). The CVAD allows for easy access to a vein from which blood can be taken or through which drugs, blood products or other fluids can be given. The CVAD prevents the trauma of repeated injections for the child. The tip of the CVAD is placed into the major veins of the heart. The inferior vena cava is one of the main blood vessels which returns deoxygenated blood from the lower part of the body, whilst the superior vena cava returns deoxygenated blood from the upper body to the heart (Peate and Gromley-Fleming, 2015). The main types of CVADs are Port-a-Cath or Hickman lines. They are inserted in a regional centre under general anaesthetic and can be left in place for months with no problems if cared for carefully. It is also worth mentioning that there are associated risks and potential complications which include those listed in Table 3.3.

Table 3.3 Risks and potential complications of surgery

Risks and potential complications	Explanation
Septicaemia	Septicaemia is a term used to describe poisoning of the blood. It is caused by bacteria entering the bloodstream. The child may exhibit symptoms such as high temperature, increased breathing, fatigue and general feeling of malaise (Great Ormond Street, 2016).
Catheter occlusion	The central venous access device may become blocked. If this happens then the device cannot be accessed for any treatment regimes. The child in this situation must attend hospital for assessment of the device and for treatment to address the blockage.
Air embolism	An air embolism is extremely serious and occurs as a result of air being trapped in a blood vessel, leading to a blockage. The child will become unwell, displaying signs of difficulty breathing such as increased breathlessness, chest pain, weakness of the limbs and irregular heartbeat. If the child is displaying any of these signs an ambulance should be called immediately (NHS, 2016).
Displacement and dislodgement	These terms refer to when the catheter becomes dislodged or displaced. It is highly unlikely but may occur under extreme conditions. All children and families will have a safety kit with details on what to do if this happens. For the teacher caring for the child in school this aspect of care should be clearly detailed in the child's individual health care plan. Further information concerning CVAD can be located at the following web site: http://www.gosh.nhs.uk/health-professionals/clinical-guidelines/central-venous-access-devices-long-term#Safety aspects

Reflective activity

- Does your school have a protocol for caring for a central venous access device?
- How would key risks and potential complications be identified in school?
- How would they be addressed?

Surgery is also used for removing solid masses (tumours). Surgery can be used in isolation but is mainly used in combination with chemotherapy and/or radiotherapy. If the child is receiving any of these forms of treatments, it will probably mean periods of time away from school and their peers. The teacher will need to ensure that they are aware of the planned periods of absence, what educational work may be missed and what could potentially be followed up at the hospital either through the hospital school or the hospital teachers, provided the child's condition allows for study. Peer contact could also be maintained and encouraged through the use of social media if the parents allow.

Reflective activity

- What would your school need to be aware of if a child with cancer had surgery?
- What provision would you put in place?
- Who would be involved?
- How can it best be achieved?

Radiotherapy

'Radiotherapy' is the administration of high-energy radiation to produce changes in the body. High-energy rays can kill the cancer cells. There are short-term and long-term side effects associated with radiotherapy. These are dependent on the organ receiving the treatment and the type of radiotherapy being administered. Radiotherapy is usually given in a series of short sessions over the duration of a set period of time. One of the main side effects experienced by the child will include extreme tiredness. If the child is attending school, activities may be best suited to short teaching sessions with periods of rest in between (Children's Cancer and Leukaemia Group, 2016).

Chemotherapy

Chemotherapy involves the administration of cytotoxic (cell-killing) drugs which prevent cancer cells from multiplying, invading and spreading. It is administered by many different routes: orally, intravenously, intrathecal (by lumbar puncture between the interspaces between the lumbar vertebrae) and subcutaneously (injection under the skin; Coyne et al., 2010) depending on the protocol. Chemotherapy affects not only the cancer cells but the body's naturally occurring cells and normal blood cells made in the bone marrow (Children's Cancer and Leukaemia Group, 2016). This contributes to adverse side effects which include those listed in Table 3.4.

Reflective activity

- How can teachers support children, young people and their families receiving treatment for malignant disease?
- What key information does the school and teacher need to know and understand when supporting a child with cancer or leukaemia?
- How will you identify and find the information that you need to know?
- Who will you liaise with?
- What plans or provisions will need to be set up to meet the needs of a child with cancer or leukaemia?

Table 3.4 Side effects of chemotherapy

Side effect	Explanation
Nausea/vomiting	The child may experience periods of feeling extreme sickness and may also vomit as a result of the treatment. It may be useful for the child to have access to personal facilities if this is the case. Normally they will be receiving anti-sickness medicine to reduce the side effects. It may be worth reporting to parents if the child has been unwell at school so their treatment can be reviewed.
Anaemia	This results in a reduced number of red blood cells. The child may be very tired and pale and have increased breathlessness.
Anorexia/weight loss	As a result of the treatment, the child may have a reduced appetite.
Alopecia	This side effect is when hair loss occurs. This can lead to feelings of anxiety for the child and also episodes of embarrassment amongst their peers.
Neutropenia	Neutropenia is a reduction in the number of neutrophils (granulocytes) as a percentage of the total white cell count. When a child is neutropenic, they are much more susceptible to infections.
Thrombocytopenia	This results in a low number of platelets, which are the blood cells which assist with the blood-clotting process. The child may be more susceptible to bruising and episodes of bleeding if they have a reduced number of platelets within their blood.
Sore mouth	Children may develop a sore mouth 5 to 7 days post-treatment. Their mouth may appear dry/pale, and pain may already be present. Whilst at school the child should be encouraged to undertake regular mouth care as prescribed/advised. Information on mouth care should be included as part of the child's individual health care plan.

Cerebral palsy

Cerebral palsy is a motor disease caused by non-progressive brain damage in early life with a prevalence of 2.5 per 1,000 children. Although it is a motor function disorder, damage to other parts of the brain can be expected to a greater or lesser extent, including speech disorders, impaired cognitive functioning, hearing and visual problems and epilepsy (Stephenson et al., 2002). The needs of children with cerebral palsy will be different at different ages. The educational needs of the child are a crucial part of the long-term management. Children with cerebral palsy may get more easily tired than their peers, as motor impairment means that they have to use more energy to undertake tasks. Teachers should be aware that difficulties may be encountered, especially in physical education and practical subjects and with writing.

Duchenne muscular dystrophy

Duchenne muscular dystrophy (DMD) affects 1 in 3,500 male infants in the UK and is characterised by progressive loss of function due to muscle fibre degeneration. The condition is variable, but most boys lose the ability to walk at between 8 and 10 years of age. Progressive respiratory insufficiency begins early in the second decade of life. Scoliosis, which is the term to describe abnormal twisting and curvature of the spine, develops in 90% of boys who use a wheelchair full time and is likely to require surgery within 2 years. As the child's physical needs increase over time, additional equipment within the school may be needed, such as a hoist-manual handling device, and support provided for toileting and personal hygiene. Most children will also find writing increasingly difficult. It may be that additional time for exams and alternative methods for the recording of taught sessions including the use of a computer are worth considering. It is important that school is a good experience for the child, so inclusion in physical activity is also key (Muscular Dystrophy UK, 2015).

Cystic fibrosis

Cystic fibrosis is one of the UK's most common life-limiting inherited conditions, with 1 in 2,500 live births in the UK resulting in cystic fibrosis. Cystic fibrosis is an inherited condition caused by a genetic mutation. In 1985 researchers discovered it was a faulty gene on chromosome 7 that caused cystic fibrosis. This was referred to as the Cystic Fibrosis Transmembrane Regulator. Cystic fibrosis is prevalent in any ethnic group, with a higher proportion in white populations. It is just as common in boys as girls and, sadly, each week two young lives are lost to cystic fibrosis. Improvements in treatment and management have resulted in an average life expectancy of 43.5 years (Cystic Fibrosis Trust, 2013).

The associated symptoms of cystic fibrosis are predominantly found within the lungs. Children with cystic fibrosis have smaller airways and are predisposed to frequent viral infection and increased amounts of thick respiratory secretions, contributing to infection. The mucous is difficult to clear from the respiratory tract and creates a medium for pathogens to grow in, leading to infection. These infections contribute to tissue damage and eventual scarring of the lungs (Glasper et al., 2015). A child attending school will have daily prophylactic oral antibiotics to help prevent infection. Children with cystic fibrosis will have pathogens within their lungs, and whilst these are not harmful to children without cystic fibrosis, they can be harmful to other children with cystic fibrosis. Thus it is important that if there are several children within the school community with cystic fibrosis, they are not together. This requires careful consideration, and a risk-management plan should be put in place with the cystic fibrosis multidisciplinary team (Cystic Fibrosis Trust, 2013).

Whilst at school, children with cystic fibrosis may also require regular physiotherapy which helps clear the lungs of mucous alongside possible nebulizer therapy (Glasper et al., 2015). A nebulizer is a device that is designed to enable drugs to turn into a fine mist for the purpose of inhalation into the lungs (Coyne et al., 2010). If physiotherapy is required when at school, then the child's family or cystic fibrosis physiotherapist can support the school in advising about the different techniques which can be employed. Older children may be allowed more independence with postural drainage and special breathing techniques. Regular vigorous exercise should also be encouraged, as this will strengthen the airway muscles and prevent accumulation of secretions. Schools should therefore understand that physical exercise is good for children with cystic fibrosis (Cystic Fibrosis Trust, 2013).

Pancreatic dysfunction is also a common feature of cystic fibrosis. The pancreas is an accessory organ within the gastrointestinal system which produces insulin that regulates the amount of sugar in the blood. The pancreas also produces digestive enzymes which pass into the small intestine, where they aid the digestion and absorption of food. It is for this reason that the children may require Creon (enzyme capsules) to aid the digestion and absorption of vitamins and minerals (Glasper et al., 2015). It is important that at school, children with cystic fibrosis maintain a high-calorie diet and have Creon with every meal. Enzymes are not drugs; they are supplements that should be taken by the child immediately before meals/snacks and sometimes during meals. They are often taken in large numbers. In most schools, the child can carry these enzymes in a suitable container – this should be reflected in the school's policy and in the child's health care plan. No special consideration for storage is required. Children with cystic fibrosis also produce sticky, foul-smelling stools and, as a result, whilst at school, they may need to go to the toilet very quickly, so they should be allowed to leave the class when they request it. Some children may feel self-conscious, so it is important that they have privacy and access to a toilet close by (Cystic Fibrosis Trust, 2013).

Despite the administration of these enzymes, children with cystic fibrosis are malnourished and will often require enteral feeding to boost their nutritional and calorific content. Enteral feeding is an artificial form of supplying the child with nutrients via a tube into the gastrointestinal tract (Coyne et al., 2010).

Enteral feeding

Many children with life-limiting or life-threatening conditions experience some level of feeding difficulties, and in most cases this can be managed by supplementing their diet orally through high-energy drinks and medication. However, some children may experience more complicated feeding difficulties, resulting in them being unable to eat/drink to maintain their normal growth and development. Enteral feeding tends to be considered for children with life-limiting or life-threatening conditions when there has been unsatisfactory weight gain and progressive decline on the centile chart.

Nasogastric feeding

Nasogastric feeding is the most common form of enteral feeding. A nasogastric tube is a polyvinylchloride or polyurethane tube that is passed through the nose and into the stomach (Glasper et al., 2015). The tube can stay in for up to 6 weeks at a time, dependent on guidelines from the manufacturers.

Gastrostomy feeding

Gastrostomy feeding requires a surgical opening to be made through the abdominal wall into the stomach through which a feeding tube can be passed (Cunningham and Best, 2013). There are different types of feeding tubes such as: PEGS (percutaneous endoscopic gastrostomy), balloon types, muttons, mickey and mini.

The main life-limiting or life-threatening conditions which require the insertion of a feeding tube include:

- cystic fibrosis
- renal failure
- childhood cancers
- neurological degenerative conditions

It is worth noting that there may be complications associated with enteral feeding. Those that tend to occur are usually minor and include local skin irritation, infection, granulation of tissue and leakage. With good management, these complications are preventable or manageable.

Reflective activity

- What would the school need to know about in order to meet the needs of a child who needs enteral feeding?
- What provision would need to be put in place?
- Who would you liaise with?
- Are there any educational implications?
- What policy would you need in place to safeguard staff and the well-being of the child?

The school will need to liaise with the child's family, community children's nurse and dietician for clear guidance and for advice regarding the child's care whilst at school.

Children with cystic fibrosis also require oral and intravenous antibiotics to manage chronic and acute lung infections. These antibiotics may be given orally, inhaled via nebulizer therapy or given intravenously over a period of 10 to 14 days, either in hospital or at home. If a child has an intravenous line, they may attend school, but in this case the line must be securely bandaged. Children with cystic fibrosis may also have a CVAD in place to assist with the administration of the intravenous antibiotics. If the child needs to stay in hospital for antibiotic therapy, then the school and hospital will consider whether it is appropriate for the child to have lessons whilst in hospital if their health allows (Cystic Fibrosis Trust, 2013).

Effective management of a child with cystic fibrosis within a school requires a multidisciplinary approach. The key professionals involved in caring for a child with cystic fibrosis should include:

- community children's nurse
- outreach nurse
- physiotherapist
- dietician
- paediatrician
- diabetic nurse specialist
- family
- social worker
- psychologist
- a cystic fibrosis specialist centre

Practical resources

In this section, the following practical resources are provided:

1 List of useful web sites
2 Shared care principles

1 Useful web sites

The Children's Cancer and Leukaemia Group (CCLG) publishes a range of very useful publications which will explain a range of issues relating to cancer and leukaemia. They can be accessed at http://www.cclg.org.uk/Publications/All-publications.

West Midlands Paediatric Palliative Care Network (2016): West Midlands Children and Young People's Palliative Care Toolkit: http://www.togetherforshortlives.org.uk/professionals/externalresources/2918westmidlandstoolkit

Children with Cancer UK/Resources: http://www.childrenwithcancer.org.uk/resources

Resources to help students, parents and teachers manage cystic fibrosis in the classroom: Living with CF, CF and School (Cystic Fibrosis Foundation, 2016): https://www.cff.org/Living-with-CF/CF-and-School/

Education matters: A teachers' guide to Duchenne muscular dystrophy: http://www.parentprojectmd.org/site/DocServer/EdMatters-TeachersGuide.pdf?docID=2403

2 Shared care principles

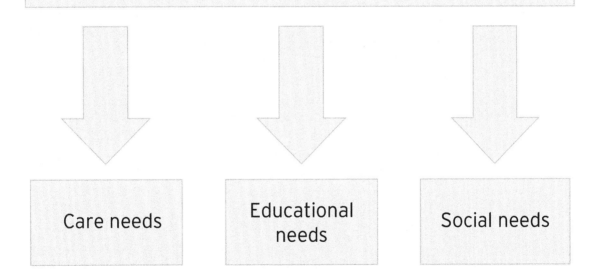

Shared care principles:
Clearly identify what the key principles for the individual are.

Health care and social care professional involved:
Clearly identify who the key health care and social care professionals involved with the child are.

Child and family needs across the team:
Collaboratively identify how the child's and their family's needs can be supported across the team.
Consider:

Care needs

Educational needs

Social needs

This diagram may be a helpful prompt of the key aspects of care to be focused upon when collaborating with other health and social care professionals. It may act as a gentle reminder to clarify roles and responsibilities around each of the areas when caring for a child with a life-limiting or life-threatening condition within the school environment.

Concluding comments

School is an important part of the child and young person's life, and it is essential that as much as possible is put in place to enable them to succeed. Teachers have an important role to play and can be supported, through the use of some additional information, to have an initial understanding of the life-limiting or life-threatening conditions they may encounter in schools.

The numbers of children attending mainstream schools with common life-limiting or life-threatening conditions is increasing. This chapter has provided an outline of the more common conditions and treatments. Teachers need to use this information to help them to understand and meet the needs of children in school.

4 Medical treatment and health care practices in school

In this chapter, we:

- Discuss how to develop an individual health care plan
- Explain consent for medical treatment
- Consider planning for transition into school
- Consider key health care areas to address in staff training
- Introduce infection control and the importance of handwashing techniques
- Discuss principles for storage and administration of medicines within the school environment

Introduction

Health care refers to maintaining or improving health using disease prevention, diagnosis, care or treatment (e.g. medicines, surgery, exercises, emotional support, physical examinations, health education, therapy, touch). It is the professional work of health care professionals, but of course almost everyone carries out simple acts of health care for themselves and others.

Medical care technically relates to the work of doctors, who care for an individual using medical knowledge and medical procedures. Medical treatment comprises medicine and surgical/invasive procedures. Some health care professionals provide medical treatment under the guidance of a doctor or if they have had specific training. For example, many nurses administer medicines that have been prescribed by a doctor. Some school nurses have undertaken specific training that allows them to prescribe certain medicines. Some teachers provide medical treatment when they give a child medicine through an inhaler, tablet or injection.

Fifty-one percent of the teachers who were surveyed had experience of providing medical treatment to a pupil with a life-limiting or life-threatening condition, with many reporting experience of multiple procedures. Anxiety was expressed by teachers, relating to dealing with the medical needs of these children in school, usually in relation to 'getting it wrong':

"I think people would be scared of getting something wrong or making a situation worse or not dealing with something in the correct way."

Many of the teachers were concerned about schools being able to accommodate the children's needs in terms of changes to the timetable:

"Thinking about putting things in place, do they need extra support? Are they in a wheelchair? Are they only here in school for half days? Can they cope with whole days? What

about trips? PE lesson? Playtimes? All the things that perhaps they would need some extra things in place, or not?"

Many teachers focused on issues relating to physical difficulties and toileting difficulties rather than actual medical treatment:

"Mobility, how that would affect the classroom set up, toileting and things like that."

The teachers highlighted the importance of training in relation to medication:

"Obviously, you'd have to have the correct training depending on how the medication was administered and have to make sure the parents were okay with a non-medical person administering it. But if parents consented and if the correct training had been undertaken it would probably be okay."

Half of the respondents to the questionnaire had received formal training about the medical treatment and health care needs of pupils with a life-limiting or life-threatening condition. Yet throughout the research, concerns about administering medication were prevalent:

"They're frightened quite often to do certain things because they've got that fear of doing it wrong, not doing it correctly, at the wrong time."

Summary

Teachers identified high levels of anxiety about the issue of administering and being responsible for the medical treatment of a child with a life-limiting or life-threatening condition. This was not because they did not want to provide high levels of support and do everything that they could to meet the child's needs. Rather, it was because they were worried about:

- Getting it wrong
- The appropriate storage of medication
- Legal aspects of giving medication in school

The teachers highlighted that they wanted more training about administering medication but made it clear that this would not be enough to allay all their anxieties, because the reality of school life is that the right person might not be immediately available to administer the medication at the time it is needed.

Policy review

The Department for Education (DfE, 2015) provides a vast amount of very clear guidance about the statutory responsibilities of governing bodies to ensure that arrangements are in place to support pupils with medical conditions.

Individual health care plans

A health care plan is a record of the health care required by a child to meet desired outcomes. It records specific tasks and services that seek to prevent, treat, cure, rehabilitate and care. When a child is able to engage with school but requires on-going health care, the health care plan becomes a document that records what will happen at school and the responsibilities of health care professionals, school personnel, the child and others. The DfE (2015) identify that:

- 'Individual healthcare plans can help to ensure that schools effectively support pupils with medical conditions.
- They provide clarity about what needs to be done, when and by whom.
- They will often be essential, such as in cases where conditions fluctuate or where there is a high risk that emergency intervention will be needed, and are likely to be helpful in the majority of other cases, especially where medical conditions are long-term and complex.
- The format of individual healthcare plans may vary to enable schools to choose whichever is the most effective for the specific needs of each pupil.
- They should be easily accessible to all who need to refer to them, while preserving confidentiality.
- Plans should be drawn up in partnership between the school, parents, and a relevant healthcare professional, e.g. school nurse, specialist or children's community nurse or paediatrician, who can best advise on the particular needs of the child.
- Pupils should also be involved whenever appropriate.
- The aim should be to capture the steps which a school should take to help the child manage their condition and overcome any potential barriers to getting the most from their education and how they might work with other statutory services.
- Partners should agree who will take the lead in writing the plan, but responsibility for ensuring it is finalised and implemented rests with the school.'

(DfE, 2015: 10-11)

The DfE (2015) provides specific details about what should be included in a health care plan, suggesting that the following key information should be included:

- 'The medical condition, its triggers, signs, symptoms and treatments;
- The pupil's resulting needs, including medication (dose, side effects and storage) and other treatments, time, facilities, equipment, testing, access to food and drink where this is used to manage their condition, dietary requirements and environmental issues – eg crowded corridors, travel time between lessons.
- Specific support for the pupil's educational, social and emotional needs – for example, how absences will be managed, requirements for extra time to complete exams, use of rest periods or additional support in catching up with lessons, counselling sessions.
- The level of support needed (some children will be able to take responsibility for their own health needs) including in emergencies. If a child is self-managing their medication, this should be clearly stated with appropriate arrangements for monitoring.
- Who will provide this support, their training needs, expectations of their role and confirmation of proficiency to provide support for the child's medical condition from a healthcare professional; and cover arrangements for when they are unavailable.
- Who in the school needs to be aware of the child's condition and the support required.
- Arrangements for written permission from parents and the headteacher for medication to be administered by a member of staff, or self-administered by the pupil during school hours.
- Separate arrangements or procedures required for school trips or other school activities outside of the normal school timetable that will ensure the child can participate, eg risk assessments.

- Where confidentiality issues are raised by the parent/child, the designated individuals to be entrusted with information about the child's condition.
- What to do in an emergency, including whom to contact, and contingency arrangements.'

(DfE, 2015: 11-12)

The DfE (2015) identifies that the health care plan should clearly set out what constitutes an emergency with details about what should happen.

Managing and administering medicines

The DfE (2015) also provides very clear details and information about procedures for managing medicines on school premises:

- 'Medicines should only be administered at school when it would be detrimental to a child's health or school attendance not to do so.
- No child under 16 should be given prescription or non-prescription medicines without their parent's written consent – except in exceptional circumstances where the medicine has been prescribed to the child without the knowledge of the parents.
- In such cases, every effort should be made to encourage the child or young person to involve their parents while respecting their right to confidentiality.
- Schools should set out the circumstances in which non-prescription medicines may be administered.
- A child under 16 should never be given medicine containing aspirin unless prescribed by a doctor.
- Medication, eg for pain relief, should never be administered without first checking maximum dosages and when the previous dose was taken. Parents should be informed.
- Where clinically possible, medicines should be prescribed in dose frequencies which enable them to be taken outside school hours.
- Schools should only accept prescribed medicines if these are within the expiry date, labelled, provided in the original container as dispensed by a pharmacist and include instructions for administration, dosage and storage. The exception to this is insulin, which must still be in date, but will generally be available to schools inside an insulin pen or a pump, rather than in its original container.
- All medicines should be stored safely.
- Children should know where their medicines are at all times and be able to access them immediately.
- Where relevant, they should know who holds the key to the storage facility.
- When no longer required, medicines should be returned to the parent to arrange for safe disposal.
- Sharps boxes should always be used for the disposal of needles and other sharps.
- A child who has been prescribed a controlled drug may legally have it in their possession if they are competent to do so, but passing it to another child for use is an offence. Monitoring arrangements may be necessary.
- Schools should otherwise keep controlled drugs that have been prescribed for a pupil securely stored in a non-portable container and only named staff should have access.
- Controlled drugs should be easily accessible in an emergency.
- A record should be kept of any doses used and the amount of the controlled drug administered.
- School staff may administer a controlled drug to the child for whom it has been prescribed.

- Schools should keep a record of all medicines administered to individual children, stating what, how and how much was administered, when and by whom.
- Any side effects of the medication to be administered at school should be noted in school.
- Governing bodies should ensure that written records are kept of all medicines administered to children. Records offer protection to staff and children and provide evidence that agreed procedures have been followed.'

(DfE, 2015: 20-21)

Although the school should identify a named individual responsible for providing health care to pupils in school, importantly, the DfE (2015) provide additional advice on the role of school staff, identifying that

- 'Any member of school staff may be asked to provide support to pupils with medical conditions, including the administering of medicines, although they cannot be required to do so.
- Although administering medicines is not part of teachers' professional duties, they should take into account the needs of pupils with medical conditions that they teach.
- School staff should receive sufficient and suitable training and achieve the necessary levels of competency before they take on responsibility to support children with medical conditions.
- Any member of school staff should know what to do and respond accordingly when they become aware that a pupil with a medical condition needs help.'

(DfE, 2015: 14)

Training

The DfE (2015) highlights that school staff will require training in order to meet their statutory responsibilities for meeting the needs of children with medical conditions, including those with life-limiting or life-threatening conditions. The importance of clearly identifying the level of training required by which member of staff to ensure that the child's medical needs are fully supported is highlighted. This should 'specify how training needs are assessed, and how and by whom training will be commissioned and provided' (DfE, 2015: 17).

The following key principles are therefore useful to consider when reviewing training needs:

- 'Suitable training should have been identified during the development or review of individual healthcare plans.
- The relevant healthcare professional should normally lead on identifying and agreeing with the school the type and level of training required, and how this can be obtained.
- Training should be sufficient to ensure that staff are competent and have confidence in their ability to support pupils with medical conditions, and to fulfil the requirements as set out in individual healthcare plans.
- They will need an understanding of the specific medical conditions they are being asked to deal with, their implications and preventative measures.
- A first-aid certificate does not constitute appropriate training in supporting children with medical conditions.
- Healthcare professionals, including the school nurse, can provide confirmation of the proficiency of staff in a medical procedure, or in providing medication.
- The relevant healthcare professional should be able to advise on training that will ensure that all medical conditions affecting pupils in the school are understood fully.

- This includes preventative and emergency measures so that staff can recognise and act quickly when a problem occurs.
- The family of a child will often be key in providing relevant information to school staff about how their child's needs can be met, and parents should be asked for their views. They should provide specific advice, but should not be the sole trainer.'

(DfE, 2015: 18)

The DfE (2015) explains, 'Staff must not give prescription medicines or undertake health care procedures without appropriate training (updated to reflect requirements within individual healthcare plans)' (DfE, 2015: 18).

The role of the child

The DfE (2015) also provides specific details about the child's role in managing their own health needs and medicines:

- 'After discussion with parents, children who are competent should be encouraged to take responsibility for managing their own medicines and procedures.
- This should be reflected within individual healthcare plans.
- Wherever possible, children should be allowed to carry their own medicines and relevant devices or should be able to access their medicines for self-medication quickly and easily.
- Children who can take their medicines themselves or manage procedures may require an appropriate level of supervision.
- If it is not appropriate for a child to self-manage, relevant staff should help to administer medicines and manage procedures for them.'

(DfE, 2015: 19)

The DfE (2015) also provides guidance on what to do should a child refuse to take their medicine in school:

- 'If a child refuses to take medicine or carry out a necessary procedure, staff should not force them to do so, but follow the procedure agreed in the individual healthcare plan.
- Parents should be informed so that alternative options can be considered.'

(DfE, 2015: 19)

Liability and indemnity

Having the right insurances in place to cover the needs of children with medical conditions is vitally important. The DfE (2015) highlights the following key principles for practice:

- 'Governing bodies of maintained schools and management committees of pupil reference units (PRUs) should ensure that the appropriate level of insurance is in place and appropriately reflects the level of risk.
- Proprietors of academies should ensure that either the appropriate level of insurance is in place or that the academy is a member of the Department for Education's Risk Protection Arrangement (RPA).
- It is important that the school policy sets out the details of the school's insurance arrangements which cover staff providing support to pupils with medical conditions.
- Insurance policies should be accessible to staff providing such support.

- Insurance policies should provide liability cover relating to the administration of medication, but individual cover may need to be arranged for any healthcare procedures.
- The level and ambit of cover required must be ascertained directly from the relevant insurers.
- Any requirements of the insurance, such as the need for staff to be trained, should be made clear and complied with.
- In the event of a claim alleging negligence by a member of staff, civil actions are likely to be brought against the employer.'

(DfE, 2015: 23–24)

Practical considerations

Developing the individual health care plan

When a school hears that a child has a life-limiting or life-threatening condition or any medical condition requiring care at school, the first step is to communicate with the family to find out how the child's health care needs are currently being met. A copy of an exemplar letter inviting parents to contribute to the development of an individual health care plan is provided in the Practical Resources section.

Reflective activity

- Prior to the meeting, what information would you want to know about the child's care at home?
- Is there any pre-reading you could undertake regarding the child's condition in preparation for meeting with the child/family?

The needs of the child need to be identified, and some of these will be health care needs. Others will be wider educational or support needs, but they are often interdependent. Information will need to be collated from the child, family and any other health care or other services that are currently involved with this child (see Chapter 5). The aim is to provide an individualised, comprehensive and coordinated plan that puts the child at the centre of a multi-disciplinary team. The family is likely to already have a named key worker/lead professional who is the central point for coordinating the child's care. This may be a children's community nurse. Care planning is an ongoing process that will require regular review, evaluation and updating (Glasper et al., 2015).

An effective individual health care plan will address the following key sections (see also the exemplar individual health care plan provided in the Practical Resources section):

- Child's name, date of birth, address
- Medical diagnosis or condition
- Date
- Review date
- Family contact information
- Clinic/hospital contact details
- Who is responsible for providing support in school
- Description of medical needs, including details of the child's symptoms, triggers, signs, treatments, facilities, equipment or devices, environmental issues etc.

- Name of medication: dose, method of administration, when to be taken, side effects, contra-indications, administered by/self-administered with/without supervision
- Daily care requirements
- Specific support for the child's educational, social and emotional needs
- Arrangements for school visits/trips
- Describe what constitutes an emergency and what action needs to be taken
- Who is responsible in an emergency
- Plan developed with
- Staff training needed/undertaken – who, what, when

A flow chart setting out the model process for developing individual health care plans (DfE, 2015: 26) is provided in the Practical Resources section.

The individual health care plan should be written in an objective manner. It records when medication or health care is given. These records should be accurate and concise, providing a clear account of the child's time within the school environment. Keep in mind:

- Clarity is essential regarding the information provided.
- All information provided should be intelligible.
- All information should be accurate (Glasper et al., 2015).

The individual health care plan acts as a conduit between the school, the child, the family and other professionals, and it should be signed by all to confirm agreement. Thereafter it is important that all are aware of any changes in the child's condition or care to be delivered. Good practice would involve a regular review of the individual health care plan. This could be daily when a child is settling back within the school environment after a break and then weekly or monthly dependent on the child's situation.

Good communication is vital, and as confidentiality must be maintained at all times, it is important to establish that the child and their family are happy for information to be disseminated to relevant staff whilst the child is at school (see Chapter 7).

Consent to medical treatment

According to the Fraser Guidelines, children who are 16 and over are entitled to consent to their own medical treatment. Children under 16 can consent if they are believed to have 'enough intelligence, competence and understanding to fully appreciate what is involved in their treatment' (NHS, 2016). This is known as being 'Gillick competent' after a landmark legal case whereby Mrs Gillick took her local health authority to court and lost (British and Irish Legal Information Institute, 1985). If a child is not 'Gillick competent', a parent or someone with parental responsibility consents for them. Under this ruling, therefore, in 2008, a 13-year-old girl's right to refuse lifesaving medical treatment was upheld by a local authority, her parent and doctors (Waller & Davis, 2014).

Medical treatment comprises the taking of medicines and surgical/invasive procedures. For children under 16 the following people can give consent for medical treatment:

- the child's mother
- the child's father, if he was married to the mother when the child was born
- for children born before December 1 2003 – the child's father, if he marries the mother, obtains a parental responsibility order from the court or registers a parental responsibility agreement with the court

- for children born on or after December 1 2003 – the child's father, if he registered the child's birth with the mother at the time of the birth, or if he re-registers the birth (if he is the natural father), marries the mother, obtains a parental responsibility order from the court or registers a parental responsibility agreement with the court
- the child's legally appointed guardian
- a person with a residence order concerning the child
- a local authority that is designated to care for the child
- a local authority or person with an emergency protection order for the child

(NHS, 2016: http://www.nhs.uk/chq/Pages/900.aspx, accessed 29/10/16)

Planning for transition into school

A child's health care plan may need to include or be complemented by procedures for entering or re-entering school after a diagnosis. Where a child requires specific health care, school staff will either need to be trained or recruited before the child can attend school. This process may take time and requires timelines. Parents must be kept informed of progress, as this is an integral part of the child transitioning into school.

As part of the planning, it is important to establish what equipment the child will require, as well as any adaptations to the school physical layout or social environment that may be needed. The planning needs to consider the child's involvement in classroom and extra-curricular activities. The school needs to consider where equipment will be stored and, in some cases, whether a dedicated safe space within the school may be required.

Staff training

Reflective activity

- What key practical skills do you think you and/or other staff in school will need to be aware of to ensure that the health care needs of a child with a life-limiting or life-threatening condition are fully supported?
- What systems and processes do you have in place in school to meet these requirements already?
- Are there any obvious gaps in current knowledge, skills or provision in relation to your health care practices?
- How could these be addressed?

For children with life-limiting or life-threatening conditions to access school, it is important that all staff directly involved in health care are properly trained and assessed to have achieved competence. No member of school staff should deliver any aspect of health care until properly trained, assessed and signed off as being competent to undertake the skills by a relevant health care professional such as a school nurse or community children's nurse. The child's individual health care plan should itemise any training that is required, who will provide it, when and that competence has been achieved.

Table 4.1 illustrates some examples of health care which might be required by a child who has a life-limiting or life-threatening condition when in school. It includes who might be able to provide the training.

Table 4.1 Health care issues and training

Practical considerations	Factors to consider within a safe school environment	Who may deliver the training	Practical skills required as part of the child's care
Prevention of infection	School infection-control policy Access to equipment such as hot water, soap, alcohol gel, microbial hand wash Paper hand towels in situ Waste bins that are foot operated to avoid contamination of hands when opening the bin Separate bins for clinical waste and normal school waste Correct storage and cleaning of equipment A risk assessment must be in place.	Community children's nurse School nurse	Correct handwashing techniques Safe disposal of sharps Use of personal protective clothing Safe disposal of clinical waste
Mobility	How does the child normally mobilise? Does the child use any mobility aids such as wheelchair, walking aids, crutches, hoist? Is the school environment layout conducive to assisting with the mobility of the child? Does transport to and from school need to be given consideration? A risk assessment must be in place.	Community children's nurse Occupational therapist Physiotherapist Podiatrist School nurse (Child and parents can contribute to training.)	Safe moving and handling techniques when caring for the child Specific training of equipment in use such as wheelchairs, walking aids, hoist if required Specific training on positioning of the child whilst in lessons, attendance at extra-curricular activities How to document within individual health care plans
Personal hygiene needs	Does the child require assistance with personal hygiene? Is any specific equipment required? How can the child's privacy be maintained? A risk assessment must be in place. Does the school have adequate facilities?	Community children's nurse Occupational therapist School nurse (Child and parents can contribute to training.)	Safe moving and handling techniques when caring for the child Specific training in any equipment needed Infection-control measures How to document within individual health care plans
Enteral feeding	What type of enteral feeding is the child having? What equipment is required whilst the child is at school? Is there a need for specific storage arrangements to be put in place for the equipment needed?	Children's/paediatric nutrition nurse Community children's nurse Community dietition School nurse (Child and parents can contribute to training.)	Introduction and training in equipment to be used such as feeding pump Administering a bolus feed (this would refer to feeds given at regular intervals throughout the child's day such as breakfast, lunchtime and dinner)

Practical considerations	Factors to consider within a safe school environment	Who may deliver the training	Practical skills required as part of the child's care
	Troubleshooting if equipment is not working properly A risk assessment must be in place.		Administering a continuous feed (this refers to a feed which is running over a set period of hours throughout the child's days such as 16 hours of out a 24-hour day)
			Administering medication using the enteral feeding device such as a nasogastric tube/gastrostomy tube
			How to document within individual health care plans
Observation of signs for deterioration of the child	Effective communication is key with the child/family to understand what may happen if the child becomes unwell in school.	Children's community nurse School nurse (Child and parents can contribute to training.)	Key physical signs and symptoms to be aware of

(Coyne et al., 2010; Macqueen et al., 2012; Glasper et al., 2015)

Practical skills

Infection control

Infection control is an important aspect of care that might be covered within the individual health care plan and within considerations for the whole-school environment. Infection occurs as a result of the invasion of the body by microorganisms that reproduce and multiply, causing disease. Most children with a life-limiting or life-threatening condition are more susceptible to acquiring infection due to weakened and immature immune systems, in particular those children with acquired immunodeficiency such as childhood cancer (following chemotherapy or radiotherapy) and children with cystic fibrosis. All school staff may need to be informed about how to minimise the risks of a vulnerable child catching an infection. Health care professionals such as school nurses and children's community nurses can advise. If a child has an infection they may display the following signs/symptoms:

- elevated temperature
- lethargy
- loss of appetite
- pain

Infection can be spread by various routes of transmission such as:

- direct contact through body fluids
- indirect contact such as by people and hands
- inanimate objects such as equipment
- airborne contact through respiratory droplets/dust and through certain arthropods such as flies/bugs

Personal hygiene

Attention to personal hygiene is very important in the prevention of infection. Any member of staff who is carrying an infection and is involved in delivering a child's care is a risk to a vulnerable child. Personal hygiene includes the care of staff's clothes and routine inspections of the skin for abrasions and cuts, preferably at the beginning of each school day when they can be covered.

Handwashing and cleaning

Effective handwashing is the most important factor in reducing the spread of infection. Hands must be washed prior to any contact before and after caring for the child, in particular before a clean or aseptic procedure such as performing an enteral feed, or after any contact that may result in hands becoming contaminated such as delivering/assisting with the child's personal hygiene. It is important that within the school there is a designated area which provides hot water, soap and alcohol-based hand rub or gel antimicrobial hand wash. Soap and water can be used to clean visibly soiled hands. Alcohol-based hand rub or gel antimicrobial hand wash can be used to clean hands before performing an invasive procedure (Coyne et al., 2010). To be carried out correctly, handwashing using soap and water incorporates the stages listed in Table 4.2a. To be carried out correctly, handwashing using alcohol hand rub incorporates the stages listed in Table 4.2b. In some situations, staff directly involved in the child's care may

Table 4.2a Correct handwashing procedure using soap and water.

Wet hands thoroughly under running water.
Apply enough soap to cover all hand surfaces.
Rub hands palm to palm.
Rub back of each hand with the palm of other hand with fingers interlaced.
Rub palm to palm with fingers interlaced.
Rub with backs of fingers to opposing palms with fingers interlaced.
Rub each thumb clasped in opposite hand using rotational movement.
Rub tips of fingers in opposite palm in a circular motion.
Rub each wrist with opposite hand.
Rinse hands with water.
Use elbow to turn off tap.
Dry thoroughly with a single-use towel.
Discard paper towel in waste bin. Open bin using foot pedal only to avoid contaminating clean hands.
Your hands are now safe; the procedure for handwashing should take 40–60 secs.

(NHS National Patients Safety Agency, 2008)

Table 4.2b Correct handwashing procedure using alcohol hand rub.

Apply a small amount of the product in a cupped hand, covering all surfaces.
Rub hands palm to palm.
Rub back of each hand with palm of other hand with fingers interlaced.
Rub palm to palm with fingers interlaced.
Rub with backs of fingers with fingers interlaced.
Rub each thumb clasped in opposite hand using rotational movement.
Rub tips of fingers in opposite palm in a circular motion.
Rub each wrist with opposite hand.
Your hands are now safe; the procedure for using alcohol hand rub should take 20–30 secs.

(NHS National Patients Safety Agency, 2008: 2)

need to wear protective personal equipment such as disposable aprons or gloves. All clinical waste, that is waste potentially contaminated with infectious substances from body fluids, will need to be disposed of in a yellow plastic bag, tied at the neck and labelled with the source prior to infection (RCN, 2012).

Storage and administration of medicines

The governing body needs to ensure that the school has a clear policy and procedures in place for managing medicines (DfE, 2015). The medication management for a child with a life-limiting or life-threatening condition needs to be clearly reviewed in alignment with the school's policy and procedure for managing medicines. All medicines should be stored safely within the school environment, with the child knowing at all times where their medication is located. This will normally be a locked cupboard or a locked non-portable container.

The administration of medicines is a complex process, and it is essential that school staff do not administer medication without appropriate training. It is worth noting the caution issued by the Nursing and Midwifery Council (2010) that medication administration should not be seen purely as a mechanistic act but one that demands thought and professional judgement. All staff agreeing to administer medication should have received appropriate training specific to the task they will be performing. This information must be clearly documented. An example of an Administration of Medicines Record is included in the Practical Resources section. It is expected that the member of staff administering the medication should know the child and that a process for clearly identifying the child before medication is given is followed.

When administering medication, it is important to adhere to the five rights (Rs) of medication administration:

- right medication
- right child
- right dose of medication
- right route for administration
- right time

(NMC, 2008)

A record of when and what medicines were administered to the child and by whom must be clearly documented. See exemplar templates within the Practical Resources section.

In some situations, when a child is able to, and after discussion with parents, the child can be encouraged to take responsibility for managing their own medicines and procedures. Where this is the case, this should be reflected within the individual health care plans. Where a child will need help or supervision with the administering of medication, this should also be clearly recorded on the health care plan, along with details of who will provide the child with support to administer their medication.

It will be important to ensure that the teacher, SENCO, headteacher and office staff all have access to the family's contact details including mobile, home and work telephone numbers. A central record of the child's appointments, medicines and emergency procedures also needs to be accessible to all these staff and regularly updated. Use of IT rather than paper should facilitate this to enable a centrally controlled version-labelled record to be kept. To ensure rights to confidentiality and data protection are maintained, however, this should be password protected.

Practical resources

In this section, the following practical resources are provided:

1   Example letter inviting parents to contribute to the development of an individual health care plan for their child
2   Model process for developing individual health care plans
3   Example individual health care plan
4   Example parental agreement for setting to administer medicine form
5   Example record of medicine administered to an individual child form
6   Example record of medicine administered to all children form
7   Example staff training record
8   Handwashing diagram

1 Example letter inviting parents to contribute to the development of an individual health care plan for their child

Dear Parent,

Developing an individual health care plan for your child

Thank you for informing us of your child's medical condition. I enclose a copy of the school's policy for supporting pupils at school with medical conditions for your information.

A central requirement of the policy is for an individual health care plan to be prepared, setting out what support each pupil needs and how this will be provided. Individual health care plans are developed in partnership between the school, parents, pupils and the relevant health care professional who can advise on your child's case. The aim is to ensure that we know how to support your child effectively and to provide clarity about what needs to be done, when and by whom. Although individual health care plans are likely to be helpful in the majority of cases, it is possible that not all children will require one. We will need to make judgements about how your child's medical condition impacts their ability to participate fully in school life, and the level of detail within plans will depend on the complexity of their condition and the degree of support needed.

A meeting to start the process of developing your child's individual health care plan has been scheduled for xx/xx/xx. I hope that this is convenient for you and would be grateful if you could confirm whether you are able to attend. The meeting will involve [the following people]. Please let us know if you would like us to invite another medical practitioner, health care professional or specialist and provide any other evidence you would like us to consider at the meeting as soon as possible.

If you are unable to attend, it would be helpful if you could complete the attached individual health care plan template and return it, together with any relevant evidence, for consideration at the meeting. I [or another member of staff involved in plan development or pupil support] would be happy for you to contact me [them] by email or to speak by phone if this would be helpful.

Yours sincerely,

2 Model process for developing individual health care plans (DfE, 2015)

Parent or health care professional informs school that child has been newly diagnosed, or is due to attend new a school, or is due to return to school after a long-term absence or that needs have changed.

Headteacher or senior member of school staff to whom this has been delegated co-ordinates meeting to discuss child's medical support needs and identifies member of school staff who will provide support.

Meeting to discuss and agree on need for Individual Health Care Plan to include key school staff, child, parent, relevant health care professional and other medical/health clinicians as appropriate (or to consider written evidence provided by them.

Develop individual health care plan in partnership - agree who leads on writing it. Input from health care professional must be provided.

School staff training needs identified.

Health care professional commissions/delivers training and staff signed off as competent review date agreed.

Individual health care plan implemented and circulated to all relevant staff.

Individual health care plan reviewed annually or when condition changes. Parent or health care professional to initiate.

3 Individual health care plan (DfE, 2014)

Name of school/setting	
Child's name	
Group/class/form	
Date of birth	
Child's address	
Medical diagnosis or condition	
Date	
Review date	

Family Contact Information

Name	
Phone no. (work)	
(home)	
(mobile)	
Name	
Relationship to child	
Phone no. (work)	
(home)	
(mobile)	

Clinic/Hospital Contact

Name	
Phone no.	

G.P.

Name	
Phone no.	
Who is responsible for providing support in school	

Describe medical needs and give details of child's symptoms, triggers, signs, treatments, facilities, equipment or devices, environmental issues etc.

_____

_____

Name of medication, dose, method of administration, when to be taken, side effects, contra-indications, administered by/self-administered with/without supervision

_____

_____

Daily care requirements

_____

_____

Specific support for the pupil's educational, social and emotional needs

_____

_____

Arrangements for school visits/trips etc.

_____

_____

Other information

_____

_____

Describe what constitutes an emergency and the action to take if this occurs.

_____

_____

Who is responsible in an emergency *(state if different for off-site activities)*?

_____

_____

Plan developed with

_____

_____

Staff training needed/undertaken – who, what, when

_____

_____

Form copied to

_____

_____

4 Parental agreement for setting to administer medicine (DfE, 2014)

The school/setting will not give your child medicine unless you complete and sign this form and the school or setting has a policy that the staff can administer medicine.

Date for review to be initiated by	
Name of school/setting	
Name of child	
Date of birth	
Group/class/form	
Medical condition or illness	

Medicine

Name/type of medicine (*as described on the container*)	
Expiry date	
Dosage and method	
Timing	
Special precautions/other instructions	
Are there any side effects that the school/setting needs to know about?	
Self-administration – y/n	
Procedures to take in an emergency	

NB: Medicines must be in the original container as dispensed by the pharmacy.

Contact Details

Name	
Daytime telephone no.	
Relationship to child	
Address	
I understand that I must deliver the medicine personally to	[agreed member of staff]

The above information is, to the best of my knowledge, accurate at the time of writing, and I give consent to school/setting staff administering medicine in accordance with the school/setting policy. I will inform the school/setting immediately, in writing, if there is any change in dosage or frequency of the medication or if the medicine is stopped.

Signature(s) _____   Date _____

5 Record of medicine administered to an individual child (DfE, 2014)

Name of school/setting	
Name of child	
Date medicine provided by parent	
Group/class/form	
Quantity received	
Name and strength of medicine	
Expiry date	
Quantity returned	
Dose and frequency of medicine	

Staff signature _____

Signature of parent _____

Date	
Time given	
Dose given	
Name of member of staff	
Staff initials	

Date	
Time given	
Dose given	
Name of member of staff	
Staff initials	

(Continue overleaf as needed)

6 Record of medicine administered to all children (DfE, 2014)

Name of school/setting

Date	Child's name	Time	Name of medicine	Dose given	Any reactions	Signature of staff	Print name

7 Staff training record – administration of medicines (DfE, 2014)

Name of school/setting	
Name of staff	
Type of training received	
Date of training completed	
Training provided by	
Profession and title	

I confirm that [name of member of staff] has received the training detailed above and is competent to carry out any necessary treatment. I recommend that the training is updated [add date for review of training].

Trainer's signature _____

Date _____

I confirm that I have received the training detailed above.

Staff signature _____

Date _____

Suggested review date _____

8 Handwashing

National Safety Patient Agency (2008).

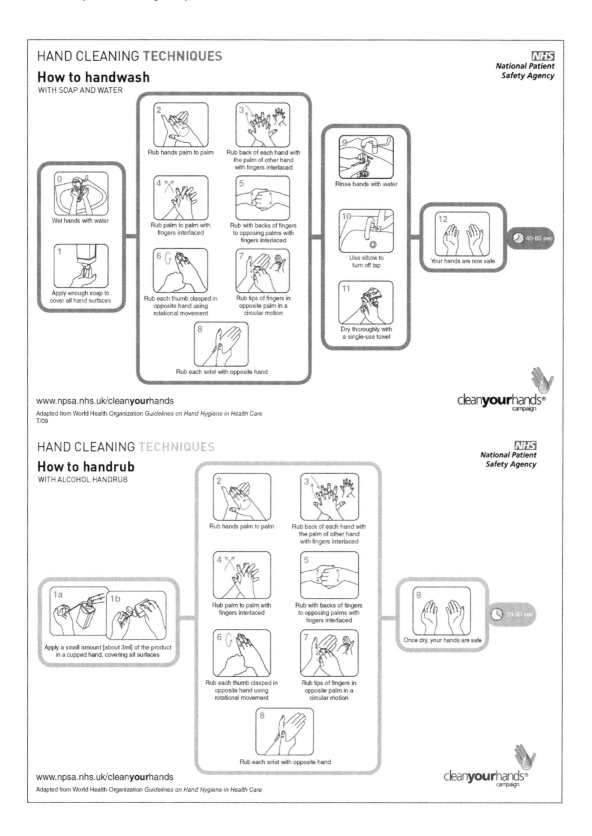

Concluding comments

This chapter has provided an overview of some important health care principles and practical skills which may be carried out by a teacher or key nominated member of staff for a child with a life-limiting or life-threatening condition while attending school. Each child is unique and will have their own health care plan. The health care plan must be child and family centred. Teachers and the multi-disciplinary team collaborate and communicate around the child. Teachers will be guided by the child or their family; they may require formal training from a health care professional in order to ensure their competence to carry out many health care tasks.

5 Communicating with the child and their family

In this chapter, we:

- Consider effective ways to communicate with a child with life-limiting or life-threatening conditions
- Consider the particular needs of siblings of children with a life-limiting or life-threatening condition and ways to communicate with them effectively and sensitively
- Consider effective ways to communicate with the parents of a child with life-limiting or life-threatening conditions
- Explore why communication is difficult
- Provide some key principles and strategies for communicating effectively with the child and their parents
- Consider ways to complete risk assessments collaboratively with the child and their parents
- Explore ways to communicate sensitively in writing to parents of a child with a life-limiting or life-threatening condition

Introduction

The Teaching for Life research showed that many teachers lacked confidence when communicating with a child with a life-limiting or life-threatening condition and their family. The teachers reported that they often heard about a child who had a life-limiting or life-threatening condition from the child's parent, but that many parents were not emotionally able to talk further:

> "Some days they could talk about it – some days they couldn't. The child had a brother so the mother had to stay strong."

and

> "Liaison with the parents, that's the thing that is just so critical, to talk to the parents all the time. It's the most hideous time for them, but pretending it's not happening or ignoring it is just the worst thing."

When seeking information about the needs of a child with a life-limiting or life-threatening condition, teachers cited parents more than anyone else. This was partly because teachers had received useful ongoing information from parents in the past or because they assumed that the parents would have the information they needed. They wanted to respect parents' wishes, and some recognised how parents may need differing types of support from a school, as one explained:

> "I think it's going to be very dependent on the parents, because if you've got proactive parents who are confident communicators with professionals it's probably going to be more cohesive, but if you have parents who are less confident, younger, who are not able to ... manage significant issues in their lives themselves, it's going to fall more to the school to be the ones going out looking to see what's out there because if it isn't coming from the medical people then the school is going to have that responsibility because they're the people seeing the child on a day-to-day basis."

Teachers described how overwhelmed and exhausted parents can be, recognising that parents were coping with their own emotional trauma and were simply unable to provide teachers with all the information they needed.

> "[H]is parents didn't want to really even discuss it, because I think the parents were so devastated and angry."

Teachers were clear that parents' needs and choices needed to be respected, but sometimes teachers found themselves in the unenviable position of not knowing what they could say and not say. For example,

> "You have to check that you're not saying something they don't want you to say and that they haven't broached with the child. Yeah, eggshells all the time, isn't it?"

Two thirds of the teachers in the research identified the pupil with a life-limiting or life-threatening conditions as a key source of information. Teachers provided many examples about their observations and perceptions of children's experiences. However, this remained complex as, apart from sharing a few examples of children not wishing to talk about their needs, they provided no examples of children who had. A typical comment was,

> "He didn't want to really even discuss it,"

Teachers were particularly anxious about how to communicate about death, for example,

> "I'd be concerned about how I would talk about this to the student and their family."

Summary

The research concluded that in addition to needing information about life-limiting or life-threatening conditions, teachers also needed support with and reassurance about:

- the principles and skills required for communicating with the child about serious illness, death and bereavement
- ways to sensitively and professionally discuss the needs of the child with the child's parents
- ways to communicate with siblings of children with life-limiting or life-threatening conditions.

Policy review

The Department for Education (DfE, 2015) recognise that open, honest, sensitive and respectful communications between the school and the parents and family of a child with medical conditions are essential to be able to support them as effectively and fully as possible. The DfE (2015) also acknowledge that this relationship and the communication between home and school will often be impacted by difficult emotions:

> Parents of children with medical conditions are often concerned that their child's health will deteriorate when they attend school. This is because pupils with long-term and complex medical conditions may require ongoing support, medicines or care while at school to help them manage their condition and keep them well.

(DfE, 2015: 5)

The DfE (2015) highlight that:

- '[I]t is therefore important that parents feel confident that schools will provide effective support for their child's medical condition and that pupils feel safe. In making decisions about the support they provide, schools should establish relationships with relevant local health services to help them.
- It is crucial that schools . . . listen to and value the views of parents and pupils.'

(DfE, 2015: 5)

In relation to the role of parents to provide information to the school, the DfE (2015) identify the following key points:

- 'Parents should provide the school with sufficient and up-to-date information about their child's medical needs.
- They may in some cases be the first to notify the school that their child has a medical condition.
- Parents are key partners and should be involved in the development and review of their child's individual healthcare plan, and may be involved in its drafting.
- They should carry out any action they have agreed to as part of its implementation, e.g. provide medicines and equipment and ensure they or another nominated adult are contactable at all times.'

(DfE, 2015: 13)

The DfE (2015) also acknowledge the importance of the role of the child themselves in being a key information sharer:

- 'Pupils with medical conditions will often be best placed to provide information about how their condition affects them.
- They should be fully involved in discussions about their medical support needs and contribute as much as possible to the development of, and comply with, their individual healthcare plan.'

(DfE, 2015: 13)

In addition to the DfE (2015) guidance, the need to communicate and engage effectively with all children and their parents, including those with life-limiting or life-threatening conditions, is also embedded within the Teachers' Standards (DfE, 2011). This explicitly states that a teacher is expected to maintain high standards of ethics and behaviour by:

- treating pupils with dignity
- building relationships rooted in mutual respect
- having regard for the need to safeguard pupils' well-being
- showing tolerance and respect
- ensuring that personal beliefs are not expressed in ways which exploit pupils' vulnerability

A teacher must also:

- have a clear understanding of the needs of all pupils, including those with special educational needs . . . those with disabilities . . . to engage and support them.
- communicate effectively with parents with regard to pupils' achievements and well-being.

Practical considerations

Communicating effectively with a child with a life-limiting or life-threatening condition

Reflective activity

- What key issues do you think you would need to be aware of when communicating with a child with a life-limiting or life-threatening condition?
- What approach would you take to setting up effective communications?
- Are there any aspects that you are concerned about?
- Would you consider talking directly to the child about their condition?
- Or do you think that this would be addressed solely by the medical professionals?
- Are there others in the school who would be able to support you with this or be able to advise you about the best ways to interact and communicate with a child with a life-limiting or life-threatening condition?

A good principle for all teachers who are engaged in any health-related education or communication is to 'start from where children are'.

- Cognitively: What does the child know?
- Affectively: How does the child feel?
- Behaviourally: What is the child doing?

What does the child know?

Most countries of the world understand health in terms of a person experiencing balance and harmony inside the body, something that can only be achieved if a person is similarly in harmony with the spiritual and physical universe outside of the body. Illness is the result of imbalance. Beyond the Western world, what the UK calls the complementary therapies that seek to restore balance are mainstream, and concepts of germs, bacteria, viruses and physiological malfunctions requiring surgery may be relatively alien in some countries. Understandings about an illness will be influenced by a family's culture, friends' beliefs and experiences, their own experiences and what they hear through the media. In addition, children's understandings may be affected by their stage of cognitive, emotional and social development.

Piko and Bak (2006) report that children think that their illnesses are caused by cold air; icy drinks; bacteria and viruses from other people, dogs, classmates, not washing hands; sudden change in climate; cats' hair; exhaust fumes; alcohol and smoking; too much spicy food, chips and hamburgers and not enough fruit. Some think that their illness is a punishment for a misdemeanour or, because their previous experience of ill health was an infection, that they are now infectious. If they don't understand the purpose of a medical treatment, they may view it as negative and useless.

The children in Knighting et al.'s (2010) study found that children viewed cancer in a negative way from an early age. Children thought that it was caused by cigarettes, sun and sunbeds, illness, drugs, pollution from cars, gas, microwaves, television, fires and mobile phones, alcohol, sugar, lack of exercise, plastic surgery, sex and violence. They thought that the consequences of having cancer were immobility (needing to use wheelchairs or crutches or being bed bound), hair loss, pain, death, cure and spending a lot of time in hospital.

Teachers need to find out what a child knows and what a child does not know, and they need to be informed about the culture and beliefs of the child's family. From this dialogue, a teacher has a baseline on which to build a relationship and good communication.

What does the child feel?

Children with life-limiting or life-threatening conditions experience symptoms from their illness; symptoms from their treatment; symptoms related to the time and effort required to keep appointments and comply with treatment, being absent from school and juggling the rest of life; and symptoms post-treatment. Robinson and Summers (2012) summarise:

- Physical symptoms could include difficulties in eating, seeing, walking, hearing, hunger, nausea, poor sleep, sensitivity to light, pain, weight loss or weight gain, hair loss and many children will feel very fatigued.
- Mental/cognitive symptoms could include difficulties with concentration, slowing down of information processing, memory loss and a general decline in intellectual abilities.
- Social symptoms could include difficulties keeping up with peers, missing 'building blocks of learning' through absence, separation from school and peer activities, being teased or bullied due to changes in appearance or ability, changes in relationships and social isolation.
- Emotional symptoms could include anxiety, sadness, stress, repression and loss of control as parents decide for them, feeling a need to please parents/others, feeling left behind, changed self-concept, lowered self-confidence, feeling and looking different and feeling inferior.

In summary, a life-limiting or life-threatening condition and the related treatment and upheaval 'made me look different, feel different and act differently' (Joanne, aged 11, in Chambers, 2008: 73).

What is the child doing?

If a child cannot communicate, that is 'take in' or 'give out' words, teachers need other strategies. Teachers can learn a lot about a child's feelings from observing them. Geldard and Geldard (2002) note signs of emotional distress include whether a child's speech is unclear, silent, stumbling, interrupted by breath holding, sighing or gasping or whether a child's behaviour is unusually:

- quiet, careful, self-absorbed, flat, constricted, repetitive, solitary, limited
- loud, risky, without boundaries, aggressive
- needy, defensive, avoidant of others, trusting or mistrusting
- regressive, that is appropriate to a younger age (this is about obtaining feelings of security from re-living a time when life felt safer)

Once we have a better understanding of the starting point for the child (what they know, how they feel and what they are doing), we can then develop more effective approaches to communicating effectively with them both about their condition and about them as a child. In this, a key central principle is to embed an understanding of the fact that there is more to the child than just the condition. Often children with life-limiting or life-threatening conditions can become very frustrated and/or withdrawn, as they feel that they as a person or individual have become lost or forgotten about as a result of the dominant discussions about the condition and their treatment. Make sure, therefore, that time is made for relaxed communications and interactions with the child which are not focused on the condition and/or medical treatment plans.

Communicating effectively with siblings of a child with a life-limiting or life-threatening condition

The three questions listed earlier (What does the child know? How does the child feel? What is the child doing?) also apply to siblings of a child with a life-limiting or life-threatening condition. Siblings may not have the medical and physical experiences, but they have significant emotional needs. Siblings can get neglected, and yet they often shoulder a huge burden of trying to be strong and 'not needy' for their families. Teachers may be a vital support system for siblings.

> I clearly remember the day the school secretary walked into our class with a message for Miss Johnson. They both looked in my direction with sad faces and their heads slanted in sympathy, a look I have come to resent with a passion! My stomach immediately tied into a knot and my mouth felt dry with fear. All I could think was that my brother had died and that my parents were too busy and upset to tell me. I was trembling with pure terror when Miss walked towards me. She bent down and whispered, "Your neighbour rang to say that she will collect you half an hour later, same place." I had a hard time holding back the tears of relief!
>
> (Michael's sister, aged 11, in Chambers, 2008: 19)

As with the discussions about ensuring 'normal' conversations and interactions with the child with a life-limiting or life-threatening condition which are nothing about their condition and/or health care plan, the same is again hugely relevant to siblings of a child with a life-limiting or life-threatening condition. Whilst it is important that staff are aware and that they engage with the child with sensitivity and understanding, it is also important for the child to be seen as an individual and not just the brother/sister of the child with a life-limiting or life-threatening condition. As with the child themselves, siblings can become frustrated, angry or withdrawn if the attention that they receive is only focused on the needs of their brother/sister.

Make time to get to know the sibling as an individual in their own right, and ensure that opportunities are available for them to relax and pursue/talk about their own hobbies, interests and aspirations. Ensure that this is done in a supportive and positive context that helps to reassure the sibling that it is okay for them to continue to want to enjoy life and have their own aspirations and that they should not feel guilty or upset with themselves for having these natural feelings.

Communicating effectively with parents

Reflective activity

- What do you think would be the barriers to effective communication with parents?
- Can these be overcome?
- How?

- What approaches could you develop/extend/enhance to make communication with parents as easy and supportive as possible?
- What would you be most worried about?

As the teachers in our research recognised, communications with the parents of a child with a life-limiting or life-threatening condition can be very difficult, for a number of reasons. These include:

- the stage of the emotional cycle that the parent is experiencing at that time
- time availability – parents will be exhausted with the emotional intensity of supporting their child, as well as trying to maintain and sustain a 'normal' family life. They may also have a number of time-consuming medical appointments to attend, many of which may be some distance from their home.
- Parents may wish school to be seen to be the place of 'normality' and may therefore be reluctant to bring the difficult details of the medical condition into the school environment.

The emotional cycle

Grief, including before actual bereavement, is a complex and difficult process which often includes a number of different stages, including:

- denial
- anger
- bargaining
- depression
- acceptance

The grief process, however, is not a simple linear process. It is not as straightforward as going through each of the stages identified above. Individuals will typically go through each of the stages but may do so in different ways, with each stage taking a different length of time to go through. Communicating with parents who are currently at any of the stages of the cycle will be difficult and challenging, and teachers will need to be mindful of the emotional sensitivity of the situation and, most importantly, ensure that they do not take any emotional outbursts from parents personally.

Why communication is difficult

Teachers, parents and children find it incredibly difficult to communicate with one another about the distressing subject of a sick child who could die because of how our brains work. The lowest part of our brains, the brain stem, has been with humans since we evolved from reptiles. Its function is to protect us and enable us to survive. If we sense danger such as the appearance of a tiger running towards us, our brain stem sends out a message to fight, flee or freeze in order to keep us safe. This does not involve any thought; it is a quick, instinctive, immediate behavioural response.

Unlike reptiles, mammals including humans have a middle brain, situated above the brain stem, that deals with emotion and memory. Sometimes when we sense danger, we are ready to fight, flee or freeze, but we pause for a millisecond as the middle brain springs into action. It appraises the danger by accessing our unconscious memories and core feelings. It tells us that our body is feeling fear, but it also tells us that the tiger is actually a placid large cat and is not dangerous, it is not frightening, and we start to feel calmer and we need not run. The middle brain is our emotional regulator.

The middle brain works closely with the upper and largest part of our brain, the neocortex. The neocortex is our conscious self, and its huge size distinguishes us from other mammals. This is where the brain reasons, problem solves, reflects, empathises and thinks. This part of the brain will only work well if all is emotionally and chemically calm in the brain. When the brain is calm it releases chemicals such as oxytocin and opioids, and our whole being feels alert and content. We can rationally work out what we think and need to do; we can put our thoughts and feelings into words.

Teachers will know that one cannot reason with a child who is in a high state of anxiety, per-haps frozen with fear. With time and space, a child may be able to consciously self-regulate. The child is able to get their middle brain and upper brain to work together; the middle brain is able to calm down the impulse to freeze coming from their brain stem. As the feelings of fear reduce, the child becomes less frozen, the chemicals in their brain re-balance, their upper brain is able to function and the child can think, listen and communicate with the teacher.

Some situations are so stressful, either in one short sharp burst such as a serious accident or the chronic ongoing stress of worrying about a child who is very ill and could die, that the middle brain (emotion) and upper brain (thinking) do not work well together. People are unable to consciously self-regulate and calm down their own emotions sufficiently to think because they are so overwhelming. The brain stem urges us to flee, fight or freeze, the middle brain identifies the strong feelings of fear, the upper brain's functions are overridden. Problem solving, reflection, empathy, thinking and words become almost impossible. The whole body is in a chronic state of high alert. Parents and children are simply too frightened to be able to communicate in words.

> Cancer ... tears families apart, breaking bonds. Causing pain and fear to all families who ... watch a family member fight it.
>
> (child in School 4, in Knighting et al., 2010: 295)

Reflective activity

- Think of a time or situation in which you may have experienced an emotionally stress-ful situation. This does not need to necessarily be directly linked to working with a child with a life-limiting or life-threatening condition; it may have been as a response to other personal circumstances.
- Calmly reflect on which instinctive responses were triggered and how you then coped with the situation.
- Is there anything that you could have done differently?
- Could you have coped with the situation in any other way?
- What key issues/responses would you want to be aware of for the future?
- Is there any support you could access and which would be useful in coping with stressful situations to enable all parts of the brain to function effectively?

How to communicate with a child and their parents

The primary aims of communication between a teacher and an anxious child or parent are to promote calm and trust and to keep it simple. Preparation includes finding a safe, private environment and an occasion when there is sufficient time. It is often better to delay communication until both of these are available, perhaps at the end of a day.

Being there

The most important communication a teacher can give to a vulnerable child and their parent is 'being there'. Do not underestimate the power of physical presence, as opposed to avoidance. No words, and certainly no special words, are required. Even if a child is away from school, be around, be close, be present, be near.

> The teachers and my mates kept in constant contact. Phone calls, letters, visits and e mail. They were brilliant.
>
> (Jerome, aged 14, in Chambers, 2008: 15)

Mirror body language

Mirroring body language, if done with subtlety, provides a non-verbal, sub-conscious message to the child's or parent's brain that helps them feel that the teacher is 'with' them. Matching the tone and speed of speech and eye contact can also promote feelings of oneness and comfort.

Listening without words

Words are not the natural communication medium of children. Expressing themselves in words, both orally and in writing, is the task of development, socialisation and education. The task is made much harder when the subject is highly sensitive and emotional because of what happens in the brain. Most adults find this extremely difficult. Non-verbal communication through media such as art, clay, plasticine, sand, drawing, movement/non-verbal behaviour and so forth is much easier, and simply providing sensory opportunities for child-led play/creativity can provide really helpful opportunities to enable a child to 'get the feelings out of themselves' within a safe place. Without such opportunities, a child's difficult feelings do not go away; they are stored within the brain and body. They build and build until a child is so weighed down that they become completely non-communicative and shut down, or the feelings build to such a high pressure that they erupt out of the body in the form of inappropriate behaviour.

Words are not needed, but a teacher could provide a very simple task such as, 'Imagine a rabbit has come to school today. Paint a picture of the rabbit at school'. A child is unlikely to realise that they have projected something of themselves into their depictions. A teacher simply acknowledges the task and thanks them, or they could show an appreciation of the care or skill that has gone into the picture. Unconsciously, the child has released some feelings through the process of creating their picture, and this is good. They do not have to talk about it for good to have been done, but of course a teacher can listen if they wish to. These are not pictures/artefacts for public display. A child might be encouraged to take them home.

Releasing feelings, a very little at a time, can help the child's brain to calm, their upper brain to function, and maybe, if a teacher has 'been there' and has built trust in non-verbal ways, a child might be able to begin to communicate a little in words.

Teachers' communication

When a child or adult is communicating difficult feelings or information, the teacher needs to give the appearance of a calm, safe place into which a person can put their problems and know that they are being held by a safe, strong pair of hands. Parents and children need to know and feel that the teacher can 'cope'; they will not confide in a teacher if they think the teacher is too vulnerable to handle the information. It is not about having a 'stiff upper lip'; being non-emotional is a sign of not coping. A teacher can be kind, caring and concerned, but they need to try not to crumble whilst the child is going through treatment, and the family needs the teacher to be emotionally steady and strong. They need the teacher to gently help them with the thinking they are unable to do for themselves. Teachers must have opportunities to release the feelings from themselves too, so it is important that they can share with an appropriate colleague or use a teachers' counselling service.

Active listening

If a parent or child is able to talk, the golden rule is,

> Be prepared to listen – again and again and again!
>
> (Mr Wright, form teacher, in Chambers, 2008: 68)

Reflective activity

- Which key principles would you identify as key to active listening?
- Do you think that you are a good active listener?
- What strategies/approaches do you use to be an effective active listener?
- Is there anything further that you think you could do to develop the skill of being an active listener?
- How could you support others in your school to understand the key principles of active listening and be able to incorporate those within their own approaches to communication with others?

Active listening comprises:

- good, quiet, calm, attentive listening, allowing the child or parent to finish what they want to say
- use of encouraging body language by the teacher such as good eye contact, nodding, smiling, an open posture, open hands, leaning forward
- reflecting the content of what has been said by paraphrasing, 'So you think you are falling behind . . .'
- reflecting the feelings that have been expressed, such as 'It seems to me that you are understandably very anxious'.

Helpful talking

If the time is right or necessary to initiate a question, teachers need to keep in mind:

- A verbal question is always received alongside non-verbal communication, so expression, intonation, tone, emphasis, eye contact, posture and gestures matter.

- Keep the language direct, clear and simple. Always seek clarification of any medical jargon picked up from health care professionals, and take care to avoid educational jargon.
- Remember that the child or parent's upper thinking brain is not working properly. Be prepared to speak slowly and to repeat. Acknowledge that it is difficult to think and to remember when one is so tired and worried. Offer to clarify and repeat further. Offer to write points down.
- Keep questions to a minimum and space them out over time.
- Ask about one issue. Decide what the priority issue is, and focus on that one.
- Try out questions with a colleague to see if they think that the phrasing is clear and unambiguous.
- Focus on questions which impact the child's learning or school experience or the experience of others within the school. If a teacher comes across as being unnecessarily intrusive, this will reduce trust within the relationship. It is for the parent or child to choose if they wish to share other information. For some families, school might represent the only 'normal' and consistent part of their lives. The family's strong need to keep it that way might explain a reluctance to bring this difficult issue into the school environment. A teacher might need to clearly acknowledge this wish and reassure a family that 'normality' is something they can strive for together.
- Open questions can encourage a person to express themselves in the way that they can help a teacher to understand more fully the situation and can show a child or parent that a teacher is open to listening.
- Closed questions may be useful for specific information when time is limited but can shut a potential communication down before it has begun and can give the message that the questioner cannot cope/does not want to hear more.
- Ask about a family's cultural beliefs about health, illness, treatment, death and bereavement. It demonstrates genuine interest and care. Use this understanding to ensure that questions are culturally appropriate and sensitive.
- Encourage feedback, such as, 'Are we agreed? Is that clear?' and offer future support.

Communicating about death

All the communication techniques discussed in this chapter, starting with being there, body language, listening without words and active listening and helpful talking, are important building blocks that continue through to discussions about death. Should a child with a life-limiting or life-threatening condition choose to talk to a teacher about their own potential death, it is natural for a teacher to want to avoid the subject or protect the child, but it is a great compliment to a teacher that a child has chosen to talk to them.

> Children can deal with the truth, no matter how difficult or traumatic, what they find hard are untruths.
>
> (Adams, 2010: 1)

If a child initiates a conversation:

- The maxim, of 'start from where the child is' stands, so be guided by the child. They will ask only what they are ready to hear.
- Answer them, but don't overload the child.
- Be honest about what you don't know; perhaps ask the child what they think.
- Use simple words and real words such as 'dead', not euphemisms.

If a parent initiates a conversation, almost the same applies:

- Be guided by the parent. They will only tell what they are ready to tell. They will ask only what they are ready to hear.
- Answer them, but don't overload them.
- Be honest about what you don't know; perhaps ask them what they think.
- Use simple words, use their words.

If a teacher needs to initiate a difficult conversation, sentences starting with 'I' can be helpful:

- 'I am saddened to hear that . . .'
- 'I was sorry to hear . . .'
- 'I heard . . . '

Then:

- 'I understand that this is very difficult . . .'
- 'I can see that you . . .'
- 'I imagine . . .'
- 'I'd like to . . .'
- 'I'm wondering whether . . .'

Followed by a gentle exploratory question:

- 'Could you tell me a little . . .'
- 'How can I . . .'
- 'Tell me more about . . .'

Be careful of 'you must be', as if it is not an accurate perception, it can backfire and irritate.

There are many children's books that can help both a dying child and other children to understand and navigate serious illness, death and bereavement. These can be used with children or recommended to parents to read with their children at home (see Practical Resources section).

Confidential conversations

If a child tells a teacher something about their condition, their fears and hopes, they are likely to assume that this will not be shared with others, including their parents. Where confidentiality conflicts with safeguarding, safeguarding must be take priority. However, in other cases it is a matter of professional judgement. If in doubt, a teacher should tell the child that they might have to share the content of the conversation with others and/or seek advice. At the point when a teacher decides they are definitely going to share with another, they should tell the child beforehand so that the child knows that the teacher is always open and trustworthy.

Similarly, a teacher should avoid being put into the lonely position of 'keeping secrets' for parents. A parent who asks a teacher not to divulge to a child that they have a life-limiting or life-threatening condition needs to know that the teacher respects their wishes but will need to inform the headteacher and work within the school policy. Teachers need to explain that they cannot promise to stop a child finding out about their condition themselves or from others; children have access to the Internet. In addition to teachers' support, parents can be directed to useful books and web sites. They need to talk with their health care professional, and they need to take things one step at a time and be led by their child.

Completing risk assessments collaboratively with the child and their parents

At times a risk assessment will need to be developed in collaboration with the child and their parents. This will detail what the child can and cannot reasonably be expected to participate in, what reasonable adjustments need to be made, by whom and when. This will require consultation with parents and pupils and should be developed in conjunction with other specialists (e.g. school nurse and occupational therapists). The risk assessment can be completed to address day-to-day participation and engagement in school or for specific activities such as school trips and visits. Once complete, this document should be kept in a central location, accessible by all those who need access (bearing in mind confidentiality) and updated regularly. This should be seen as a crucial document which will be regularly reviewed and updated to ensure that it reflects changing circumstances for the child. In this:

> A risk assessment is not about creating huge amounts of paperwork, but rather about identifying sensible measures to control the risks in your workplace.
>
> (HSE, 2014: 1)

It is therefore central to thinking about what risks there might be and minimising or removing the potential hazards, in this case for the child with a life-limiting or life-threatening condition. As part of the process, it may be helpful to consider the following key prompts:

1 **Identify hazards.**
   Either by walking around and observing how people use equipment and spaces or through discussion (parents, school nurse, occupational therapists), identify any hazards for the child. This may be in relation to physical spaces or activities, training for key staff, access to medication and so on.

2 **Think about who might be harmed.**
   In this instance, this is primarily the child with a life-limiting or life-threatening condition. However, it is important to also consider whether there are any associated risks to other children or staff that also need to be identified and addressed – for example, safe storage of medication; safe disposal of sharps and the like.

3 **Evaluate the risk.**
   Consider the likelihood of risk and the potential harm that would occur. In this it is important to bear in mind the following:
   'Risk cannot be eliminated what needs to be considered is what is 'reasonably practicable' to protect people from harm. This means balancing the level of risk against the measures needed to control the real risk in terms of money, time or trouble. However, you do not need to take action if it would be grossly disproportionate to the level of risk. Your risk assessment should only include what you could reasonably be expected to know – you are not expected to anticipate unforeseeable risks.'
   (HSE.gov.uk, accessed 21/10/16)

4 **Complete a risk assessment** (see exemplar form in Practical Resources section).
   A risk assessment must be suitable and sufficient; that is, it should show that:

   • 'a proper check was made
   • you asked who might be affected
   • you dealt with all the obvious significant hazards, taking into account the number of people who could be involved

- the precautions are reasonable, and the remaining risk is low
- you involved your employees or their representatives in the process'

(HSE, 2014: 4)

Some practical steps that school staff could take include:

- 'trying a less risky option
- preventing access to the hazards
- organising your work/environment to reduce exposure to the hazard for yourself and others
- issuing protective equipment
- providing welfare facilities such as first aid and washing facilities
- involving and consulting with workers/users (this is likely to include parents, the child themselves and other pupils)'

(HSE, 2014: 3)

At this point, it will be absolutely essential to ensure that the child and their parents are fully involved in the process of identifying and reviewing the level of risk associated with attendance and engagement in school and a variety of school-based activities. Try to plan a suitable time when parents are able to review this with relevant school staff so that the plan is collaborative, relevant and accessible to all, including the child. It may also be useful here to involve health care professionals in developing the risk assessment so that it fully reflects the range of perspectives and understandings about actual risks that the child can face whilst in school (see discussions about communicating with other professionals in Chapter 6). Having completed the risk assessment form, it will then be absolutely essential to distribute it to all relevant parties. Do not just file it away or keep it in an office where it is not referred to.

5   Review and update.
The specific risk assessment needs to be regularly reviewed and updated, since risks can increase or diminish. In addition, the organisation needs to learn through the process of how to understand and minimise risks over time.

Communicating in writing with parents

Teachers need to be mindful not only of verbal communications with parents but also of the importance of positive and supportive written communications with parents. There will be times when the school is requested to provide written reports on the child for various multi-professional meetings, and there will be times when the school will need to contact the parent in writing to take forward appropriate levels of support within the school. As with verbal communication, it is essential to ensure that a clear, straightforward and supportive approach to all written communications is used.

Reflective activity

A school is needing to write to a parent. Consider the following communication styles.

1. *We understand from the communication received on 2nd May that your child may be in need of an EHC plan to respond to the diagnosis of Duchenne muscular dystrophy, and this will be dealt with under the school's Inclusion Policy, section 2.* (long and ambiguous)

Or

I was personally reviewing Peter's needs at school, and as an inclusive school we have structures already in place we can use to support him. (active and succinct, but uses educational jargon)

Or

Following the letter that I received about Peter having muscular dystrophy, I have looked into what he is going to need when he is at school. We already have some support in place and would like to meet with you to take this forward. (no jargon)

2. *The school has been apprised of action it may wish to take in regards to Peter's illness, assuming that the appropriate medical information is furnished.* (third person, lacks ownership or clarity about responsibility)

Or

I have been informed of Peter's condition. Please contact the secretary to arrange a meeting. It would be very helpful if you could bring with you all relevant medical records and information pertaining to Peter so we can discuss his needs whilst at school. (clear, direct and is unambiguous about who is supposed to do what, but a very long sentence with long words).

Or

I have heard about Peter's condition. Please could you contact the secretary to arrange a meeting with me. Please could you bring Peter's medical records and any other information that you think is important. We will discuss how we can best support him. (short words, short sentences)

3. *We will consider the matter of responding to your child's medical condition shortly.* (passive)

Or

We will be taking action very soon in regard to your child's medical condition, as it is a high priority. (active)

Or

We understand that your child's medical condition is very important. We will be taking action very soon. (starts by acknowledging that the parent has been heard and then says what the school is doing)

4. *I understand your son has a terminal condition due to progressive degeneration of his autonomic nervous system, and as such we are required to introduce palliative care.* (full of technical language that a reader may be unfamiliar with; even words like 'terminal' could be misinterpreted)

Or

I understand that Peter's condition is very serious and that it would be helpful if we could put measures in place to manage likely changes. (gentler, shorter and more proactive)

Or

I understand that Peter's condition is very serious, and we need to plan for likely changes in his health. (shorter words)

5. *You may like to come to a meeting where we could consider ways forward, and it would be helpful to have more information.* (ambiguous in terms of next steps and responsibility)

Or

Please contact the secretary, Mrs Jones, in the next few days to arrange to visit the school, and please bring with you a list of appointments and medications for Peter. (direct and clear)

Or

Please contact the secretary, Mrs Jones, in the next few days, to arrange when you can visit the school. Please bring Peter's list of appointments and medications. (shorter sentences)

6. *We have had a discussion about this matter.* (ambiguous and use of nominalisation).

Or

The senior leadership team discussed this yesterday. (clearer in terms of what was done, by whom)

7. *In the meeting, it would be useful to discuss Peter's condition, his medical history and its impact on his schooling. We also need to consider his medication and how a nurse might better work with him.* (long, rambling, unclear)

Or

For the meeting, please could you bring

- *a list of Peter's medications*
- *a list of hospital visits and appointments*

I will bring

- *Peter's school records*
- *the school nurse's report*

(list that indicates tasks and makes them clear)

Practical resources

In this section, the following practical resources are provided:

1   A list of children's books about experiencing illness, death and bereavement
2   Example of a risk assessment form
3   Example of a supportive and effective letter home to parents

1 Children's books about experiencing illness, death and bereavement

Bickford-Smith, C. (2015) *The Fox and the Star*. London: Particular Books.   Loss and learning to accept change
Brown, L. K., and Brown, M. (1998) *When Dinosaurs Die: A Guide to Understanding Death*. New York: Little Brown Books for Young Readers/Hachette Book Group.   Explores lots of reasons people die
Crossley, D. (2000) *Muddles, Puddles and Sunshine: Your Activity Book to Help When Someone Had Died (Early Years)*. Stroud: Hawthorn.   Activities for children to remember a loved one
Durrant, A. (2013) *Always and Forever*. London: Picture Corgi, Random House.   Bereavement, loss and grief
Heegaard, M. (2003) *Living Well with My Serious Illness*. Manhattan: Taylor Trade.   An activity book
Jeffers, O. (2010) *The Heart in the Bottle*. London: Harper Collins.   A book about loss and grief
Rosen, M. (2011) *Michael Rosen's Sad Book*. London: Walker Books.   A book that acknowledges the feelings of sadness
Schulz, C. M. (2002) *Why, Charlie Brown, Why? A Story about What Happens When a Friend Is Very Ill*. London: Ballantine Books, Random House.
Stickney, D. (1997) *Waterbugs and Dragonflies: Explaining Death to Young Children*. London: Bloomsbury Continuum.
Stokes, J. (2009) *The Secret C: Straight Talking about Cancer*. 2nd edn. Cheltenham: Winston's Wish.   Explains cancer to children
Sunderland, M. (2003) *The Day the Sea Went Out and Never Came Back (Helping Children with Feelings)*. London: Speechmark.   A book about the feelings of loss
Wagner, J. (1980) *John Brown, Rose and the Midnight Cat*. London: Puffin/Penguin Books.   Learning to accept change

2 Example of a risk assessment form

Date of Assessment:		ASSESSMENT NO:	
Assessed by (Name):		DEPARTMENT code:	
NATURE OF ACTIVITY:	Health & Safety Risk Assessment	DATE OF ACTIVITY:	
LOCATION:		REVIEW DATE:	

Hazard	Persons at Risk	Current Control Measures	Severity (S)	Likelihood (L)	Risk Rating (S × L)	Additional Control Measures Required	Revised Risk Rating	Action Sign Off Date/ Responsible Person

3 Example of a supportive and effective letter home to parents

Dear Mr and Mrs Brown,

Following the letter that I received about Peter having muscular dystrophy, I have looked into what he is going to need when he is at school. We already have some support in place, and I would like to meet with you to take this forward. We need to plan for likely changes in his health. Please could you contact Mrs Smith, the school secretary, to arrange a meeting with me.

Please could you bring:

- a list of Peter's medications
- a list of hospital visits and appointments
- and any other information that you think would be helpful

I will bring:

- Peter's school records
- The school nurse's report

Yours sincerely,

Concluding comments

Communicating effectively with both the child with a life-limiting or life-threatening condition and their parents is an essential yet very sensitive and complex issue for teachers in schools. Many teachers in our research expressed concern about 'getting it wrong' and therefore needed reassurances about the best way to manage these sensitive conversations.

This chapter has explained why communication is so difficult and yet so important. Communication starts with being there, listening without words, active listening, helpful talking and clear writing.

6 Communicating and collaborating with other professionals

In this chapter, we:

- Review who is responsible for providing services to support the needs of children with life-limiting or life-threatening conditions
- Consider the role of different professionals
- Explore ways to establish effective communication and collaboration with other professionals
- Emphasise the importance of multi-professional input into the health care plan

Introduction

Our Teaching for Life research showed that teachers were strongly committed to doing their best to support children with life-limiting or life-threatening conditions and that this started with being as informed as possible. In our research, we asked teachers where they had obtained or where they thought they would obtain information about the medical and non-medical needs of a child. Parents and the pupil themselves were cited the most frequently, followed by health professionals (see also Chapter 5). However, experience showed that none of these sources were fully providing what teachers needed, and many teachers supplemented their knowledge by turning to the Internet. In the research, teachers identified the following as key sources of information about the medical needs of children with life-limiting or life-threatening conditions:

Table 6.1a Sources of medical information identified by teachers

Sources of information	% of respondents identifying this as a key source of information
Parents/carer	83.3%
Paediatrician	75.6%
School nurse	70%
Occupational therapist	65.5%
The pupil themselves	62.2%
Web sites	60%
Physiotherapist	57.8%
General practitioner	55.6%
SENCO	37.8%
Textbooks	24.4%
Siblings	11.1%
Other	8.9%

Teachers then identified the following as key sources for finding information about the non-medical needs of children with life-limiting or life-threatening conditions:

Table 6.1b Sources of non-medical information identified by teachers

Source of Information	% of respondents identifying this as a key source of information
Parents/carer	76%
The pupil themselves	66%
Web sites	56%
Paediatrician	49%
School nurse	50%
Occupational therapist	42%
SENCO	36%
Physiotherapist	36%
Textbooks	33%
General practitioner	32%
Siblings	17%
Common Assessment Framework Assessment	1%
Educational psychologist	1%
Friends/family/colleagues with specialist experience/training	1%
School counsellor	1%
Specialist teachers	1%
Staff at other schools	1%
Specialist Teacher Service	1%
Early intervention team	1%

Teachers looked to health care professionals to be able to provide them with information about a child's medical and non-medical needs, but a barrier mentioned by many was poor communication and delays in receiving information, for example:

> *"I don't feel that I have a good, free and easy access to therapists. I'm very frustrated . . . how slowly the wheels turn."*

and

> *"We've got a couple of children where they're not life threatening, but they are significant conditions and they just fall through the gap. They didn't meet the criteria for this, they didn't meet the criteria for that and they need something more than we can offer them as a school, we need that other support and it isn't until you get to crisis point that anything seems to happen. And it doesn't seem fair for these children, that you are getting to crisis point and it's not fair for the school to not be able to support these children in the best way. Feeling like school is failing them, when in fact it's the external services."*

Teachers identified risks associated with delays in communication:

> *"It's a concern with children with significant difficulties that it took some time for the epilepsy nurse to contact us to say that she needed to come in to do training and the child had*

actually been in school for about 6 weeks with this medicine that no one had been trained in administering."

Teachers' concerns about delays in getting what they needed and when they needed it from health care professionals led to some describing feelings of powerlessness and that they were failing the children.

Another barrier to getting the information and support teachers needed from health professionals was understanding which professionals could help and how. Teachers who had experienced working with a child with a life-limiting or life-threatening condition had greater awareness of other health professionals, notably general practitioners, physiotherapists, occupational therapists and paediatricians, than those who had not.

School nurses

Seventy percent of teachers identified school nurses as a key source of information about the medical needs of a child with a life-limiting or life-threatening condition. Yet experiences and perceptions of the role of the school nurse were very variable, with some teachers identifying that they now have very little contact with a school nurse and that the service has been dramatically cut over recent years. Others identified that the school nurse may not have the professional expertise to know about and effectively address the complex medical care needs of children with life-limiting or life-threatening conditions. Some teachers shared positive experiences:

"I've just had a child in my class diagnosed with a condition, it's not life threatening, but the school nurse took a big role and he has to have medication at school and it was all done by them, they arranged to come in and see me and explain what had happened and what the diagnosis was and how that was going to affect him and what my role in that would be. It was an automatic thing."

More typically, others described working with school nurses as being very mixed. One explained,

"So the school nurse knows the children very well for a long time, but hasn't got the expertise, so when we're having the discussions about, 'Is the skin as it should be?' or other issues going on she always says, 'It's beyond my expertise. . . .' So I think school nurses will sometimes . . . have lots of general knowledge about things, but not necessarily specific knowledge. I think if it's a rare condition or something where there are going to be lots and lots of complications, you would need someone who really is able to give you as much advice as possible, because then you feel confident about where you're going and what you need to do."

Often, therefore, teachers reported working with school nurses as

quite 'hit and miss'.

Some teachers also reported having almost no contact with a school nurse, concluding that it often came down to the personal character of the nurse and goodwill. There were no clear procedures or structures to follow.

Summary

Whilst communication with parents and the child was recognised as paramount, teachers needed more professional support. Collaboration in this research was therefore all about sourcing the right sort of information from the right person and knowing how to build more effective collaborations with key professionals. In this,

- knowing what services are available and the roles and responsibilities of each;
- understanding different professional roles;
- knowing how to directly access additional services to support the child and their family; and
- developing high-quality and effective approaches to secure meaningful professional collaboration

were all seen as key themes.

Policy review

Supporting Pupils at School with Medical Conditions (DfE, 2015) is clear about the importance of collaborative working to support the needs of children with medical conditions in school, highlighting that:

- 'Supporting a child with a medical condition during school hours is not the sole responsibility of one person.
- A school's ability to provide effective support will depend to an appreciable extent on working co-operatively with other agencies.
- Partnership working between school staff, healthcare professionals (and, where appropriate, social care professionals), local authorities, and parents and pupils will be critical.
- An essential requirement for any policy therefore will be to identify collaborative working arrangements between all those involved, showing how they will work in partnership to ensure that the needs of pupils with medical conditions are met effectively.'

(DfE, 2015: 12)

The Department for Education (DfE, 2015) identifies that all providers of health services should:

- 'Co-operate with schools that are supporting children with a medical condition'
- Provide effective communication and liaison between themselves including "liaison with school nurses and other healthcare professionals such as specialist and children's community nurses" and the school
- 'Participate in locally developed outreach and training.'

(DfE, 2015: 16)

The DfE (2015: 16) also highlights that 'Health services can provide valuable support, information, advice and guidance to schools, and their staff, to support children with medical conditions at school'. Local authorities are identified as having a responsibility for ensuring the effective sharing of information and collaboration between health services and schools. As the DfE (2015) notes:

- 'Under Section 10 of the Children's Act 2004, they have a duty to promote co-operation between relevant partners – such as governing bodies of maintained schools, proprietors of academies, clinical commissioning groups and NHS England – with a view to improving the wellbeing of children with regard to their physical and mental health, and their education, training and recreation.'

(DfE, 2015: 15)

Despite the experiences of the teachers in this research, the DfE (2015) identifies the following key features of the role of school nurses in supporting schools to meet the medical needs of their pupils. They advise that:

- 'Every school has access to school nursing services . . .
- They are responsible for notifying the school when a child has been identified as having a medical condition which will require support in school . . .
- They would not usually have an extensive role in ensuring that schools are taking appropriate steps to support children with medical conditions but may support staff on implementing a child's individual health care plan and provide advice and liaison, for example on training.
- School nurses can liaise with lead clinicians locally on appropriate support for the child and associated staff training needs . . .
- Community nursing teams will also be a valuable potential resource for a school seeking advice and support in relation to children with a medical condition.'

(DfE, 2015: 15)

The Department for Education also state:

- 'Other healthcare professionals, including GPs and paediatricians, should notify the school nurse when a child has been identified as having a medical condition that will require support at school.'

(DfE, 2015: 15)

Practical considerations

Who is responsible for providing which services?

For collaborative practices to develop meaningfully, it is essential that teachers understand the role and responsibilities of both individual professionals and broad services.

Reflective activity

- Who do you think is responsible for providing services to:
  - The child with a life-limiting or life-threatening condition?
  - The child's family?
  - The school?
- How do you think you would access those services?
- Which services do you think you would need to collaborate with?

The Integrated Personal Commissioning Emerging Framework (NHS England/LGA, 2016) has emerged out of a recognition that coordinating services around a child needs to be underpinned by financial and legal directives and practical support. It will provide a completely new approach to planning and purchasing services for those with complex, ongoing needs such as children who have life-limiting or life-threatening conditions. Collaboration is a thread that runs from government departments to the individual child.

Integrated Personal Commissioning (IPC)

- has emerged from a national partnership between NHS England and the Local Government Association;
- seeks to join up health care, social care, education and other services;

- is underpinned by collaborative leadership and common, co-designed approaches;
- includes the introduction of IPC support teams who will help with planning and coordinating professionals and volunteers; and
- enables an individual to receive an integrated personal budget, which they choose to be used for health care, social care and educational services.

Health care and public health

The local National Health Service (NHS) has a statutory responsibility to provide health care services for its local population. Health care includes services that seek to prevent, treat, cure, rehabilitate and care. Most health care professionals work with the ill or disabled population. They offer clinical care and the observation and treatment of patients and comprise clinicians such as paediatricians, community child nursing services, doctors, physiotherapists and occupational therapists.

The Local Authority has a statutory duty to provide public health services for its local population. Public health includes communication, education and policy development and includes services that seek to prevent ill health and promote good health. Most of the public health workforce works with the whole, including the 'healthy' population. They include smoking-cessation advisers, healthy-weight teams, health visitors and school nurses. Teachers who lead on healthy schools or personal, social and health education are carrying out public health work.

The Department for Education (2015) explain that the local NHS has a duty to ensure that health services, that is both health care and public health services, are responsive to children's needs and are set up to co-operate with schools who are supporting children with medical conditions. Under Section 10 of the Children Act 2004, the local authorities and the local NHS must work together to allow the purchasing of education, health and care for children with SEN or disabilities.

Social care

Social care is the provision of protection, personal care, social support or social work services to individuals who are at risk, to include children with life-limiting or life-threatening conditions. The social care workforce, comprising social carers and social workers, can be found in many public services including Children's Services. Their work spans support for families and children with special educational needs and/or disabilities, child protection, adoption and much more. Children and family social workers have a statutory responsibility for 'keeping children safe, and making the right decisions about their future' (DfE, 2016: 4).

The roles of different professionals

Reflective activity

- Which health care professionals are you already aware of?
- What do you know about their role and the support they could provide to:
  - The child with a life-limiting or life-threatening condition?
  - The child's family?
  - The school?

- Review again Tables 6.1a and 6.1b which show where the teachers in the research went for sources of information about the medical and non-medical needs of a child with life-limiting or life-threatening conditions.
  - o Which of those sources would you prioritise?
  - o Why?
  - o How?
  - o Who would you contact, and what information would you want from them?
- How would you find out more about which services and professionals were providing support to the child and their family?

Local authorities, Children's Services and the National Health Service and others such as the voluntary sector will employ health care, public health and social care professionals. Some professionals work independently. It is always important to advise families to check that professionals are 'registered', meaning that they are approved by a reputable professional body such as the Healthcare Professions Council, Registration Council for Clinical Psychologists, the Nursing and Midwifery Council, the General Medical Council or, for counsellors, psychotherapists and complementary therapists, see the accredited registers listed by the Professional Standards Authority. Registration can be checked by asking the professional to provide proof directly or by looking up the register on line and searching for their name.

The team of health care and social care professionals may come together around a specialism, for example a palliative care team. They support families when a child's illness cannot be cured. It could comprise nurses, doctors, therapists and providers of social and spiritual care from a range of services. They work in homes, hospitals, hospices and other venues. They may include a chaplain, someone who has been appointed as a representative of a church or another religious authority within a hospital, hospice or another organisation. Today, they often represent all faiths and none, focusing on generic spiritual support.

Reflective activity

The range of different professionals working with a child with life-limiting or life-threatening conditions falls into the following professional categories:

- Doctors
- Nurses
- Specialist nurses
- Allied health professionals
- Psychologists and therapists
- Complementary therapists
- Social carers

Brainstorm what you know about each broad group of professionals:

- What would their role and responsibilities for the child with life-limiting or life-threatening conditions be?

- How would they liaise with the school?
- What support/advice could they provide?
- How might they work directly with the child and their family?

Doctors

Doctors practice medicine, the science-based practice of diagnosis, treatment (medicines or surgery) and prevention of disease. Except for general practitioners (GPs), doctors specialise in a specific part of the body or a specified population. Referral to any specialist doctor is normally by the family GP or another doctor.

Nurses

Nurses organise, plan and provide health care, often complementing medicine and augmented by attention to physical, psychological and social care needs.

Table 6.2 The role of doctors

Physician	Surgeon	Branch of medicine
Cardiologist	Cardiac/cardiothoracic surgeon	Heart and circulatory system
Dermatologist	Dermatologic surgeon	Skin, nails, hair
Gastroenterologist	Gastrointestinal surgeon	Gastrointestinal tract from mouth to anus
General practitioner (GP)		Common medical conditions
Haematologist	Vascular surgeon	Blood
Medical geneticist		Genes, hereditary disorders
Nephrologist	Renal surgeon	Kidneys
Neurologist	Neurosurgeon	Nervous system including brain and spinal cord
Oncologist	General surgeon or surgeons who specialise in a specific area of the body e.g. gastrointestinal surgeon and renal surgeon	Cancer
Rheumatologist	Orthopaedic surgeon	Bones, joints, ligaments
Ophthalmologist	Ophthalmologist	Eyes
Paediatrician (Paediatricians may specialise, e.g. paediatric rheumatologist, paediatric oncologist and paediatric cardiologist)	Paediatric surgeons often specialise, e.g. paediatric orthopaedic surgeons and paediatric oncology surgeons.	Infants and children to 18 years. Conditions related to growth and development, e.g. arthritis in children
Psychiatrist		Moderate to severe mental disorders which may have physical, psychological and/or social origins

Table 6.3 The role of nurses

Nurse	Role	Referral
Children's nurse/ paediatric nurse	Plans and provides holistic health care to infants and children in need and their families. Hospital-based children's nurses may work in general wards or specialist units. Roald Dahl nurses are hospital-based children's nurses who support children living with serious, rare and undiagnosed conditions. Community children's nurses work in day care centres, child health clinics and in children's homes to provide treatment, care and support. Some provide specialist care such as children's palliative care.	Normally via a health care or social care professional, or make an appointment through a private health care provider or nursing agency.
Learning disability nurse	Seeks to improve the health, well-being and social inclusion of people with a learning disability	
Mental health nurse	Works with people who have mental and emotional health concerns, including mental illness	

Specialist nurses

Specialist nurses are nurses or midwives who have taken additional, often postgraduate education to provide a high level of expertise in health care or public health.

Table 6.4 The role of specialist nurses

Specialist nurse	Role	Referral
Clinical specialist nurse	Specialises in one acute field such as children's nursing, cancer, stoma care or epilepsy	By doctor or other health care professional
Practice nurse (a specialist community public health nurse)	Delivers health care, often with a disease-prevention focus	Most GP practices employ a practice nurse, and appointments can be made with the receptionist.
School nurse (a specialist community public health nurse)	Promotes healthy lifestyles and disease prevention among children of school age. They are the link between school, home and the community. They can undertake health assessments, provide information on common childhood conditions and refer to other services such as community children's nursing services.	See local NHS web site and make an appointment, or referral by a school teacher, or some areas offer 'drop-in' services.

Allied health professionals

Registered health care professionals who are not nurses, doctors or pharmacists are collectively known as the allied health professionals.

Table 6.5 The role of allied health professionals

Allied health professional	Role	Referral
Audiologist	Assesses and provides support for problems related to hearing and balance	Free online or telephone hearing checks or by a GP
Diagnostic radiographer	Uses x-rays, scans, imaging and ultrasound to provide images that can help diagnose an injury or disease	By a doctor
Dietition	Assesses, diagnoses and treats nutritional problems. A registered dietition can provide special diets for medical conditions; a registered nutritionist cannot.	By a health care professional, or contact an independent dietitian through the British Dietetic Association Freelance Dietitians web site
Occupational therapist	Identifies strengths and difficulties that a child may have in carrying out everyday activities such as dressing. Teaches a different way of carrying out the activity and/or provides resources in order to promote independence. Works holistically with physical, social and psychological challenges.	By a health care or social care professional, or contact the local authority's Children's Services, or contact an independent occupational therapist through the Healthcare Professions Council (HPCP) on-line register
Optometrist	Performs eye examinations, vision tests, prescribes corrective lenses, detects abnormalities and prescribes medicine for certain eye diseases	By a GP or another health care professional
Orthoptist	Specialises in problems related to eye movements	By a GP or another health care professional
Paramedic (senior ambulance service)	Assesses patients in an emergency and provides essential treatment	Telephone: 111 non-emergency medical number for when life is not threatened, but advice is needed about what to do. 112 is the same service, but it will work on any mobile phone throughout the world. 999 emergency such as a child struggling to breathe.
Physiotherapist	Helps restore function and movement through tailored exercise. Focuses on bones, joints and soft tissues including brain/neurological and breathing problems.	Make appointment with physiotherapist working at local GP practice, or referral by GP, or contact an independent physiotherapist through the online Physio2u web site.
Podiatrist/chiropodist	Provides specialised foot care and treatment	See local NHS web site to make an appointment, or referral by a health care professional, or contact an independent practitioner through the Institute of Chiropodists and Podiatrists web site.

(Continued)

Table 6.5 (Continued)

Allied health professional	Role	Referral
Speech and language therapist	Helps with speech, language, communication and swallowing	See local NHS, Local Authority/Local Offer web site to make an appointment, or referral by a health care professional, or contact an independent practitioner through the Association of Speech and Language Therapists in Independent Practice web site.
Therapeutic radiographer	Provides radiotherapy and related support for children with cancer and other conditions	By a doctor

Psychologists and therapists

Psychologists and therapists use psychological theories to underpin their work.

Table 6.6 The role of psychologists and therapists

Psychologist/therapist	Role	Referral
Arts therapists (art therapist, music therapist, drama therapist, dance therapist)	Uses the arts to process emotional/psychological concerns	See local NHS, Social Services/Children's Services web sites and, if available make an appointment, or referral by a health care or social care professional, or independent practitioners can be contacted through the British Association of Art Therapists web site.
Child psychotherapist	Uses talking therapy to help with a range of complex emotional/psychological concerns. Tends to work on longer-term concerns than counsellors.	By a health care or social care professional, or independent practitioners can be contacted through the Association of Child Psychotherapists web site.
Child psychologist	Assesses thinking, learning, behaviour and social skills and provides support for emotional, language and learning needs	By education, social care or health care professional, or independent practitioners can be contacted through the Association of Child Psychologists in Private Practice web site.
Counsellor	Uses talking therapy to help with a range of emotional/psychological concerns. Tends to work on shorter-term concerns than psychotherapist.	By a health care, social care or education professional, or independent practitioners can be contacted through the British Association for Counselling and Psychotherapy web site
Play therapist	Uses play, the natural language of children, to process emotional/psychological concerns. Often includes a range of creative arts, e.g. art, clay, sand, puppets and music. Normally for 3- to 11-year-olds.	See local NHS, Social Services/Children's Services web sites and if available make an appointment, or referral by a health care, education or social care professional, or independent therapists can be contacted through Play Therapy UK or British Association of Play Therapists web sites.
School counsellor	Uses talking therapy to help with emotional/psychological concerns and to promote mental health and well-being	If available within a school, children can often self-refer. Schools may have arrangements with the local authority or local charities.

Complementary therapists

Complementary therapies and alternative medicines are treatments that fall outside mainstream health care. Some are based on a different understanding about the body and health than the medical approach which underpins most mainstream health care in the UK.

Table 6.7 The role of complementary therapists

Complementary therapist	*Role*	*Referral*
Acupuncturist	Inserts fine needles into the body to restore equilibrium. Sometimes used alongside Chinese herbs.	See local NHS web site to see if available at a local GP practice or hospital and make an appointment. Sometimes provided in hospices. Most are independent and can be contacted through the British Acupuncture Council web site.
Aromatherapist	Uses natural oils, for example within a massage in palliative care	See local NHS web site to see if available at local GP practice or hospital and make an appointment. Sometimes provided in hospices. Most are independent and can be contacted through the International Federation of Aromatherapists web site.
Chiropractic	Manipulates joints to restore mobility and function	See local NHS web site to see if available at local GP practice or hospital and make an appointment. Sometimes provided in hospices. Most are independent and can be contacted through the General Chiropractic Council web site.
Healer	Aims to provide well-being, balance, alleviation of symptoms or sometimes cure. May involve 'non-contact therapeutic touch', placing of hands, meditation or prayer.	See local NHS web site to see if available at local GP practice or hospital and make an appointment. Sometimes provided in hospices. Independent practitioners can be contacted through the Healing Trust or Complementary and Natural Healthcare Council web sites.
Homeopath	Uses very small amounts of substances to treat symptoms	Independent practitioners can be contacted through the Society of Homeopaths web site.
Hypnotherapist	Uses hypnosis, an altered state of consciousness, to treat anxiety, phobias, pain management, stress and produce relaxation. Hypnosis does not work if someone does not want it to.	By a GP or another doctor; may be available at a hospice. Independent practitioners can be contacted through the Complementary and Natural Healthcare Council or UK Council for Psychotherapy web sites.
Nutritional therapist	Uses nutrition to promote optimum health and prevent ailments. It is based on the belief that nutritional and biochemical imbalances lead to ill health.	Independent practitioners can be contacted through the British Association for Applied Nutrition and Nutritional Therapy web site.

(Continued)

Table 6.7 (Continued)

Complementary therapist	Role	Referral
Osteopath	Moves, stretches and manipulates muscles and joints. Can help with digestive issues, circulatory problems, problems with sleeping, head- and backaches, and a range of symptoms that might not be obviously joint or muscle related.	By GP if it is available in the local NHS area. Independent practitioners can be contacted through the General Osteopathic Council web site.
Reiki	Provides spiritual healing by the gentle placing of hands. Used for stress reduction and relaxation.	By a health care professional if it is available in the local NHS area. Sometimes provided in hospices. Most practitioners are independent and can be contacted through the UK Reiki Foundation web site.

Social carers

Social care comprises personal care, protection and social support services.

Table 6.8 The role of social carers

Social carer/social worker	Role	Referral
Key worker	Provides and helps coordinate health care and social care services around a family	Agreed at the point of finalising a Continuing Care package, care plan or Education, Health and Care Plan.
Social worker	Helps individuals and communities develop their skills and abilities to resolve problems. Social justice, human rights and respect for diversity are central values of the work.	Contact local Children's Services in the Local Authority or via the Local Offer to make an appointment, or contact an independent social worker through the British Association of Social Workers web site.
Youth worker/youth and community worker	Supports 12- to 21-year-olds through individual relationships, creating and delivering local projects and using a wide range of communication skills	Contact local Youth Service or Local Authority/Local Offer.

Reflective activity

- Having now reviewed a range of information about different categories of health care and social care professionals who may be able to provide information and support to the child with a life-limiting or life-threatening condition, their family and the school, identify which professionals you would most value working with.
- How would you make contact with them to seek their support and collaboration?
- Research how to contact those different professionals in your own locality.

Communicating and collaborating effectively with other professionals

As the practitioner working closely with the child and their family, it is essential to be aware of effective communication and collaboration strategies and approaches so that the very best support and service can be put in place around the child and their family. In this, it is important to acknowledge the number of embedded potential barriers to current effective multi-agency working. These include:

- Time
- Professional identities and professional hierarchies
- Differing expectations of roles and levels of need
- Different professional discourses/terminology

Reflective activity

- How would you seek to overcome the potential barriers that have been identified:
  - Time?
  - Professional identities and professional hierarchies?
  - Differing expectations of roles and levels of need?
  - Different professional discourses/terminology?
- Are there any other potential barriers you can identify that need to be considered?

Time

Finding times when all professionals are able to attend meetings to collaborate effectively will always be difficult. It will therefore be important for the educational practitioner to seek a range of flexible strategies to encourage collaboration. Some or all of the following strategies may be helpful:

- Make sure that key meetings are booked well in advance to give all professionals plenty of time to book them into their working diaries.
- Consider holding key meetings in different locations to help busy practitioners fit in a collaborative multi-professional meeting about a child within a busy schedule.
- Use Skype or conference calling to enable professionals to input into multi-professional meetings without having to actually travel to the meeting location. This is particularly important where the child may be receiving treatment from one of the key national care centres, which may be located some way from their home and school area.
- Use emails to encourage direct communication between professionals. Try to make sure that everyone is always copied in to all communications, as this will help ensure that open lines of communication are maintained, and the teacher does not end up receiving conflicting advice or support from different professionals. Open emails will help all professionals gain a much deeper understanding of the actual needs of the child outside of the hospital or treatment centre, and this will help them evaluate the impact of the condition and treatment on the child's ongoing development and care needs.

Professional identities and professional hierarchy

Unfortunately, due to years of separate practice and a lack of cohesive and structured collaborative practices, professional identities have evolved in isolation. As a result, whilst there are perceptions about the professional identities of different professionals, these are rarely well understood. When a multi-professional care team is set up around the child with a life-limiting or life-threatening condition, it will therefore be important to allow some time for information sharing about each professional role and to ensure that this understanding is continuously checked and reviewed to ensure that everyone understands the different roles of each practitioner. The following strategies and approaches may help address this in practice:

- Include brief introductions (by email or in person) each time a multi-professional care team is set up to support a child and their family. Ensure that this is shared with everyone and that everyone (even if not able to be present at the meeting) has a good understanding of the range of different practitioners involved with the care and treatment of the child.
- Try to establish some clear understandings of the different roles of each professional. Here it may be useful to develop a simple flow chart to outline the different professionals that are involved with the care and treatment of the child and who will make decisions and provide advice to whom.
- It is helpful to identify one key lead from the multi-professional team. In this, the previous concept from Every Child Matters (H.M. Government, 2003) of the lead professional is helpful. Discussions within the team about the best person to take on this role will help develop clearer understanding of the active role that each person will take within the care and treatment of the child. Whilst teachers, for example, may be the professional that sees the child most regularly and therefore provides the most direct contact with the child, they will not have the medical expertise to lead on treatments, so decisions will need to be made about who would be best to take on the role of lead professional.
- Be aware that professional teams can change, so you may establish a good working relationship with one consultant or particular professional only to find that they then move into a different team and are no longer involved in the treatment and care of the child. Find ways to ensure a smooth transition from one professional to another, and this may best be secured through contacts with administrative assistants.
- Professional practices can seem or can become rather hierarchical, and this can obstruct the development of really meaningful and effective collaborative professional practice. Where possible, try to avoid any potential barriers caused through a hierarchical understanding of professional roles by maintaining at all times a respect of each professional, emphasising the need to work together collaboratively to ensure the best service and support for the individual child.

Differing understandings of roles and levels of need

Truly effective collaborative professional practice can be undermined when professionals do not fully understand the situation from the perspective of another. Taking time to ensure a full and open understanding of each other's roles and ways that teams can work together is therefore crucial. In this, the following approaches and strategies may be helpful to utilise:

- Make sure there is time to understand the different roles of the professionals that are attending meetings.
- Try to find out more about the level of support they will provide to the child and their family, that is, the differences between the involvement of a consultant and that of a nurse.

- Find ways to brainstorm, as a collaborative team, roles and responsibilities in relation to a multi-professional team approach to meeting the needs of the child and their family. Try to clearly outline responsibilities: actions to be taken, by whom and by when, but make sure that this is fully agreed and fits within the broader context of the professional roles and time availability.

- Ensure that there are open discussions about professional expectations and perceptions of levels of need. To the educational practitioner unfamiliar with the condition, it may seem that the level of need for the child is high, but this may not be the case for the consultant or allied health professional who is more familiar with the condition and perceives the level of risk or need to be low.

- Ensure that a detailed health care plan is drawn up with input from all professionals involved in the collaborative team. This should provide specific details about roles and responsibilities and who should be contacted to provide what level of support and service at what times. Emergency procedures as well as day-to-day routines should be clearly set out. Where possible, try to include direct contact details.

- Ensure that all care plans and information about the needs of the child are written in accessible language. Make sure professional jargon is avoided (see below) so that all professionals involved in the care and support of the child are able to fully understand all of the details across education, health care and social care.

Different professional discourses and terminology

Due to the separate and specialist ways different professionals work, one key barrier to effective multi-professional working can be the different language and discourse that is used. This can include the very specialist medical terminology that will be used by health professionals to describe the condition and the treatment of the child but can also include broader terms relating to types of services and support available to access and ways of working. It is therefore essential to ensure that professional jargon is avoided as much as possible, and, where it is absolutely essential, that all professionals are given the opportunity to check and clarify meaning.

- Where specialist medical terms need to be used and understood, try to draw up – in consultation with the medical professionals – a glossary of key terms, and attach this to the child's health care plan. This can then be used by teachers and the parents to help them access and understand key medical terminology.

- Where it is needed, also provide a glossary of educational terms for health professionals, and add this as an attachment to the health care plan for use by the health professionals.

- Make sure that when you receive reports from professionals or when they attend meetings and you do not understand any of the terminology being used, you directly ask for further clarification. In all of our professional roles, jargon is embedded into our practice and we can become oblivious to it as we are so accustomed to what it means and how to use it in our day to day work. It is therefore essential to enable all professionals to interrupt and ask for further clarification where needed.

- The glossary of terms provided in the Additional Resources section at the end of this book may also be a useful starting point to explain some of the key health terms that can be used.

Multi-professional input into the health care plan

As discussed in Chapter 4, a key part of the support needed for a child with a life-limiting or life-threatening condition is the development of a clear and comprehensive individual health care plan. In this, it is essential that the range of professionals involved in the child's health care are actively involved in inputting into, reviewing and agreeing on the detailed plan that will then be implemented within the school context. As the listed points highlight, this may need to be completed by email or Skype in order to enable the key health professionals working with the child to actively participate and contribute to the development of an effective plan.

Practical resources

In this section, the following practical resources are provided:

1   A format for developing a multi-professional contact list
2   Key principles for effective multi-agency working

1 Developing a multi-professional contact list

Specialism	Name and contact details	Services provided	Costs/hours worked	Comments
Education				
Health				
Social care				

2 Key principles for effective multi-agency working

Effective multi-agency working has been characterised as follows (adapted from Walker, Jackson & Turnbull (Multi-agency working for children and young people) from ESCalate, accessed 30/10/16).

- **Clearly agreed and defined functions** - everyone is clear about their role and that of others so there is no confusion.

- **Tasks with agreed boundaries** - this avoids duplication of work, people stepping on one another's toes etc.

- **Well organised and established communication** - workers know how and when to get hold of people, how to make referrals for services and so on.

- **Well developed local relationships** - workers from different agencies have met before they engage in 'crisis' work, and they know each other and understand each other's roles.

- **Overcoming of ignorance and prejudice about each other's work** - workers from different agencies understand the various aspects of each others jobs and the pressures that each worker is under. They avoid making assumptions about others, e.g. that all teachers finish work at 3.00 p.m. and have long holidays.

- **Defining of common goals** - time is taken at the beginning of a joint piece of work for workers to define what it is the joint work is trying to achieve so that everyone shares a common aim.

- **Using common language** - workers avoid using jargon or abbreviations; or, if they do, this is explained. They should not make assumptions that workers from other agencies will know what certain terms mean, e.g. a social worker may not know what age Key Stage 1 covers or what being dis-applied from the National Curriculum means.

- **Respecting different skills** - the contribution of every worker engaged in the joint task should be recognised. It is particularly important that those with lowest status in the hierarchy who may be closest to the child (e.g. a teaching assistant) have the opportunity to share their knowledge and are not overlooked in favour of workers with little knowledge but with more status (e.g. a doctor).

- **Ensuring all know what the local arrangements are** - the systems for seeking support or making referrals should be clear to all. Similarly, arrangements for getting hold of people should be clear to all.

Concluding comments

Collaborating effectively with other professionals can be difficult because of the embedded differences between and across different professional roles. Staff in the school setting may therefore have to work flexibly and creatively to ensure high levels of active involvement and contribution by the wide range of health care and social care professionals working with the child and the family.

Where this is achieved, the impact for the family and the child, in terms of a successful, fully integrated understanding of needs, provision and support is substantial.

7 Communicating and sharing information with others

In this chapter, we:

- Review key principles around confidential data and confidentiality
- Consider the importance of ethical practice
- Consider key principles and guidelines for sharing personal information
- Explore appropriate and sensitive ways to share information with others

Introduction

Schools are communities in which what affects one child will affect all those whose lives have been touched by that child. Teachers have a duty of care to children who have life-limiting or life-threatening conditions but also to others within the school community, their families and colleagues. Within the Teaching for Life research, many teachers were concerned about what they could say to others about a child with a life-limiting or life-threatening condition, to whom and when.

> "Depending on what it was, how much it was appropriate for the other children to know, how much they needed to know. How much they would have to know, because of obvious things that they would notice, or how much it wasn't really necessary for them to be fully aware."

> "I'd be thinking . . . as that illness progresses how I would cope, but also the other students in the class and an understanding that is obviously dependent upon your setting and the students you work with and an understanding that is relevant to them about that other student and what that will look like. It might be their first experience of bereavement; it might be someone they're close to. It might be actually how I would understand that, but also how I would help them to understand that would be really, really challenging."

> "I'd be concerned about how I would talk about this to the student and their family. Also with the other students, how I'd integrate them into the class and what I'd need to do to make them feel comfortable and also the other students feel comfortable. How much the other students need to know and what information is vital for everyone to know, other members of staff as well."

An inclusive school is one that meets the needs of all pupils, whilst diversity acknowledges that these needs are diverse. The research showed that there can be tensions between respecting the rights of one child with a life-limiting or life-threatening condition and their parents and meeting the needs of the other children in school and their parents.

The impact of the experience of grief and bereavement on the development of other children in their care at the school was therefore a key concern to the teachers:

"It's not just his class and his friends, it's also, he's got siblings, so it's them and their friends . . . So I think when it does happen it's going to be very, very difficult and it's going to affect the whole school and we haven't got that support. I don't think we're prepared for it, I think it's going to be quite devastating to the staff and probably the children, because it is going to hit them in such a big way in school and also their home environment."

"If he was to pass away under our care he would have been a classmate of 28 other 8-year-old children. How are we going to, how are we gonna manage that positively and enable the children to grieve? . . . If a child in the class were to die, how do you . . . I don't think I'd even know where to start with that."

The impact of managing the range of emotions and juggling the emotional responses of a wide range of different people was also identified by teachers in the research:

"When the first child died quite a while ago there was absolutely no support, I was busking it and I felt very vulnerable. The teachers very upset, the parents very upset, obviously devastated. The other children were very upset and I was making it up as I went along and somehow, sort of got most of it right."

Summary

Teachers in the research identified a number of key concerns that they had about communicating information about the condition of a child with life-limiting or life-threatening conditions to others. These included:

- Knowing how much information to share, when and how so as not to make the situation more difficult for others, particularly young children who may be in the same class as the child with a life-limiting or life-threatening condition
- Being aware of the tensions that exist between the rights of the individual child and the rights of everyone else within the school setting
- The impact of knowledge and information about a child's life-limiting or life-threatening condition on others
- The impact on themselves of having to juggle the emotional needs of a range of people

Policy review

Whilst *Supporting Pupils at School with Medical Conditions* (DfE, 2015) provides a wealth of information about how schools should meet the needs of children with a life-limiting or life-threatening condition, there is no advice given about the difficult issue of when and how information about the child's life-limiting or life-threatening condition should or could appropriately be shared with others. There are, however, a number of key considerations to take into account. The Data Protection Act (1998) regulates the processing and disclosure of information about identifiable, living individuals. It explains that everyone who is responsible for using data has to follow data-protection principles. Information must be:

- used fairly and lawfully
- used for limited and specifically stated purposes

- used in a way that is adequate, relevant and not excessive
- accurate
- kept for no longer than is absolutely necessary
- handled according to people's data-protection rights
- kept safe and secure
- not transferred outside the European Economic Area (European Union countries and Iceland, Liechtenstein and Norway) without adequate protection

These can be summarised as only using data for the purpose for which it was collected and only sharing it with the permission of the person whom it concerns. There is also an obligation on schools and health care professionals to ensure that stored information is accurate and kept securely.

Practical considerations

Implications of policy

In summary, current government and professional policies point to common practical considerations. These are:

- The child and the family are always at the heart of any decisions. As far as possible, all decisions are child led/family led and respected.
- Written data about the child needs to follow the data-protection principles. All those who have access to the child's records or knowledge of the child's condition have a duty to keep this information confidential, unless they have clear permission to share it or there is a child-protection issue.
- At Local Authority level, a protocol needs to clearly explain how information is to be shared between agencies.
- At school level, clear guidance/policy about the communication of confidential information about a child's condition would be helpful, and this needs to be considered by the governing body.
- A child has rights to confidentiality, but if a practitioner believes it is in the child's best interest to disclose a child's confidential information to another, they should share this with the child first.
- If in doubt, discuss with other professionals, and keep written records.
- Communication, communication, communication.

Reflective activity

Review the key principles outlined earlier.

- Which of these do you think are already well embedded, understood and established in your school context?
- Which of them do you think your school needs to develop further?
- How can this be achieved?
- Consider ways these aspects can be developed, either as a whole staff working collaboratively to address any key issues, by having one person or a working party take responsibility for the development of the key issue or by drawing in the advice or support of others to help the school.

Confidential data

Confidential data might include:

- details of the child's conditions, including reasons for absence or medical appointments
- treatment given within the school, such as changing dressings
- how the class- or school-based activities, such as sport, may need to be missed or adjusted
- details of a child's home life, such as details of their death and funeral arrangements
- risk assessments carried out by the school which focus on what the child can and cannot be reasonably be expected to participate in, what reasonable adjustments need to be made, by whom and when. This should be developed in conjunction with other specialists such as a school nurse or an occupational therapist.

Confidentiality

Nurses, like all health care professionals, have a legal duty of confidentiality to children. Their professional code stipulates that they may be liable to disciplinary proceedings if they breach medical confidentiality. The Royal College of Nurses advise the following for school nurses:

- 'The pupil has rights to confidentiality, which depend on their level of development, intelligence and ability to understand.
- The nurse will always seek the child's consent to disclose confidential health information to parents and, in appropriate circumstances, the school head teacher.
- If consent is withheld, there is a prima facie legal duty of confidentiality that forbids disclosure.
- Within a school this can cause a conflict of interest, and calls for a certain amount of understanding on both sides.
- It is necessary to establish what is reasonable information to divulge to a third party on a 'need to know' basis.
- Rarely, if the nurse considers that it is in the pupils' best interests to disclose information to the school or parents, they must inform the pupil before doing so and be prepared to fully justify their actions at a later date if necessary.'

(RCN, 2014: 47)

- 'Every school should have a policy, of which parents and teaching staff are aware, that covers the nurse's professional and ethical obligations, including confidentiality.
- It is important to remember that the duty of confidentiality to the patient is greater than that owed to the school which employs the nurse.
- The only times when this confidentiality may be breached are if:
  - the child consents to disclosure in writing
  - a Court of Law requires disclosure
  - disclosure is justified in the public interest or in the child's best interests, as in the case of child protection issues.'

(RCN, 2014: 48)

A child with a life-limiting or life-threatening condition is likely to have a health care plan, a record of the health care that is required to support them. This may be part of a broader Education, Health and Care Plan for some children. The health care plan needs to be accessible to all who need to see it 'while preserving confidentiality' (DfE, 2015: 10). The Department for Education (2015) explain that the governing body of a school should consider 'where confidentiality issues are raised by the parent/child, the designated individuals to be entrusted with information about the child's condition' (DfE, 2015: 12).

Ethical practice

Clearly there are many ethical issues to consider when working with anyone affected by life-limiting or life-threatening conditions. First and foremost, there is a duty of care to the pupil affected by these issues, but of course the duty of care also extends to the whole school community. It is a complex issue, as some of these ethical considerations can appear to be in tension: for example confidentiality and the need for disclosure. At all times, appropriate professional, ethical practice must be upheld. It may be wise for schools to explicitly revisit and share their understanding of appropriate ethical practices. For teachers, the Teachers' Standards (DfE, 2011) highlight, amongst other expectations, the need to:

- treat pupils with dignity, build relationships rooted in mutual respect, and at all times observe proper boundaries appropriate to a teacher's professional position
- have regard for the need to safeguard pupils' well-being, in accordance with statutory provisions

Reflective activity

- What ethical issues do you think you may experience when meeting the needs of a child with a life-limiting or life-threatening condition in your school context?
- How will you respond to those within the boundaries of your professional standards for conduct?
- How regularly do you review whole-staff shared understanding of professional ethical practices?

Whilst teachers and other staff will have their own understandings about appropriate professional ethics, it may be helpful to invite health care professionals in to work with staff when reviewing key principles and guidelines for professional ethical practice in school. They will have alternative and useful professional perspectives to share.

Starting to communicate and share information with others

When teachers are meeting with a child who has a life-limiting or life-threatening condition and their family, they need to listen in order to gauge the child's and parents' level of knowledge and understanding about the condition and the impact it is having on the child cognitively, socially and emotionally. This requires much patience and skill. A teacher may focus on supporting communication between a parent and their child first (see Chapter 5). Once a partnership of parent, teacher and child is established, it is easier to collectively discuss wider communication. In this, the following key points should be discussed and agreed:

- what information to share with others (e.g. perhaps start with a child being unable to join in an activity because of not feeling well)
- how to share with information others (e.g. within a personal, social and health education (PSHE) class during a lesson about friendships/relationships; appearance/body image; what makes us feel well, what makes us feel poorly; difficult feelings; social skills. How would the child like to share information with others?)

- the consequences of sharing information with their class or others in the school
- consider the pros and cons (e.g. children and other parents may provide much-needed social, emotional and practical support; parents will ask questions; it will not be private anymore)
- that many facets of having a life-limiting or life-changing condition are difficult to hide, no matter how much a child and their family may wish to. The child may change appearance, be absent from school for short or extended periods, may need to opt out of school activities such as sport.
- the 'reasonable adjustments' that a school needs to put in place. Once in place, some of these 'reasonable adjustments' will be noticed by others.
- one step at a time, it is a journey. A child's life-limiting or life-threatening condition is not always incurable. Conditions such as cancer can often be cured. Some conditions become acute and then get better (go into remission) and repeat. Some conditions can be lived with for long into adulthood. Other conditions become increasingly debilitating. Keep in the present and the near future.

Sharing personal information

> **Reflective activity**
>
> - What do you know already about how to appropriately share personal information?
> - What sort of personal information can be shared?
> - In what ways?
> - Under what circumstances?
> - With the consent of whom?
> - Do you have a clear school policy in place to support this?
> - Are all members of staff aware of this and the implications of putting the policy into practice?

The Special Educational Needs and Disability Code of Practice (DfE/DH, 2015) discusses the sharing of information between education, health care and social care providers.

> Local authorities with their partners should establish local protocols for the effective sharing of information which addresses confidentiality, consent and security of information . . . Local authorities must discuss with the child and young person and their parents what information they are happy for the local authority to share with other agencies.
>
> (DfE/DH, 2015)

The Code of Practice (DfE/DH, 2015) refers teachers to further guidance (H.M. Government, 2015) about the sharing of personal information to practitioners who work with children.

The seven golden rules to sharing information (H.M. Government, 2015: 4)

1. Remember that the Data Protection Act 1998 and human rights law are not barriers to justified information sharing but provide a framework to ensure that personal information about living individuals is shared appropriately.
2. Be open and honest with the individual (and/or their family where appropriate) from the outset about why, what, how and with whom information will or could be shared, and seek their agreement, unless it is unsafe or inappropriate to do so.

3   Seek advice from other practitioners if you are in any doubt about sharing the information concerned, without disclosing the identity of the individual where possible.

4   Share with informed consent where appropriate and, where possible, respect the wishes of those who do not consent to share confidential information. You may still share information without consent if, in your judgement, there is good reason to do so, such as where safety may be at risk. You will need to base your judgement on the facts of the case. When you are sharing or requesting personal information from someone, be certain of the basis upon which you are doing so. Where you have consent, be mindful that an individual might not expect information to be shared.

5   Consider safety and well-being. Base your information sharing decisions on considerations of the safety and well-being of the individual and others who may be affected by their actions.

6   Necessary, proportionate, relevant, adequate, timely and secure: Ensure that the information you share is necessary for the purpose for which you are sharing it, is shared only with those individuals who need to have it, is accurate and up-to-date, is shared in a timely fashion, and is shared securely.

7   Keep a record of your decision and the reasons for it – whether it is to share information or not. If you decide to share, then record what you have shared, with whom and for what purpose.

The flowchart of when and how to share information (H. M. Government, 2015: 12) provided in the Practical Resources section of this chapter is also a very helpful tool to support teachers to think through the issues around sharing information. It may be helpful for the school to include this within their school policy.

Communicating information

It is vital that communication with colleagues, health care professionals, parents and children is as clear and accessible as possible. The Plain English Campaign provides online helpful advice about communicating in plain English. Key points are:

- Keep your sentences short.
- Use active verbs as much as possible.
- Use 'you' and 'we'.
- Use words that are appropriate for your audience.
- Use everyday English.
- Prefer short words.
- Do not be afraid to give instructions.
- Avoid nominalisations.
- Use lists where appropriate.
- Apologise well.
- Be concise.
- Stop and think before you write.
- When writing, imagine you are talking to your reader.
- Check that your writing is clear, helpful, human and polite.

Empathic communication

Teachers who need to work closely with other teachers, practitioners or parents need to not only be able to communicate information clearly, but they need to support one another emotionally using empathy. Being empathic means being able to understand another's own internal frame of reference. It is about being able to imagine and appreciate their unique experience, but it is not about experiencing their emotions, which is sympathy (Hough, 1998). Jacobs (1985) suggests that if a teacher is caught up in sharing the same emotional response as the parent/colleague/child, they will find it very difficult to remain objective and to listen really well. When a teacher is able to maintain a persona of calm and emotional stability, this gives the message that the teacher can cope and also that the teacher believes that the children, parents and colleagues can also cope. The value of empathy lies in the 'received' empathy that someone experiences from the teacher. It promotes their self-worth and counters their feelings of helplessness. At about 3 or 4 years old, children start empathising with others, and when they do, they largely take their cues from adults (Hoffman, 1989). Teachers who can express themselves empathically are role modelling the skills of helpful emotional and social communication which are vital to the healthy processing of emotions related to chronic worry, stress, death or bereavement.

Some examples of empathic sentences are provided below:

To a class

- I understand that you are feeling disappointed. You thought that Jemma would be able to help us today.
- I imagine, like me, you are feeling very sad today.
- I think we are all feeling anxious today.

To parents

- I realise that this is very painful to talk about.
- I can see that you are very worried about how Jack's illness might be affecting your own child.
- I understand your very reasonable concerns.

To health care or social care professionals

- I realise that you are extremely busy and have very many other commitments, but I am feeling very anxious about Sam.
- I understand that you are trying your best for us. Is there anything that the school can do to speed things along?
- I see that you are very rushed today and what I'm asking is difficult for you.

Taking into account the needs of others

Obviously, the needs and wishes of the child with a life-limiting or life-threatening condition and their family are just one side of the issue. Teachers will also need to make difficult decisions, as recognised by the teachers in our research, about when and how to communicate about the condition (with the permission of the child and their parents) with other parents and children in the school. Issues relating to the emotional needs of other children and ways to communicate appropriately with them about life-limiting or life-threatening conditions, death and bereavement are discussed in Chapter 9. Decisions about the right time and approach to use will need to be made on the basis of a number of key factors, including:

- the developmental age of the children
- any cultural issues which may need to be considered and respected

At other times, the school may need to send general information out to all parents, particularly, for example, in the case of infection control, which is key for children going through treatments for cancer. The example letter provided in the Practical Resources section can therefore be adapted, in consultation with parents, the child and the professionals involved, to provide clear information to other parents.

Practical resources

In this section, the following practical resources are provided:

1   Flowchart of when and how to share information (H. M. Government, 2015: 12)
2   Guidelines for communicating in plain English
3   Example letter to parents about the risk of infection in school

1 Flowchart of when and how to share information

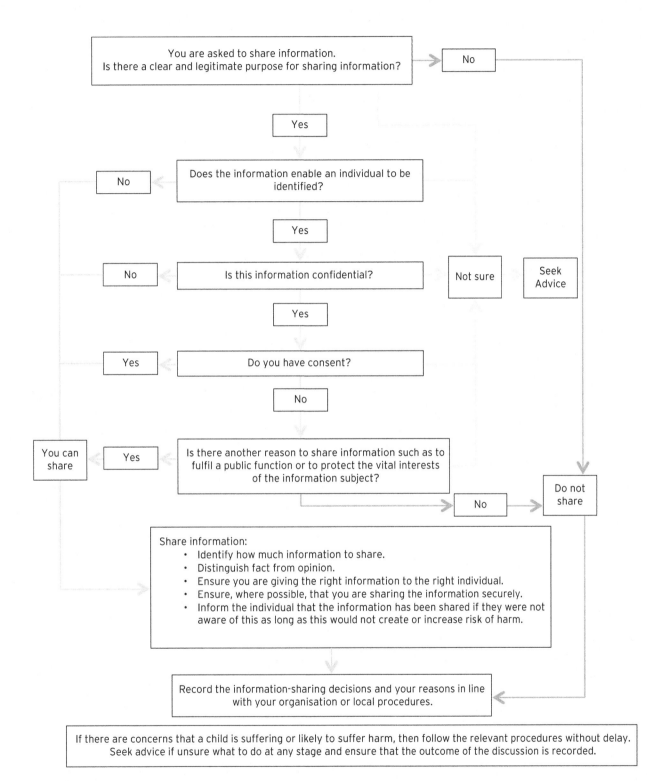

You are asked to share information.
Is there a clear and legitimate purpose for sharing information? → No

Yes

No ← Does the information enable an individual to be identified?

Yes

No ← Is this information confidential?   Not sure   Seek Advice

Yes

Yes ← Do you have consent?

No

You can share ← Yes ← Is there another reason to share information such as to fulfil a public function or to protect the vital interests of the information subject? → No → Do not share

Share information:
- Identify how much information to share.
- Distinguish fact from opinion.
- Ensure you are giving the right information to the right individual.
- Ensure, where possible, that you are sharing the information securely.
- Inform the individual that the information has been shared if they were not aware of this as long as this would not create or increase risk of harm.

Record the information-sharing decisions and your reasons in line with your organisation or local procedures.

If there are concerns that a child is suffering or likely to suffer harm, then follow the relevant procedures without delay. Seek advice if unsure what to do at any stage and ensure that the outcome of the discussion is recorded.

2 Communicating in plain English

Guidance	Explanation
Keep your sentences short.	Clear writing has an average sentence length of 15 to 20 words. Be punchy. Mix shorter sentences with longer ones.
Use active verbs as much as possible.	Consider the order of the subject, object and verb. Using a passive verb: The television (object) was watched (verb) by Peter (subject). Using an active verb: Peter (subject) watched (verb) the television (object).
Use 'you' and 'we'.	Using 'you' or 'we' is like speaking directly to a person, it personalises it, and it can be useful in making clear who holds responsibility.
Use words that are appropriate for your audience.	Say exactly what you mean, using the simplest words that fit.
Use everyday English.	Avoid jargon.
Prefer short words.	Long words will not impress your audience or help your writing style.
Don't be afraid to give instructions.	Be clear about what is to happen. Start the sentence with 'please' e.g. Please stand aside.
Avoid nominalisations.	These are formed from verbs e.g. to complete becomes completion; to fail becomes failure; to arrange becomes arrangement. Use the active verb rather than a nominalisation.
Use lists where appropriate.	Lists are excellent for splitting information up.
Apologise well.	Put yourself in your audience's shoes. Be professional, not emotional. Apologise at the start. Apologise completely, concisely, sympathetically and sincerely. Then move on to what you can do for them.
Be concise.	
Stop and think before you write.	Organise your points into a logical order.
When writing, imagine you are talking to your reader.	Write sincerely, personally, in a style that is suitable with the right tone of voice.
Check that your writing is clear, helpful, human and polite.	

Adapted from *How to Write in Plain English*. Plain English Campaign. Available at www.plainenglish.co.uk/files/howto.pdf. Accessed 18th October 2016.

3 Example letter to parents about the risk of infection in school

To alleviate undue stress and anxiety for staff, parents and the child about the potential for the child to become more ill due to infection within the school environment, it may be helpful to adapt the example letter that follows to send home to all pupils and families:

Dear Parents,

Measles, chicken pox and shingles

Please may we ask for your co-operation in an important matter.

One of our pupils is receiving medical treatment for cancer, which puts them at risk if they are exposed to measles, chicken pox or shingles.

Please let us know immediately if your child is suspected of having measles.

Our pupil is also at risk from chicken pox and would need to be given an injection within three days of contact. If your child is suspected of having chicken pox, you should let us know.

It is also important that you let us know if there is shingles in your household.

Your child is not at any risk whatsoever from this situation. However, the health and well-being of our pupil who is at risk does depend on the co-operation of all other parents, and we hope you can help us.

With many thanks.

Yours sincerely

Head Teacher

(Taken from CCLG, 2015).

Concluding comments

Knowing when and how to share information about the needs of a child with a life-limiting or life-threatening condition is crucial. In this, the statutory requirements and protocols around data protection must be understood and upheld. For effective communication with everyone, school staff will need to carefully consider their use of language, ensuring that jargon and specialist terminology are avoided so that meaning is as clear as possible.

8 Teaching and learning approaches

In this chapter, we:

- Consider ways medical conditions, treatments and other health care interventions can impact upon a child's ability to learn
- Consider ways for teachers to work flexibly within the context of the child's medical regime
- Reflect on the impact of social skills and/or social isolation on the learning process
- Introduce provision mapping as a way to plan for and record additional strategies and interventions that are needed for the individual or whole class
- Consider ways to link with other schools to support the needs of a child with life-limiting or life-threatening conditions

Introduction

Reflecting on appropriate teaching and learning approaches is a natural and significant part of the daily role of the teacher; it is something teachers are familiar and confident with. Our Teaching for Life research found that when faced with teaching children who have life-limiting or life-threatening conditions, teachers lacked confidence about how to manage this. Some, teachers started to question the relevance of education itself for a child who might not survive to adulthood:

> "How do you make education relevant to someone with a life-limiting illness? What's it for? What am I learning about? So much of what you feel you're driven towards in education is about the future, just as a general agenda. Of course it should be a bit more about the enjoyment of learning and all of that, but actually school is for qualifications, qualifications are for work, work is to earn money for your life and that might not be a stage that they ever reach."

For these teachers, questions were raised about the intrinsic purpose of and motivation for learning and education. Schools are held accountable for qualifications and standards which a child with a life-limiting or life-threatening condition may never reach or use. Teachers therefore started to reflect on the broader moral and ethical purpose of education:

> "I think there's a lesson for us all here, that it is that love for learning itself, rather than what the next step is. Throughout the whole of life, it's the value in the here and now, so perhaps it's looking at what we're doing in that respect as well."

The teachers also raised practical concerns such as worrying about how to stick to the curriculum when it may include references to death:

> *"Some topics, PSHE for example in year 4/5 one of the topics is death and how you're going to approach that with a child in your class that's facing that is going to potentially totally change how you deal with it or whether you deal with it at all. But I'd imagine that also has consequences in other topics, history and things like that, I'd feel apprehensive about approaching the topic of death a lot more I think. So even when you're talking about Henry VIII or beheading wives and things like that, you're still going to have connotations to not only that child but other children in the class and they'll know about this child that could die."*

> *"It's also when you're reading stories and the curriculum that you choose, you sometimes find yourself in the middle of a story and think, oh I don't want to see how this ends."*

The teachers also reflected on other practical considerations, such as how to make their teaching and learning approaches fun, to make the most of every hour and day that the child had left:

> *"My goodness, if I had a child like that in my class I'd want to make sure every lesson was really exciting, that was my initial thought. If a child had 6 months to live, it would be a massive influence on how you were teaching day to day I think. But I don't think a family would put a child in school if they only had 6 months to live, would they?"*

> *"So have you got to make it fun? And then how are you going to make it good without making things too different, so they're feeling more different than they do already?"*

Clear concerns from the teachers can be seen here: with fear about whether parents would really send children to school if they only had a limited time to live and how they would be able to cope with balancing a really spectacular, fun teaching and learning approach with the demands of the curriculum and accountability focus, with the continued focus on standards and the need for teaching to be 'OFSTED good or outstanding'.

> *"I feel like we're having to justify things a lot. So when you get an education welfare officer come in, they're looking at your attendance data and then [we're] having to . . . almost on the defensive justify what you're doing. Whereas actually you should be praised and supported for the fact that your student is in for 50% of the time, because the decision could be made actually what's the point of education? He's not got long with us, the parents could make that decision . . . because there isn't a framework saying what the recommendations and advice should be."*

Others thought that a framework to provide pastoral support was needed:

> *"That [type of] framework is simply absent for the pastoral side of things, the care side of things. It's the sense that the teacher has to be everything; the carer, the educator, the social worker. But there isn't a framework for it."*

Teachers also identified that they needed to develop bespoke and individualised approaches to meet the needs of the child and their family and that these would need to be flexible and responsive to the changing needs of both the child and their family over time:

> *"And then you have to do a bit of bespoke, catch-upy teaching, you just do it, you have to find the time. So their profiles tend to be a little bit spikey."*

"We've done a lot more working with Mum, so she does quite a lot with him at home. . . . She was very keen to make sure that what he couldn't necessarily do in school, she could take on a home tutoring type role."

The teachers identified that the educational experience became secondary to the medical/ health perspective and that this was a complex and difficult perspective for teachers and schools (often focused on raising standards and increasing attainment levels) to respond to. They identified that:

"They [parents] will say, yes we want them to have some work, no they're sick as a dog this week it's pointless."

"Her learning was almost on hold for quite a large portion of time, which we were aware of but it became secondary really. It was the health need that had to become our primary concern."

Yet within the concerns that were expressed by teachers anxious to 'do the right thing' for children in their care with life-limiting or life-threatening conditions, teachers also reflected on and recognised that school was a necessary and normalising influence on the life of the child and their family. Many recognised, therefore, that the school may act as a stable and 'normal' environment for a child amongst all their hospital visits and treatment. It could be a place where they could feel 'normal' within their routine:

"The school's providing the stable environment, where they're just one of everybody else, whereas at home, in hospital, they're not getting that."

Summary

Whilst the medical and health needs of children with life-limiting or life-threatening conditions were a primary focus, teachers naturally started to reflect and consider more practical pedagogic issues which would impact the teaching and learning approaches they develop within schools. In this, teachers identified a number of challenges and tensions, with the following key themes therefore emerging as significant:

- The broad relevance of education
- The challenge of making learning fun versus maintaining high standards of teaching and learning
- Education as secondary to medical needs
- School as providing normality for children and their families

Policy review

Local authorities are ultimately responsible for arranging suitable education for permanently excluded pupils and for other pupils who, because of illness or other reasons, would not receive suitable education without such arrangements being made (DfE, 2013). This requirement, however, is then passed to the individual school.

Thus, all schools, including maintained schools, academies and PRUs (Pupil Referral Units) are required, under Section 100 of the Children and Families Act (DfE, 2014) to ensure that appropriate arrangements are in place to meet the needs of children at their school with medical conditions (DfE, 2015). Schools must, therefore, ensure that the educational needs of children with life-limiting or life-threatening conditions are understood and met, even when the child is not able to physically attend school. *Supporting Pupils at School with Medical Conditions* (DfE, 2015) highlights the following key points:

- 'Pupils at school with medical conditions should be properly supported so that they have full access to education, including school trips and physical education.'

(DfE, 2015: 4)

- Children with medical conditions should be 'properly supported in school so that they can play a full and active role in school life, remain healthy and achieve their academic potential.'

(DfE, 2015: 5)

- Schools need to ensure that 'children with medical conditions fully engage with learning and do not fall behind when they are unable to attend.'

(DfE, 2015: 5)

- The arrangements that the school puts into place to meet the needs of a child with life-limiting or life-threatening conditions 'should show an understanding of how medical conditions impact on a child's ability to learn.'

(DfE, 2015: 7)

- 'Schools, local authorities, health professionals, commissioners and other support services should work together to ensure that children with medical conditions receive a full education. In some cases this will require flexibility and involve, for example, programmes of study that rely on part-time attendance at school in combination with alternative provision arranged by the local authority.'

(DfE, 2015: 7)

- Schools will also need to carefully consider how children will be 'reintegrated back into school after periods of absence.'

(DfE, 2015: 7)

Reflective activity

- What is your understanding of the term 'full access to education'?
  - Is this currently achieved in your school setting?
  - How?
  - Are there any remaining barriers?
  - Do you think that the child and/or their parents would also consider that they have 'full access to education'?
- What does 'properly supported' mean in practice?
  - How can this be achieved?
  - What could be the barriers, and how could these be overcome?
- How can the school ensure that a child with life-limiting or life-threatening conditions is 'fully engaged'?
- How can the school ensure that a child with life-limiting or life-threatening conditions does not fall behind when unable to attend school?

- What implications does this have for different teaching and learning approaches that the child can access even when not in the school?
- Are these different approaches still providing the child with an equitable experience of education? Or are they missing out on some elements of the curriculum or teaching?
- Does your school have an understanding of how medical conditions impact a child's ability to learn?
- How is this demonstrated?
- How effective is this understanding?

One of the concerns teachers and school leaders may have, although they may not wish to it voice explicitly, is the impact of low levels of attendance and low rates of academic progress on the school's overall attendance and attainment/progress figures. School staff are also often concerned about the scrutiny of OFSTED where overall school trends and patterns of attendance and attainment may be skewed by the inclusion of a child or children with life-limiting or life-threatening conditions.

Attendance

It is a legal requirement in Britain that all children must receive an education between the school term after their fifth birthday and the last Friday in June in the school year that they turn 16. For parents, this means:

> You must make sure your child gets a full-time education that meets their needs (e.g. if they have special educational needs). You can send your child to school or educate them yourself.
> (Gov.UK, 2016)

As part of both their pre-inspection and inspection reports, OFSTED monitors a child's pupil attendance, since research has clearly shown it has an impact on attainment (DfE, 2015): as part of 'Personal development, behaviour and welfare', inspectors will make judgements on 'prompt and regular attendance' (OFSTED, 2015). However, children can be excused from attending school if they are too ill to attend or have received prior permission. In these cases, OFSTED will want to know how pupils with absence due to long-term medical needs are supported. The school will be expected to have:

- up-to-date attendance and absence figures
- comparative attendance and absence figures for the current year and previous years
- the trend in the rate of absence over the previous 3 years
- data about the proportion of permissible absence

The school will also be expected to have a breakdown of attendance and absence by:

- gender
- absence code
- year group
- Key Stage

- vulnerable groups, e.g. special educational needs (SEN), English as an additional language (EAL), new arrivals, Pupil Premium
- attainment, e.g. under-performing groups from RAISEonline
- 'at-risk' groups, e.g. young carers, child in need

Progress

For those children with life-limiting or life-threatening conditions, the school is expected to keep accurate records of their attendance and progress as they would with any other pupil. They must also show that they have supported the child with a life-limiting or life-threatening condition to make progress; this is not without its challenges when a child may have long periods of absence from the school setting. Whilst schools are still accountable for end of Key Stage attainment data, there is now an increased focus on rates of progress against baseline starting points. In this, both the Department for Education and OFSTED acknowledge that for any pupil, progress is not always linear. When a child or group of children do not show age-expected progress or are not reaching 'floor/minimum standards', schools will be expected to show that they:

- are aware of these
- have an understanding of why
- are proactively attempting to address it

The situation for a child with a life-limiting or life-threatening condition, who previously may have been making age-related progress and attainment, will therefore need to be carefully explained, and the school will need to be very clear about the positive steps they are taking and responsible for in relation to putting in place focused and appropriate support to enable the child to make progress in school. For children with serious illnesses affecting their attendance and ability to concentrate, the school may find it helpful to adopt a 'blended' approach to learning, consisting of but not limited to:

- use of the school's virtual learning environment (VLE) which can include recorded lessons which the child and their families can access at a later date
- use of Skype or some form of virtual classroom (e.g. Moodle or Collaborate) to teach children at a distance, including in hospital
- training and support through use of TA and/or SENCO in liaison with class/subject teachers to provide additional support
- working closely with parents and health professionals to understand when a child can and cannot attend
- clear record keeping in pupil progress meetings, in regard to pupil needs, progress and action being taken to address these needs. This could be recorded on a provision map or individual learning plan.

Practical considerations

There are a range of educational options available to children with a life-limiting or life-threatening condition, including education within the hospital, where it is even possible to take exams if necessary, home tuition and so forth. However, no matter how lengthy the treatment regime or how ill the child is, they are often encouraged to attend school whenever they can to enable them to retain their social relationships and interactions with peers (CCLG, 2014).

When a child is able to attend school, intermittently or permanently, it is preferable for the child to continue their education in the same classroom and with their same peers wherever possible. Withdrawal, separation or moving the child into a younger age class will simply exacerbate feelings of separation and make developing appropriate social interactions with peers more difficult.

Ways medical conditions, treatments and other health care interventions can impact a child's ability to learn

Reflective activity

- In what ways do you think medical conditions, medical treatments and other health care interventions could impact a child's ability to learn?
- How do you think those conditions/issues could be resolved?
- What impact do you think they may have on the teaching and learning approaches that you need to embed within your classroom when working with the child?
- How can you ensure that those approaches are inclusive and supportive rather than exclusive/withdrawn approaches?

Medical conditions, medical treatments (medicines including chemotherapy, surgery and radiotherapy) and other health care or therapeutic interventions can all directly impact the child's ability to access learning in a range of ways. The most obvious is that all require the child to be absent for a short or very long period of time. It is, even for just a minute, a time when the child is reminded that they have a condition, that they are different. Each child is unique, and they will be affected in different ways and to different degrees. Table 8.1 identifies some common symptoms associated with many life-limiting or life-threatening conditions or their treatment and their consequences for a child's ability to learn.

Table 8.1 Common symptoms associated with life-limiting or life-threatening conditions

Symptom	Impact	Strategies to support learning
Breathing difficulties	Lack of energy; unable to access physical activities	Ensure that the child is given the time they need to complete activities, particularly ones involving physical activity. Where the planned physical activities would not be possible for the child, plan alternative inclusive options for them to engage with, preferably with peers. Or use the child as the leader/teacher of a physical activity rather than having them participate in it directly (e.g. they can time the activity/start the race/coach peers on effective techniques).
Bruising	Self-conscious; risk of bruising in the school environment	Ensure that private changing facilities are provided where necessary and opportunities for the child to wear long sleeves and clothing that covers bruising if needed. Consider arrangements that may need to be implemented to ensure that the risk of bruising to the child (e.g. when transitioning between classrooms through busy corridors between lessons) are identified and reduced, that is, by allowing the child to leave the classroom 5 minutes before the usual transition time so that they can avoid crowded times/areas where there is more chance that they will be bumped by others.

(Continued)

Table 8.1 (Continued)

Symptom	Impact	Strategies to support learning
Eating difficulties	Weight loss, hunger, low energy, poor concentration	Ensure that a plan is agreed with the child and their parents for supporting eating within the school environment. This may include frequent opportunities for snacks to ensure that the child is able to have the energy levels required to concentrate during lessons, as well as support to eat at lunchtime. Provide the child with the time they need to be able to eat effectively, and be aware that if their mouth is particularly sore, they may need help with eating and may prefer privacy to avoid embarrassment.
Emotional rollercoaster: sadness, loss, anxiety	Inability to think	Be aware of the situation for the child, and ensure that all adults working with the child are aware. Chunk learning into smaller, more manageable amounts, with regular positive prompts to help the child achieve successfully.
Fatigue	Fatigue can be 'greatly underestimated. It is more than being a bit tired, and can affect mood as well as energy levels' (CCLG, 2015).	Allow 'short bursts of activities with regular changes in task and expectation' (CCLG, 2015). Be flexible about school attendance.
Hair loss	Self-consciousness, low self-esteem, avoidance of peers and therefore learning opportunities	Work with the child and the adults to talk openly about strategies and approaches they think will work, that is, would the child prefer to wear a wig, or a hat all the time at school? Consider ways to explain this to peers in an appropriate way (with the prior permission of parents and the child) so that it 'normalises' the approach. Consider activities that focus on identifying 'what makes us unique' which can emphasise differences as a positive aspect rather than as a negative difference. Talk with the child about whether it would support their self-esteem if all children were asked to wear a hat for a day to again 'normalise' the difference.
Lack of sleep, insomnia	Tiredness; lack of concentration	Be aware of this and ensure that all learning is chunked and as active as possible. Identify with the child and their family times when they are most able to concentrate.
Lethargy/tiredness	Inability to focus or concentrate	Identify with the child and family when the best time to access learning may be. It may be best to focus on mornings only to allow time in the afternoon to rest. Or perhaps the child needs to sleep in in the morning and then has more energy after lunch.
Long-term or frequent absence	Gaps in knowledge Inability to concentrate for long periods of time; out of the 'habit' of learning	Send work home, where/when appropriate, to help the child retain previous learning.
Loss of appetite	Low energy levels, inability to concentrate for long periods of time	Allow frequent opportunities for the child to 'snack-eat' to gradually build up reserves of energy to be able to access teaching and learning activities.

Symptom	Impact	Strategies to support learning
Loss of confidence/ self-esteem	Lack of confidence and ability to participate effectively in learning.	Provide structured support focused on building self-esteem - this could be through a 1:1 mentoring approach and/or whole class confidence and self-esteem-building approaches.
Memory loss or slow information processing due to fatigue, absences or head-related condition and treatment	Slower learning and processing speed	Ensure that learning is chunked into smaller activities and that there is regular repetition, consolidation and reinforcement of learning. Do not assume that because the child has 'learnt' something one day, they will necessarily be able to retain that to another day.
Nausea	Poor concentration	Plan provision/support for when a child is feeling like this. Make sure that the child knows where they can go if they feel sick and/ or provide a sick bowl. Provide frequent rest breaks and/or small chunks of learning.
Pain	Unable to concentrate, unable to be still	Ensure that you are fully aware of the timings on the painkiller regime and that learning fits in in tandem with that regime. Ensure regular reviews of painkiller regimes with appropriate medical professionals to ensure full understanding of the implications of it for learning.
Shortened attention span	Unable to concentrate for prolonged periods during whole-class or group teaching and learning activities	Find ways to chunk learning into smaller, more manageable steps. Make learning as active and multi-sensory as possible to support shortened attention spans.
Skin breakdown (e.g. injection sites, radiotherapy)	Sore and sensitive skin	Ensure that dressings are safe and clean within the school environment. Be aware of key busy transition times during the school day and provide opportunities for the child to avoid busy and over-crowded corridors or areas where possible, as if the child gets bumped by others in a crowded corridor, this could exacerbate skin sensitivity. Consider carefully physical activities that the child is expected to engage in and ensure that the child is able to do these - or find an alternative activity, for example using the child as the teacher, lead or coach - if the activity itself would exacerbate skin sensitivity.
Weak ankles, aches and pains	The treatment that the child receives may impact their muscles, causing weakness or pain. They may have weakened coordination skills and/or not be able to carry school bags and equipment around school.	Implement a 'buddy system' so that the child has someone who will carry their equipment and bags around school for them. Put in place support and additional/alternative systems for enabling the child to record written work.

It is essential for teachers to be flexible and proactive, to anticipate needs and to communicate effectively with the child's parents, the child and the team working with the child and their family. Additional needs, such as the need for extra time in formal exams (e.g. GCSE and A Level exams), should be anticipated, planned for and put in place in plenty of time to support and reassure the child.

Working flexibly to respond to the child's health care plan and medical regime

Reflective activity

- If you already have or have had a child with a life-limiting or life-threatening condition in your school, how aware were/are you of the child's health care plan and medical regime?
- Was/is this shared with you?
- Who by?
- What sort of information would you hope to be included on the child's health care plan?
- What sort of information about the medical treatment regime would be helpful for you to have?
- How do you think that this would help you understand and respond more effectively to the child's teaching and learning needs?

The child's individual health care plan, or Education, Health and Care Plan if they have special educational needs or a disability, drawn up by the family and multi-professional team, needs to make reference to dates and types of health care or therapeutic interventions such as surgery, physiotherapy or counselling so that the teacher can predict (as far as possible, with parental guidance if possible) whether a child is likely to be very tired, emotional or physically unwell at different times. It should also identify and plan for all possible/potential problems, allowing staff to feel more prepared and less anxious about any issues that may emerge such as nosebleeds or vomiting.

The child's medical regime is the sequence of medical treatments, such as surgery followed by chemotherapy followed by radiotherapy, over a period of time. Medical treatments are often the most invasive aspects of health care for both a child's body and their self-concept. For some life-limiting or life-threatening conditions, the family will know the dates of the medical regime that has been planned. The health care plan needs to include these key dates to enable teachers to consider how to provide planned appropriate teaching and learning activities. Medical regimes vary, some conditions require long stays in hospital, while others can just receive treatment on an out-patient basis. All children respond differently to medical treatment, and so even where staff are fully briefed about the expected symptoms or side effects of treatment, an individual child can respond in their own unique way. Although Table 8.1 offers a starting point, nothing can replace good dialogue with parents and health care staff where possible. Teachers need to:

- ensure that teaching and learning approaches are planned to work *with* rather than in competition with the health care plan, including the medical regime
- look at times when the child is going to have high levels of treatment and the consequences of this for the child's ability to positively access learning activities and plan lower-level, consolidation activities rather than new teaching and extension learning activities
- check with health care professionals and parents for the times when the child is likely to be more stable within the overall treatment plan, and then ensure that at those times additional provision and support is put in place to help the child make the most of times when they are able to access learning and make progress
- continue to have high expectations for the ability and progress of the child and to be able to positively demonstrate those whilst doing so within the reality of the timings of the health care plan

- ensure that the child is supported when they are well enough to make positive progress and that the learning potential of the child is not completely neglected under the excuse or justification that they are too ill

It is important for school staff to understand that they have a responsibility, as the professionals who will hopefully see the child regularly within the school context, to alert the multi-professional team if they notice any worrying changes to appearance and/or behaviour and also to alert the team if the child is absent from school.

The impact of social skills and/or social isolation on learning

Learning is a largely social process, and whilst the primary focus of the teacher will be on their teaching and learning approaches, the provision and support planned and the curriculum on offer, it is also important for staff to be mindful of the social aspects of learning and the implications of this for a child with a life-limiting or life-threatening condition. Children learn by copying and interacting with others across a range of activities during which they learn new skills then transfer and apply them in new and different ways. The greatest way to extend learning is often not by adult-led instruction but through peer-to-peer discussion and collaborative, social learning.

A child with a life-limiting or life-threatening condition who has been absent from school for some time may find re-engagement with social aspects of both school and learning very daunting. The busy and sometimes noisy environment of the teaching and learning situation may at times feel overwhelming to a child who has been isolated at home or hospital for some time. They may feel anxious and insecure within the busy classroom context where everyone else seems to know exactly what to do and how to behave. Their social links with peers may have broken down, and children who were previously firm friends may now, naturally, have moved on to form new social bonds with others in the class. The child may be left feeling isolated and unsure of how to fit in to the new social dynamics.

In addition to this, teachers also need to consider ways that all children subconsciously compare and judge themselves against the learning abilities of their peers. Children, from a very early age, are adept at understanding themselves and others in relation to their skills and difficulties. They will make conscious and unconscious judgements about themselves in relation to the abilities of others in the class. For example, they will be aware of their own gaps in learning and skills as a result of their absences from school. Staff need to be very aware of how perception can impact the child's self-concept and self-esteem. The following key strategies may be helpful for teachers who are trying to support a child to positively access and engage in social and collaborative teaching and learning activities.

- Aim for sensitive approaches that will support the child without highlighting the differences or gaps in learning.
- Try to avoid situations in which the child is, albeit in well-meaning ways, moved into younger age or lower-ability teaching groups, as this may add to the child's insecurity about their own abilities.
- Consider the social situations that are set up for learning. Make additional preparations to ensure that the child feels safe, secure and confident enough to engage in group learning situations.
- Consider buddying systems to support the child, but make sure that this is discussed fully with the child so that it is a positive strategy to support the child rather than something that can become a negative experience.

- Consider alternative or supported strategies during unstructured times at school so that the child does not experience unnecessary social isolation: could they use break times and/or lunchtimes as rest times so that they are not exposed to overly daunting unstructured social situations? Or would it be best for the child to access those unstructured social times as a way to help them engage positively with their peers and form new social relationships and then have rest breaks during some of the learning situations?
- Think about the best way to support the child to catch up and fill in potential gaps in their learning without making those gaps in learning obvious to the child and others during whole-class and group learning activities.
- Make sure that all decisions about these strategies are discussed fully with the child and their family to ensure that the best plan for the child is selected.
- The child's needs may change regularly as a result of changes to their health care and other factors. The health care plan needs to be updated accordingly. Specifically, the child's re-integration into a school after a period of absence needs to be thoughtfully planned.
- Ensure that there are regular, planned opportunities for reviewing any strategies that have been implemented. These dates/times should be noted within the child's health care plan.

Provision mapping

Provision mapping can be used as a way to record an individual's, a class's or even a year group's additional needs, the allocation of resources and their impact (Ekins & Grimes, 2009; Massey, 2013; Ekins, 2015). Provision mapping is often used for planning provision for children who have special educational needs and disabilities, but it can equally be used for planning, recording and assessing resources such as school counsellors, therapists or additional classes in social and emotional education. Keeping such records not only allows an assessment of impact and a useful record to share with other professionals working with the child of the interventions and strategies that are used to support the child in school but also provides useful evidence for OFSTED about creative approaches to deal with issues that may impact pupils' achievement (see example provided in the Practical Resources section).

Links with other schools

If a child with a life-limiting or life-threatening condition has been in hospital receiving treatment for some time, it may be that they have been able to access some education provided through the hospital. Whilst this is happening, it would be helpful for the school to be able to provide the hospital provision with an update summary of the child's academic attainment and progress levels up until that point so that the hospital educational provision can most accurately and effectively support the child with meaningful learning activities which will match their actual ability levels.

Once the child starts to re-integrate into the school context, further communication and liaison between any hospital educational provision that the child has been able to access and school will be really helpful in order to ensure that work completed is acknowledged and incorporated into any strategies for future teaching and learning activities. Remember as well that staff who provide education on behalf of a hospital will have extensive expertise in and experience of setting up supported teaching and learning activities for children with life-limiting or life-threatening conditions. School teachers are therefore encouraged to liaise with and learn from these staff.

Teachers in mainstream schools should also consider utilising the expertise that lies within local special schools. Special schools cater for a wide range of diverse needs, and many, particularly those meeting the needs of children with profound, multiple and complex needs, will regularly be working with children with life-limiting or life-threatening conditions. It will therefore be very beneficial for mainstream school staff to make approaches to local special schools asking for opportunities to learn from and observe strategies that they have developed and implemented for many years.

Reflective activity

- Identify the local schools and/or settings that you could liaise with to find out more about how to effectively meet the teaching and learning needs of children with life-limiting or life-threatening conditions.
- What information would you like to gather from a different school setting?
- How would you plan to use this information to help you effectively meet the needs of children with life-limiting or life-threatening conditions?

Practical resources

In this section, the following practical resources are provided:

1   Example Provision Mapping format

1 Example Provision Mapping format

Provision	Student name	Pupil premium	Lead person/ Frequency/duration	Starting data	Expected outcomes	End data	Evaluation of impact
Circle time/ focused PSHE input	Whole class	N/A	Class teacher. Daily for 10 mins	The class have just found out about the condition of one of their peers	To be able to understand and articulate feelings of grief. To be able to know how to ask sensitive questions. To know who to approach if feeling sad.		
Small group play therapist input	Stuart Molly Alice Ben	Y N N N	Play therapist. 1x weekly for 30 mins	High levels of grief and anxiety about their friends' condition	To be able to think about and understand their feelings of grief in different ways. To be able to talk about feelings of anxiety. To understand and use key strategies to cope with feelings of anxiety.		
1:1 play therapy	Peter	N	Play therapist 2x weekly for an hour each	Peter is in denial about his condition and showing high levels of anger and frustration.	To be able to talk about his condition. To be able to acknowledge his feelings and find strategies to cope with them.		
Medical exit card	Peter	N	First aider As needed	Peter is experiencing high levels of pain and tiredness in school.	To be able to use his medical exit card to find the named first aider to get support and a rest from class.		

© 2017 Alison Ekins, Sally Robinson, Ian Durrant and Kathryn Summers

Concluding comments

Children with life-limiting or life-threatening conditions have a right to access education, and teachers therefore need to be supported to understand and respond to this statutory responsibility in meaningful and effective ways. Having a child with a life-limiting or life-threatening condition in their class can be a worrying experience for a teacher who is not supported and does not understand the implications of the situation for both herself and the child. The findings from our research certainly suggested that where a teacher was prepared, supported and, to a large extent, reassured about the impact of a life-limiting or life-threatening condition on a child and its implications for teaching and learning, the teacher's anxiety diminished. This facilitated good communication between the teacher, family and child and enabled the teachers to confidently put effective strategies into place.

9 Understanding and supporting emotional and behavioural changes

In this chapter, we:

- Consider the emotional and behavioural needs of children with life-limiting or life-threatening conditions
- Review ways to maintain consistent behavioural expectations for children with life-limiting or life-threatening conditions
- Recognise the emotional and behavioural needs of other children at school
- Recognise the emotional and behavioural needs of siblings of a child with a life-limiting or life-threatening condition
- Consider the use of Class Profiles of Need to support information sharing so that all staff have an understanding of factors impacting a child's emotional and behavioural well-being
- Review ways that social and emotional aspects of learning (SEAL) can be used to support the emotional and behavioural needs of children
- Explore ways to help children with bereavement and feelings of loss

Introduction

Teachers in the Teaching for Life research identified particular concerns about the impact of a life-limiting or life-threatening condition on the child's emotional and behavioural development. It was recognised that the child may experience a range of emotions, including anxiety, low self-esteem, anger, isolation and/or frustration, and teachers demonstrated that they were concerned about how to manage these appropriately:

> "Are there going to be any behavioural issues? Is the stress or the trauma of what's going on going to impact on the child's behaviour and then how are you going to manage that?"

Teachers' experiences confirmed that pupils' attitudes and verbal and non-verbal behaviour could become challenging. Some children had become used to one-on-one focused attention at hospital and being able to challenge doctors and nurses. On returning to school, they seemed unsure about how to speak to teachers appropriately:

> ". . . he spent so long under medical care, talking to doctors and things where he'd be allowed to challenge them. He doesn't necessarily know how to speak to the adults in school appropriately and can come across as quite rude and quite blunt, the tone which he uses. And he also has a certain attitude of 'well you can't punish me, because I could die before you'. He tries to take advantage of it and play it on an emotional level to the teachers."

Another teacher had been confronted with comments such as: "*I'm going to be dead before you.*" The teachers described feeling vulnerable and anxious about how to deal with these situations, identifying that if information is not shared effectively, the wrong assumptions may be made about the underlying cause of any changes in behaviour:

> "*This girl had had behaviour changes, which everyone was going, oh she's got really naughty, she must have got into a bad crowd and we've only just found out, oh my goodness that's . . . now I feel awful.*"

Teachers in the research also identified the need to be aware of the effect of the needs of the child with a life-limiting or life-threatening condition on other children in the class or school. Teachers recognised the importance of thinking about the impact of the situation on all children, how other children may be feeling and the day-to-day social interactions between the children:

> "*There's been a lot of issues with bullying and peer relationships and things like that, erm, which I think is the other children's way of struggling to cope with the fact that this is something they don't see a lot of.*"

> "*The other children in the class found it quite difficult, because obviously it was quite a shock when he came in with his treatment; he had a headscarf and so on. So we had to try and prepare the children. That was the harder thing to sort of say, you know, when he comes back he won't look the same, but you need to treat him the same.*"

In the research, many teachers discussed their fears about what would happen if a child in their school died. One said,

> "*If he was to pass away under our care he would have been a classmate of 28 other 8-year-old children. How are we going to, how are we gonna manage that positively and enable the children to grieve? . . . If a child in the class were to die, how do you . . . I don't think I'd even know where to start with that.*"

Summary

The key themes to emerge from the teachers' responses were:

- anxiety and concern about the emotional well-being of the child and any behavioural changes that may be experienced
- the need for open and prompt communication to ensure that any underlying causes for changes in behaviour can be recognised and understood
- the need to be aware of the impact on other children and their emotional and behavioural well-being

Policy review

The Department for Education's guidance *Supporting Pupils at School with Medical Conditions* (2015) highlights the importance for schools to develop an understanding of the emotional and behavioural needs of children with life-limiting or life-threatening conditions: 'In addition to the educational impacts, there are social and emotional implications associated with medical conditions' (DfE, 2015: 5). In particular, the guidance identifies that the child 'may be self-conscious about their condition and some may be bullied or develop emotional disorders such as anxiety or depression around their medical condition' (DfE, 2015: 5). The guidance also notes the impact of long-term absences on the child's 'general wellbeing and emotional health' (DfE, 2015: 5), as well as the impact of 'short-term and frequent absences, including those for appointments connected with a pupil's medical condition (which can often be lengthy), [which] need to be effectively managed and appropriate support put in place to limit the impact on the child's educational attainment and emotional and general wellbeing' (DfE, 2015: 5).

Reflective activity

- How do your current whole-school policies adequately reflect the need for the school to understand and proactively plan for the 'social and emotional implications associated with medical conditions' (DfE, 2015: 5)?
- How do your current whole-school policies address how to support a child through long or frequent short-term absences from school?
- What adjustments need to be made to whole-school policies to appropriately respond to the individual needs of a child with a life-limiting or life-threatening condition?

Practical considerations

The emotional and behavioural needs of the child with a life-limiting or life-threatening condition

Teachers identified that they wanted to better understand how life-limiting or life-threatening conditions may affect children emotionally and behaviourally and wanted strategies for dealing with a range of possible changes that could be experienced.

Reflective activity

- What emotional and behavioural changes might you expect from a child with a life-limiting or life-threatening condition?
- In what ways might other children be affected (emotionally and behaviourally) by finding out that a child in their class/school has a life-limiting or life-threatening condition?
- What could be the underlying causes of those changes in emotional and behavioural well-being in the child with a life-limiting or life-threatening condition?
- What strategies/support/interventions/approaches could you consider utilising to support both the child with the life-limiting or life-threatening condition and other children in the school?
- Does anyone in the school have the skills/expertise to deliver those approaches in school already?
- If not, what support could you access to be able to ensure that effective evidence-based approaches are implemented to support the child and their peers?

Children with life-limiting or life-threatening conditions can be expected to experience a range of different emotional responses, and they may not just be limited to one or similar emotional responses. They may move from withdrawn to angry outbursts whilst they struggle to make sense of their condition and their treatment. The child may therefore experience some or all of the following emotional and behavioural responses:

- anger
- frustration
- denial
- loss of self-confidence/self-esteem
- tearful
- depressed
- anxious
- withdrawn
- extrovert
- isolation
- dependent on others

Whilst it would be natural to assume that these emotional and behavioural responses are as a result of having to come to terms with the life-limiting or life-threatening condition and its associated health care and medical treatment, it is also important to try and look beyond that to the wide range of additional factors that will be impacting the child. These may include:

- pain
- tiredness
- anxiety
- the effect of the medication, for example, steroids can make patients more emotional (CCLG, 2015) or give them a heightened or artificial sense of well-being, making them appear more extroverted
- concern about the medical treatment
- concern about the longer-term prognosis including their own sense of mortality
- worry for their parents or siblings and the impact their condition has on them

Although teachers may be focused on recognising and understanding the emotional and behavioural consequences of medical treatments, what teachers and schools also need to understand is that even when a child's medical regime has finished and has been deemed to be 'successful' in medical terms, the child may be far from being healthy, well and 'back to normal'. Both the physical and emotional experiences and memories of the condition, medical treatment, health care and the rehabilitation process are likely to have a long-lasting and possibly permanent impact on the child's self-concept. As CCLG (2015) identified, at the end of treatment:

> [M]ost children look forward to returning to their classroom's familiarity and normality but, in practice, this is the time that they can feel the most different from their peers. They have the dawning realisation that their experience has changed them.
>
> (CCLG, 2015: 14)

Building self-esteem

As discussed in Chapter 8, one of the key consequences for a child with a life-limiting or life-threatening condition may be the impact of social isolation on their self-esteem and general emotional well-being. It will therefore be essential for school to try to positively and proactively address this, not only whilst the child is in school, through buddying and anti-bullying schemes, but also through supportive measures whilst the child may not be able to attend school. In some schools, this has included a range of age-appropriate measures, including:

- letters/cards home to the child from their friends and teachers
- video messages sent home to the child from friends and teachers
- Skype calls so that the child can directly interact with their friends and teachers
- text and social media messages
- invitations to join the class for special occasions or events

A life-limiting or life-threatening condition and all the associated experiences can cruelly damage a child's own self-esteem directly and indirectly in the way they are treated by others. A child can only develop self-esteem from interactions with other people. Sunderland (2003a) explains that self-esteem does not come from telling a child to love themselves more, nor from books. A child who feels worthless has a critical internal voice that is telling them that they are not worth much. They need help from someone who takes the time to understand exactly what it is like to be them and to help them to see how it was that they came to feel like this, and to help them to develop feelings and a deep belief that 'I am OK'. A child needs to see and feel their value and loveliness in the eyes, warmth, acceptance and words of another such as a teacher.

> 'What a shame you didn't get that bit right because I know you really wanted to. Never mind. Hey, you're probably not working at your best right now. How about going for a walk and coming back later?'
>
> (Sunderland, 2003a: 60)

In this way the child's internal critical voice can be changed to one that is forgiving and self-nurturing. Similarly, parents and siblings may also be hearing an internal critical voice that is telling them that they are not good enough. They too may need to hear and feel that a teacher understands how they are feeling and communicates an empathic, nurturing, encouraging script.

Maintaining consistent behaviour expectations for a child with a life-limiting or life-threatening condition

Whilst staff in school will naturally want to ensure that the child has a positive experience at school, there may be times when the child with a life-limiting or life-threatening condition needs additional support to be able to maintain appropriate levels of behaviour within the school setting. Perceived misbehaviour could be a direct result of symptoms related to their condition or health care. For example, a child may try to avoid activities or withdraw from the teaching and learning situation because of tiredness post-radiotherapy. At other times, a child may be very highly emotional, perhaps prone to anger or tears and reacting inappropriately to peers or staff, as a direct result of their condition, its medical treatment or other health care such as doing difficult or painful exercises. Although staff need to be mindful of the Equality Legislation, which requires 'reasonable adjustments' to meet the needs of those with a disability and the child's specific health-related needs itemised on their health care or Education, Health and Care plan, children with a life-limiting or life-threatening condition should still be required to follow the same key rules and meet the same high expectations of behaviour as all other children.

To prevent or minimise the chance of concerning behaviour, it is important for the school to put in place strong pastoral support for the child. A key member of staff should be identified and named, someone who will have the time and skills to be able to listen to the child and provide pastoral support for them when needed. It may be most practical and effective for this person to be a non-teaching member of staff, someone who does not hold the formal role of teacher to the child, and someone who will be able to devote the time for one-to-one support.

Reflective activity

- Who might be appropriate to provide pastoral, nurturing support for a child with a life-limiting or life-threatening condition
- How can this be set up?
- How can you be sure that the person that you have identified will be the most effective and appropriate to work with the child?
- How will you involve the child in making decisions about who they would like to work with in this role?
- How will you involve parents in this decision making?
- What support might the identified staff member require to be able to fulfil this role effectively?

When setting up the pastoral support role with an identified member of staff, it is essential to consider their ongoing support needs. The school needs to recognise that the individual member of staff will need ongoing training to ensure that they have the skills to cope effectively with the demands of the pastoral role. Short courses related to counselling or mentoring, as well as short specific medical courses or reading materials, are often provided by charities who have a specific interest in a particular condition.

The school needs to be aware of the short- and long-term psychological impact of the pastoral role on the individual staff member. There needs to be a clear process for monitoring and reviewing the emotional burden. For example, how to act if this adult experiences grief, loss or bereavement in another aspect of their personal life. Health care and therapeutic and social care professions often have access to supportive sessions with a supervisor. These are set up to ensure that they are provided with structured opportunities to release some of the emotional stresses that they have had to absorb through working directly with complex and emotional cases. It may therefore be beneficial for a school to have a similar system in place and applied within the school context. Teachers' unions and related professional bodies can provide advice.

Reflective activity

- What systems does your school currently have in place to ensure that all staff are supported to release any emotional buildup they may experience by working directly with the complex and emotional needs of individual children?
- How could these systems be developed further?
- Who could you contact within the National Health Service, Children's Services, teachers' trade unions or teachers' professional organisations to consider more deeply the format and structure of supervision sessions and ways to effectively implement them within the school context?

Recognising and meeting the emotional and behavioural needs of other children within the school setting

Whilst staff in the school may be focused on the emotional and behavioural needs of the child with a life-limiting or life-threatening condition, it is essential to recognise the emotional and behavioural needs of other children within the class and school setting. The school's policy on supporting children with medical conditions should provide clarity about sharing information about the child's condition with other children (see Chapter 7).

All children will need support with their feelings about a classmate who is not well. Wherever possible, staff should be open and honest with the children and ensure that they are given clear and simple facts about the condition and short- and long-term prognosis, *where this is appropriate and agreed with the child and their parents*. Children can find it difficult to 'take in' and know how to respond to sad or difficult news, and staff need to try to model appropriate emotional responses, as discussed in Chapters 6 and 7, to ensure that children at all ages feel safe to be able to express concern, sadness, disbelief, guilt, blame or anger. Most important is that the feelings of those children who are close to the child with a life-limiting or life-threatening condition are not ignored.

Psychoanalytic and psychodynamic therapists and counsellors explain what might seem like an inappropriate response to something that is emotionally difficult in terms of unconscious defence mechanisms. The idea is that defence mechanisms are ways in which our mind protects us from something that could completely overwhelm us. (They are *unconscious*; we don't know that we are doing this.)

Defence mechanisms

Projection - Placing my own emotions onto someone or something else. *For example, a child who is angry may believe the teacher is angry with him.*

Repression - Preventing unacceptable desires, motivations and emotions from becoming conscious; burying them. The repressed desires may influence behaviour and induce emotional problems later. *For example, a child does not react to hearing their sibling is seriously ill. The anger or sadness is buried, only to be expressed at a later time or in a completely different situation. Quite unexpectedly, the child over-reacts to some failure or challenge.*

Reaction Formation - In an effort to reduce anxiety and repress undesirable characteristics, unacceptable wishes are changed into their opposite. *For example, a child undergoing chemotherapy, struggling with their hair loss and feeling very sad, may appear excited, silly or happy.*

Regression - Responding to anxiety by acting in a childish (younger) way. This may show itself particularly in times of stress. *For example, a 15-year-old undergoing painful medical treatment may seek out their teddy from early childhood or revert to behaviours like thumb sucking. Similarly, if an 18-year-old's mother died when he was 6 and no one ever talked about it, the young man's unprocessed emotions may 'leak out' in terms of exhibiting behaviour related to his sad 6-year-old self, e.g. seeking out his teddy or thumb sucking.*

Denial - A refusal to believe events or admit that they are experiencing emotions that provoke anxiety. *For example, refusing to believe their friend won't return. Even 'forgetting' what they have been told.*

Rationalisation (intellectualism) – Finding rational reasons (excuses) to justify actions which have unconscious motives. *For example, bullying another child but claiming they provoked it.*

Displacement – Diverting emotions from their original source to a less dangerous one. *For example, diverting one's anger with the nurse or the medical treatment into hitting or biting another child.*

Recognising and meeting the emotional and behavioural needs of siblings of the child with a life-limiting or life-threatening condition

Reflective activity

- What might be the effect or impact of the life-limiting or life-threatening condition on the siblings of the child involved?
- How might this be experienced in the school context?
- What sort of signs or symptoms will teachers need to be aware of and looking for in the siblings of children with a life-limiting or life-threatening condition?
- What support could be put in place to meet those needs?
- How will you know if it is effective?
- How will you communicate with the parents of the child and the child themselves about this?

An issue that is often overlooked when focusing on the needs of a child with a life-limiting or life-threatening condition is the impact of the whole situation on siblings who may or may not be attending the same school. Siblings can easily be ignored and their needs forgotten about. As attention is directed towards their brother or sister, the sibling will experience significant disruption to their home life and routines and to the quantity and quality of attention that they might normally receive from their parents. Teachers need to be aware that any diagnosis, ongoing condition and related additional care may 'cause strong and often conflicting feelings in siblings of the child or young person' (CCLG, 2015: 19). Siblings might feel:

- guilt because they may think that they are somehow responsible for their sibling's ill health
- guilt because they are able to do what their sibling can not
- guilt because they feel they should be able to help more or do more
- jealousy or anger because of the attention given to their sibling
- anxiety about their sibling, changes and uncertainty
- isolated because they have needs which are not being met
- conflicting emotions of guilt, anxiety, jealousy and anger
- the weight of bottled-up feelings because they are trying to avoid worrying their parents or feel they cannot safely let them out
- explosions of uncontrolled feelings as they burst out into the open
- indifferent to or jealous of peers
- ill with psychosomatic symptoms such as aches and pains

Teachers might observe:

- erratic behaviour, associated with the seesawing of emotions, from anxiety, jealousy, anger, guilt, resentment and upset
- a false persona of strength, capability and containment
- needy or attention-seeking behaviour
- withdrawal and non-communication
- poor concentration or disruptive behaviour
- increased emotionality, such as crying or outbursts of anger
- non-conformist, challenging or rebellious behaviour
- missing school
- reduced academic performance
- breakdown in relationships with peers
- non-verbal behaviour that signifies feeling unwell such as closing eyes or not eating. The sibling may try to hide their own physical symptoms of illness.

Advice about how to communicate effectively with siblings of a child with a life-limiting or life-threatening condition can be found in Chapter 5. Clear and ethical communication sharing across the school context is discussed in Chapter 7.

Reflective activity

- How are staff members in the school currently made aware of the social and emotional needs of siblings of children with life-limiting or life-threatening conditions?
- Is this process defined within the school's policy for supporting children with medical needs?

Class profiles

A Class Profile (Ekins & Grimes, 2009; Ekins, 2015) is a useful tool for recording key information about all children's educational, medical, health, social, emotional and behavioural needs. Used well, it can help all staff have a full overview of the needs of the children within a given cohort. It can be used to plan specific work and for senior leaders and teachers to strategically review the incidence and trends of needs within and across different class groups. At its most basic, a Class Profile is a register of all the children within a given class or group. It is important to include all children, not just those with identified needs. Against the class register, a range of other information is recorded:

Student Characteristics – e.g. SEN Support/SEN EHCP (Cognition and Learning (C&L); Communication and Interaction (C&I); Social Emotional and Mental Health (SEMH); Physical/ Sensory (P/S)); G&T; EAL; Health.

Description of Need – concise details about actual need. This could include the medical diagnosis for the child with a life-limiting or life-threatening condition and can also include a note to explain that an individual's sibling has a life-limiting or life-threatening condition (and name condition).

Useful Strategies – details about the 'headline' key strategies that are needed to support the child with the life-limiting or life-threatening condition (e.g. rest breaks, chunked learning) as well as strategies to support a sibling of a child with a life-limiting or life-threatening condition (e.g. 1:1 support to talk through emotions).

Table 9.1 Example of a class profile

Student name	Student characteristic	Description of need	Useful strategies
Alex	SEN with support (C&L)	Support with literacy	Writing frames and scaffolds
John			
Barmeena	Health	Abdominal cancer	Radiotherapy on Mondays (April 12th – July 5th), fatigue, nausea, low self-esteem – use rest breaks; support social inclusion
Maria			
Esme			
Lucas			
Rodney	Health	Sibling (Josh) has Duchenne muscular dystrophy, anxiety	Needs information about DMD
Frederika			
Susie			
Jac			
Sanjay			
Rita			
Noel			
Petra	SEN with Support (SEMH); Health	Anxiety; diabetes	Unable to concentrate for long periods; insulin injection before lunch Provide clear instructions and expectations, ensure she eats lunch after injection
Ravitt			
Ella			
Bobby			
Brandon			
Rosie	Health	Asthma	Ensure ready access to inhaler at all times.
Charlie			
Robert			

Social and Emotional Aspects of Learning (SEAL)

In the early years, primary and secondary school, the provision of Social and Emotional Aspects of Learning (SEAL) activities is a very effective way of helping children understand and deal with emotional events which impact themselves, their peers, siblings, family or significant others.

Reflective activity

- Which SEAL activities are you already aware of?
- How are they used within your school context currently?
- Are there ways these could be developed to provide a structured approach to supporting children to manage complex social and emotional needs linked to the news about a peer with a life-limiting or life-threatening condition?

SEAL activities are often carried out within the Personal, Social and Health and Education (PSHE) curriculum. Even though many of these activities seem simple and straightforward, it is very important to ensure that they are very carefully managed. They need to be:

- complemented by an emotionally literate whole-school culture (see Chapter 11)
- prefaced by ground rules
- followed by a debrief
- used 'lightly and carefully'. Teachers need to tread lightly across the surface of emotions, helping them be released and accepted a little at a time, in ways that keep the children and themselves safe. Facilitation, listening and reflection are the keys. Avoid actively 'digging down', and most especially in the presence of other children. Consider referral to a therapist or counsellor who can contain and support the processing of big emotions over a period of time in a private environment.

Ground rules

Activities that are dealing with sensitive subjects or emotions are serious. They always need to be prefaced by ground rules in order to keep everyone psychologically safe. These can be decided by the children and put up on a wall. They might include:

- everyone can have a say if they so wish
- you can choose not to speak if you wish
- we will listen to one another
- we will respect everyone's comments and feelings (no teasing)
- anything said in the circle stays in the circle
- you can only speak when you are holding the 'talking sticks'/ teddy etc.
- we only play on the blue carpet

Activities which support social and emotional learning for all ages include:

- circle or golden time
- persona dolls
- empty chair
- role play
- play

Circle or golden time

Circle time usually comprises asking children to sit in a circle and inviting them to make a statement about something. For example, they might be asked to make 'I' statements and say how they feel today or about something in particular. Circle time could be used to explore how it might feel to be someone else, perhaps a child who is feeling unwell, who looks different or who has been away from school for some time. It is often 'safer', and just as helpful, to focus on a character's feelings than those of the children directly. 'How do you think he might feel?' So circle time might follow or complement a fictional story or a story in the media. Later, the teacher might feel it appropriate to move towards more personal examples.

Persona dolls/puppets

The use of a doll or puppet as a 'persona' is based on the idea of projection, the transfer of a child's feelings and thoughts into the doll/puppet. The teacher might explore how 'the doll' feels in certain circumstances, such as their friend has gone away to a far-away land. The teacher may start to include the children and ask them to also consider what the doll may be thinking and feeling and what she might do. In this way, the children safely release/project onto the doll their own pent up thoughts, feelings and emotions. An alternative way to do this, when working with older children, is to ask them to consider a hypothetical other, maybe write a letter to them or story about them.

Empty chair

Similar to the persona doll is the empty chair technique. An older child is encouraged to 'address' an empty chair, either as a hypothetical other or even as themselves in a given situation. Here again the rationale is that it facilitates them in articulating their emotional conflicts and allows them to be projected outward in a safe environment. Such an activity can be undertaken in a group or one to one. A variation is to 'write yourself a letter', perhaps from your current self to your future or past self, expressing how you have coped and what you have learned.

Role play

Role play is an effective way to develop empathy for others but also to articulate hidden feelings. At its best, the facilitator not only allows it to happen but takes note of how the process develops as a social situation, full of emotions, negotiations and conflicts. Ideally, role plays should be structured. Teachers may, for example, write vignettes or 'personalities' for each person to adopt. The ground rules need to be complemented by an explanation that the children are 'acting', it is a learning exercise and nothing that is said or done should be taken as indicative of how the other child/actor feels. The facilitator needs to carefully monitor the interaction and if it does not come to a natural end, ensure it is time limited. But most importantly, time needs to be given for a thorough debrief.

Play

As part of the Early Years Foundation Stage (DfE, 2014), 'free' play is considered an essential tool to both facilitate and assess the emotional development of children. It is therefore encouraged as part of the curriculum and as a way for teachers to record appropriate developmental milestones or causes for concern in their social and emotional development. Play can be used as a window into a child's emotional world and a way to help them deal with new and confusing experiences.

> At nursery he kept taking things to the sandpit, burying them and digging them up to bring them back to life again. Then he'd say out of the blue, 'My daddy's dead'. You have to pay close attention to what they are trying to express. The nursery did a lot of work with him through play.
>
> (from an interview with a parent, from Dowling, 2014: 113)

The debrief

After engaging in social and emotional activities, the children need to go through some form of careful debrief. This is both ethical and therapeutic because it has important implications for the later well-being of the children. This might be relatively short, or it might be much more extensive. A debrief is a time when the children can explore and reflect on what was shared, what emotions were raised and how to move forward. In circle time or a role play, for example, it is very important to emphasise the confidential nature of what emerged. After an absorbing role play, it can be a good idea for the children to say their own name out loud, as a way of 'coming out of role and back into the room'. Or perhaps make clear that it was 'just play' and the actors are fictional. If necessary, time should be devoted to returning to the events. After a period of 'free play', a comment on what the teacher saw, not what the teacher thought or interpreted, will suffice. For example, "I saw that you played a lot in the sandpit."

Therapy and counselling

Play therapy

As explained in Chapter 5, finding words for difficult emotional experiences can be hugely challenging for anyone and even more so for a child. Play therapy is 'without words'. Children do not need to explain anything, and therapists do not interpret anything to the child. The child enters a safe and private play room to engage with a range of materials such as toys, puppets, paint, clay, musical instruments, dressing-up clothes, water, sand and miniature toys/artefacts that represent the 'whole world' and works through their emotions and their stories without knowing that they are doing so. Whilst the child thinks that they are 'just playing', unconscious memories and emotions are churned up, faced, sorted out and resolved. The therapist's role is to carefully observe and respond in ways that enable the child to continue their therapeutic work until the child has completed what they needed to do.

Registered play therapists often work in a child-centred/non-directive way but will also provide specific direction to a child's play in order to address a specific need, such as practicing social skills or making a memory box of someone who died. Play therapy is most frequently provided for children aged 3 to 11, both individually and in groups, often weekly, over a time period of between 6 weeks and a couple of years. Play therapy is most effective when the child is not in the middle of a deep crisis such as a massive change, because their whole being is focused on coping with the crisis, and there is no psychological space for effective therapeutic work. It makes sense to wait until life is a bit calmer, and the therapy can help with what happened. Play therapy can be helpful for a wide range of situations in which a child has suffered emotionally, for example:

- children who are living with a life-limiting or life-threatening condition, or any long-term condition
- siblings of a child who has a life-limiting or life-threatening condition or a child who requires a great deal of support for another reason
- bereaved children
- sad, angry, withdrawn, explosive children
- children who have experienced a loss, trauma or major change

Arts therapies

Art therapy, drama therapy, dance/movement therapy, music therapy, writing/story therapy and sand play therapy are all based on a similar premise to play therapy which, it should be said, has incorporated aspects of each of the individual arts based therapies rather than vice versa. Each creative medium is a vehicle through which children can work through and express difficult emotions. Registered arts therapists may be influenced by different approaches, such as those from the psychoanalytic tradition or from the non-directive/humanistic tradition, and this will influence how they work with a child. Some may use directed activities, talking, probing, reflection and interpretation much more than others.

Counselling/psychotherapy

Talking therapies are more suited to older rather than younger children. Counsellors and psychotherapists use the skills such as attending, active listening, reflection, paraphrasing, focussing, challenging, creative thinking, goal setting and action planning. Those who work within a psychoanalytic or psychodynamic tradition will identify and work with a child's defence mechanisms and the experience of transference, that is when the child unconsciously brings information of another relationship into the current child–therapist relationship. Cognitive behavioural therapy is concerned with understanding and sometimes changing a child's beliefs and thought patterns in order to promote greater well-being. Some counsellors and therapists have incorporated examples of arts-based therapies into their work to enable them to better meet the needs of younger children in particular.

Helping children with bereavement

Most research related to supporting children emotionally relates to unexpected bereavement (Black, 1998). In the case of life-limiting or life-threatening conditions, this is clearly not the case, and as such it can be harder to prepare for. The child in question is likely to have the condition for months or years and may even have left the school or education by the time their condition becomes terminal. On the one hand, this does mean that the school community has time to prepare; however, on the other, it does mean they may well witness the deterioration of the child physically and mentally, which places an additional burden on all concerned.

When a child has died, Bowlby (1998) advised that young children need to know two important things; to understand that the child who has died will never return and to know what has happened to the child's body. Children's reactions to another child's death will depend on their level of development, their relationship with the child, what else is going on at the time and their own experience of how others, especially their family, deal with and communicate about feelings. Feelings associated with bereavement may become visible in the form of sleep difficulties, sadness, anger, guilt, blaming themselves, anxiety, physical health complaints and insecurity (Dyregov, 1991). One minute children may behave normally as if nothing has happened, and the next they may become angry or upset. Dealing with difficult feelings in small, manageable pieces is the mind's way of protecting the child, and it is why adults need to allow children to grieve at their own pace. The strength of children's feelings will be influenced by the emotional depth of their relationship with the child who has died. Some children express few signs of grief because they were not close to the child. Others may experience more profound feelings.

Children's mourning is helped by the presence of consistent adults who allow and help them express their feelings. These adults may be their parents, and/or it may be their teacher, and teachers therefore need to know how to cope with a child who is mourning.

Bowlby (1973) said, 'We can only really mourn in the presence of another'. This is such a true statement for grieving children. The feelings are just too strong to unleash on their own, and besides it is far too lonely. When children like this find someone with whom they feel very safe and trusting, there can be a flood of feelings.

(Sunderland, 2003b: 21)

Feelings of loss

To a child, and an adult, loss can touch everything, it can make a child feel that they are no longer the same person. The world can become bleak or even hostile. Children can experience a range of different emotions. They may withdraw from this world, or they may become hostile themselves. Feeling angry may be easier than feeling hurt, feeling sad or feeling loss. Angry feelings overwhelm children's ability to think and erupt out of their bodies in the form of what might be called 'bad behaviour'. Children may defend themselves from painful feelings. This emotional numbing includes:

- not allowing themselves to register that the child who died mattered to them
- diminishing the impact of the death, such as saying, 'We all die sometime'.
- feeling numb
- feeling detached

(Sunderland, 2003b; 2003c)

The Child Bereavement Network web site provides some useful guidance and advice, which teachers may find helpful to access. The key principles for supporting bereaved pupils, taken from advice given from bereaved pupils themselves, are particularly helpful. The words of pupils who have been bereaved are particularly powerful and insightful here, with bereaved pupils identifying that it is important to:

- inform other teachers, especially supply teachers, about our loss, although we may not wish to talk about it. Keep this on record.
- talk to us about what has happened. We may need more information, advice and education about loss.
- arrange for us to get extra help with our work so we do not get behind, especially before exams.
- realise that we have a lot on our plate. Try not to put the spotlight on us too much. We will participate when we can.
- help us cope by treating us the same as everyone else.
- let us know about groups of children and young people who are also coping with loss and change.
- ask us how we are feeling. It may not be obvious.
- give us a note that allows us to leave class briefly, without having to explain ourselves, if we feel overwhelmed.
- understand that we will not 'get over it' or 'put it behind us', but with time we will learn to cope with the changes.
- give us encouragement for all the things we are managing to do and keep us in mind.
- find a way of getting our attention back in class, without others noticing and making us embarrassed.
- wait until we are ready to talk.
- remember that we are still us, just feeling a bit lost at the moment.
- help us find new dreams for the future and make plans.

Reflective activity

- Which, if any, of these key principles are already embedded in practice in your school context?
- How will you use these insights to help develop and improve whole-school understandings and practice for the future?

In addition to the valuable insights from the bereaved pupils' perspective, the following list incorporates a range of key skills and approaches advocated by the Play Therapy Network South East (England). These can provide a useful guide to the teacher, giving them some reassurances about appropriate approaches to use:

- Be OK with crying.
- Rather than dealing with one child at a time, provide slots in which children can all come together and share their questions and feelings.
- Have a place and time in the school for pastoral care.
- Don't be afraid to say, 'No, not now. Come back later'. It is better to say to a child that you will see them later, when you can give them the time they need to be heard properly and receive empathy, than to think you can do this in a very short time.
- Try to avoid difficult information and feelings becoming a secret. The more openly they can be understood and discussed, the better for everyone.
- If children have had opportunities to talk about a sick child or bereavement, they are likely to be fine. It is the ones who have not that may 'bottle it up' or 'let it out' in the form of inappropriate behaviour and who may then end up needing therapeutic support.
- Many children's storybooks work with metaphors for difficult feelings. Don't worry about feeling that you need to explain the metaphor; the children will 'get it'.
- If an infant or very young child undergoes a significant loss, they may not consciously remember it, but it will nevertheless be part of them. Having no memory of an event and not being able to articulate it does not lessen its pain.
- Loss, change and bereavement are different for each individual. For some, the sadness deepens over time, and it can be much later that it is revealed and the individual needs support.
- Normalise it. Illness and death are part of life.
- Do not belittle the pain. Acknowledge that it 'really hurts'.
- Be in the moment. Hear, acknowledge and then refer on to SENCO, play therapist, counsellor, educational psychologist.
- One family ensured that the hearse passed by the child's school so that all the school could watch it go by.
- Have a place of memorial at the school.
- It is important that headteachers are prepared to handle death and bereavement well by attending workshops on whole-school approaches to bereavement.

Funerals and memorials

Funerals can be a vital 'ending process' that makes the death real, and seeing others cry gives children permission to cry (Sunderland, 2003b). Children need to say goodbye. A memorial service at school can be a way of providing mutual support at a time of grief and an opportunity to celebrate a child's life and all that they gave to the school. Choosing or creating a memorial, in the form of gardens, playground equipment, murals and sports trophies and more, can provide a focal point for children and adults to remember a child.

Practical resources

In this section, the following practical resources are provided:

1 Blank Class Profile format
2 Class activities for children who have suffered a loss or bereavement
3 Resources for teachers to use with children in school
4 Books for children
5 Books for parents
6 Books and resources for teachers
7 Web sites
8 Organisations that can support teachers and schools with bereavement
9 Support for children who have suffered a loss
10 Five strategies to help children cope

1 Blank Class Profile format

Student name	Student characteristic	Description of need	Useful strategies

2 Class activities for children who have suffered a loss or bereavement

The following ideas for supporting children about loss and bereavement are based on Sunderland (2003b). Her book contains photocopiable resources.

Remember that it feels much safer for children, younger and older, to consider the feelings of a character or an animal. It can feel too threatening to be asked to directly communicate about themselves. Working with metaphors is enough; teachers should not feel that they need to explain the metaphor. The teacher needs to be guided by the children about whether they are able to use 'you' and 'name of child' OR use a metaphor.

Present a simple story, in pictures or words, of two characters who are friends. Then one dies and one is left alone. What happens to him? Draw, paint, write, talk or show (movement or miniatures) what happens to him. Create music to hear how he feels at the time of loss and how he feels later.

Provide a picture of a deserted place. It could be an empty building, an empty playground, an empty field. Ask, 'What does the world feel like when you've lost someone or something very precious? Draw, paint, write, talk or show (movement or miniatures) how it feels. Using music, what does it sound like?'

Read a story in which a character suffers a loss.

Draw, paint, write, talk or show (using miniatures) what life was like for a character 'before' and 'after' a loss. Make music to hear how it sounded before and how it sounds after.

How did it feel when the character found out? List a range of potential feelings, possibly with pictures, and allow children to tick which applied to them and discuss in a small group. Draw, paint, write, talk or show (using movement or miniatures) how it felt. Make music to hear how it sounded.

How does it feel now? Draw, paint, write, talk or show how it feels now. Create music to show how it feels now.

Similarly, questions could include feelings about:

- the first time 'the village' knew that their pet dog was going to die
- how it felt the last time 'the village' were with the pet dog

The squirrel was missing her friend too much. Draw, paint, talk or show how it feels to miss someone too much. What does it feel like in her head? What does her heart look like? How does it feel inside her body? What does the world feel like?

If the squirrel's much-missed friend was:

- a colour, what colour would he be?
- an animal, what animal would he be?
- a food, what food would he be?
- a place, what place would he be?
- a musical sound, what sound would he be?

Draw, paint, write, talk or show what the squirrel particularly liked about her friend.

Create a 'museum of lovely times'. This is a museum that has been built to exhibit all the happy memories that the squirrel has of her friend. Draw or paint all the exhibits in the museum.

Draw Badger's school. In each classroom, draw, paint or write all of the important people that help Badger at school. In the roof is an attic. In the attic, draw, paint or write all the special memories of Badger's friend who died. Next to the school, Badger's builder has built a new extension. Draw, paint or write the people, things and dreams that are going to be part of Badger's future.

NB: as discussed in Chapter 5, most of these will not be pictures/ artefacts for public display. They are, and should remain, private reflections and constructions.

3 Resources for teachers to use with children in class

Practical resources

Child Bereavement UK (2014) *Conversations about Loss and Change*. Northampton: Fink Cards

Free Spirit Publishing (2008) *Feelings in a Jar*

Wilson, P. and Long, I. (illustrator) (2008) *Feelings Blob Cards (Blobs)*. Brackley: Speechmark

Activity books for primary school

Crossley, D. (2000) *Muddles, Puddles and Sunshine: Your Activity Book to Help When Someone Has Died*. Stroud: Hawthorn Press

Heegaard, M. (1992) *Facilitator Guide for Drawing Out Feelings*. Chapmanville, WV: Woodland Press

Heegaard, M. (1991) *When Someone Has a Very Serious Illness: Children Can Learn to Cope with Loss and Change* (Drawing Out Feelings). Chapmanville, WV: Woodland Press

Heegaard, M. (1991) *When Someone Very Special Dies: Children Can Learn to Cope with Grief* (Drawing Out Feelings). Chapmanville, WV: Woodland Press

Heegaard, M. (1991) *When Something Terrible Happens: Children Can Learn to Cope with Grief* (Drawing Out Feelings). Chapmanville, WV: Woodland Press

Wilson, P. (2009) *Big Book of Blob Trees* (Blobs). Brackley: Speechmark

Books for secondary school

Grollman, E. A. (1999) *Straight Talk about Death for Teenagers: How to Cope with Losing Someone You Love*. Saint Louis: Turtleback Books

Sunderland, M. (2012) *Bothered: Helping Teenagers to Talk about Their Feelings*. Brackley: Speechmark

Wilson, P. (2009) *Big Book of Blob Trees* (Blobs). Brackley: Speechmark

4 Books for children

For children ages 3-6

I Miss You: A First Look at Death - Pat Thomas

- Addresses children's feelings and questions about death in a simple, realistic way. Introduces funerals and cultural difference.

Lifetimes: The Beautiful Way to Explain Death to Children - Bryan Mellonie and Robert Ingpen

- Explains life and death in a sensitive and natural way.

Sad Isn't Bad: A Good-Grief Guidebook for Kids Dealing with Loss - Mechaelene Mundy

- Promotes honest, healthy grief and growth by providing a comforting, realistic look at loss and life-affirming ideas for coping.

The Dead Bird - Margaret Wise Brown

- Upon finding a dead bird, a group of children perform a burial service to say goodbye.

When Bad Things Happen: A Guide to Help Kids Cope - Ted O'Neal

- Helps adults talk to children about feelings, fears and skills for coping and healing in times of change and challenges.

When Dinosaurs Die: A Guide to Understanding Death - Laurie Krasny Brown and Marc Brown

- Answers children's questions and fears about death with clarity and directness.

When Someone You Love Has Cancer: A Guide to Help Kids Cope - Alaric Lewis

- Helps adults talk to children about the illness cancer and the feelings, fears and skills for coping with a loved one's cancer.

For children ages 6-12

Badger's Parting Gifts - Susan Varley

- Badger's friends are overwhelmed with their loss when he dies. By sharing their memories of his gifts, they find strength to face the future with hope.

Ocho Loved Flowers - Anne Fontaine

- The story of a young girl who learns how to say goodbye to her beloved cat while treasuring memories. A helpful, sensitive way to support a child when the death of a loved one is anticipated.

Rachel and the Upside Down Heart: A True Story - Eileen Douglas

- A story about the grief of a young girl and her mom as they adjust to the changes of life after the death of Rachel's father.

The Invisible String - Patrice Karst

- Shares that there is a bond between children and their loved ones even when the loved one is not physically present.

The Memory String – Eve Bunting

- Invites readers to consider ways to remember family history and welcome new memories.

Tough Boris – Kathryn Brown

- Explains through the story of a rough and greedy pirate that having feelings is normal and that it is okay to be sad sometimes.

For teens

Common Threads of Teenage Grief – Janet Tyson and Teens Who Know

- Promotes an understanding of grief and healing for teens, their families and friends. Written by a middle school counsellor and nine teens.

Facing Change: Falling Apart and Coming Together Again in the Teen Years – Donna O'Toole

- Information to help teens cope, understand and grow through their losses.

Fire in My Heart, Ice in My Veins: A Journal for Teenagers Experiencing Loss – Enid Samuel-Traisman

- A journal for teens who have experienced the death of a loved one.

Healing Your Grieving Heart for Teens: 100 Practical Ideas – Alan D. Wolfelt, Ph.D.

- Written to help teens understand and deal with their unique grief.

Help for the Hard Times: Getting through Loss – Earl Hipp

- A guide that helps teens understand how they experience grief and loss; provides tools for coping with grief in healthy ways.

5 Books for parents

A Parent's Guide to Raising Grieving Children – Phyllis R. Silverman and Madelyn Kelly

- Provides a breadth of guidance regarding childhood loss, including topics such as living with someone who's dying, talking about death and dying with children, preparing for the funeral and developing an ongoing support system.

A Tiny Boat at Sea: How to Help Children Who Have a Parent Diagnosed with Cancer – Izetta Smith

- Information for parents, caregivers and professionals who are helping children adjust to the cancer diagnosis or terminal illness of an adult family member. Includes excellent ideas for parents about talking to their children when a family member is ill or dying. Available at *www.griefwatch.com* and *www.compassionbooks.com*.

Healing the Grieving Child's Heart: 100 Practical Ideas for Families, Friends & Caregivers – Alan D. Wolfelt, Ph.D.

- Provides kid-friendly ideas for helping children mourn.

Living with Grief: Children and Adolescents – Kenneth J. Doka and Amy S. Tucci

- A comprehensive guide for parents and professionals on how to deal with children's grief. Each helpful chapter is written by a different expert.

The Bereaved Parent – Harriet Sarnoff Schiff

- Offers guidance to parents who face the imminent death of a child, are shocked by accidental death or suffer post-funeral turmoil, grief and depression. Shows a way through day-to-day hardships and decisions and offers concrete, helpful suggestions for meeting the needs of the whole family.

The Journey through Grief and Loss: Helping Yourself and Your Child When Grief Is Shared – Robert Zucker

- Offers parents and other concerned adults important insights into managing their own grief while supporting grieving children.

6 Books and resources for teachers

Adams, J. (2010) *Information Sheet: Explaining Funerals, Burial and Cremation to Children*. Child Bereavement UK. Available at http://www.childbereavementuk.org/support/families/reading-and-resources/children-and-funerals. Accessed 22 October 2016

Department for Education (2015) *Mental Health and Behaviour in Schools*. Departmental Advice for School Staff. London: DfE

Frazer, H. and Maynell, H. (2005) *Memorials by Artists for Young People and Babies*. Suffolk: The Memorial Arts Charity

Morell, J. and Smith, S. (2007) *We Need to Talk about the Funeral: 101 Practical Ways to Commemorate and Celebrate Life*. Abercynon: Accent Press

National Institute for Health and Care Excellence (NICE) (2008) *Social and Emotional Wellbeing in Primary Education: Public Health Guidance*. Manchester: NICE. Available at www.nice.org.uk/guidance/ph12/resources/social-and-emotional-wellbeing-in-primary-education-1996173182149. Accessed 24 October 2016

National Institute for Health and Care Excellence (NICE) (2009) *Social and Emotional Wellbeing in Secondary Education: Public Health Guidance*. Manchester: NICE. Available at https://www.nice.org.uk/guidance/ph20/resources/social-and-emotional-wellbeing-in-secondary-education-1996230289093. Accessed 24 October 2016

PSHE Association. www.pshe-association.org.uk

PSHE Association (2015) *Teacher Guidance: Preparing to Teach about Mental Health and Emotional Wellbeing*. Available at https://www.pshe-association.org.uk/sites/default/files/Mental%20health%20guidance.pdf. Accessed 22 October 2016

Public Health England (2015) *Promoting Children and Young People's Emotional Health and Wellbeing: A Whole School and College Approach*. London: PHE

Sunderland, M. (2001) *Using Story Telling as a Therapeutic Tool with Children*. Brackley: Speechmark

TACADE/PSHE Association/Acorns (2011) *Life Changes: Loss, Change and Bereavement for Children Aged 3 to 11 Years of Age*. Manchester: TACADE

Wilson, P. and Long, I. (2010) *The Blobs Training Manual*. Brackley: Speechmark

Resources for teachers to use with children – about building self-esteem

Bruce, C. (2010) *Emotional Literacy in the Early Years*. London: Sage

Collins, C. (2002) *Because I'm Special*. Bristol: Lucky Duck

Plummer, D. (2001) *Helping Children to Build Self-Esteem*. London: Jessica Kingsley

7 Additional resources

There are a number of web sites which publish SEAL and PSHE resources.

BBC Bitesize

www.bbc.co.uk/education/clips

The BBC provide a number of short and very accessible videos for primary and secondary pupils on topics such as 'feeling sad' for younger ones and 'mental health', feelings and emotions and dealing relations for older children. These are ideal for children to watch alone or as a way to initiate an individual or group discussion.

Primary Resources.co.uk

www.primaryresources.co.uk

Resources on a variety of topics:

- all about me/thinking about others
- friendship and relationships
- bullying and discrimination
- making choices and resolving conflicts
- changes and new beginnings
- health and safety
- the world of work
- citizenship and global issues
- targets and goals/other resources

The SEAL community

www.sealcommunity.org

Provides forums, news and links to resources about social and emotional learning.

8 Organisations that can support teachers and schools with bereavement

Childhood Bereavement Network

www.childhoodbereavementnetwork.org.uk
The network has local free services to support bereaved children. Families can refer themselves directly to these; teachers can receive information and support from them.

Child Bereavement UK

http://childbereavementuk.org
Child Bereavement UK offers
- training for schools
- schools information pack
- an e-learning resource for schools
- films created by young people for teachers, parents and friends

Their web site includes a Schools section and includes:
- supporting a bereaved pupil
- a death affects the whole school
- terminally ill children at school
- school policy
- special educational needs
- lesson plans and ideas
- resources

Cruse Bereavement Care: Help for schools

http://www.cruse.org.uk/schools
Cruse Bereavement Care's Schools pages include how to deal with:
- impact of bereavement
- changes in behaviour
- death of a pupil
- returning to school
- violent deaths
- staff death
- dealing with crisis
- school bereavement policy

They also produce a Schools Pack which can be purchased.

Grief Encounter

www.griefencounter.org.uk
Grief Encounter provides support for bereaved children, young people and families. They also provide Good Grief bespoke training workshops for professionals.

Together for Short Lives

www.togetherforshortlives.org.uk
The UK Children's Palliative Care organisation

Winston's Wish

www.winstonswish.org.uk
Winston's Wish provides support for bereaved children and families and training for professionals including teachers.

Young Minds in Schools

www.youngminds.org.uk/training_services/training_and_consultancy/for_schools
The Young Minds charity provides a range of courses to support emotional well-being in schools and for teachers.

CLIC Sargent

www.clicsargent.org.uk
Produce resources about:
- returning to school: primary school children with cancer
- talking to primary school children about cancer

9 Support for children who have suffered a loss

Childline

www.childline.org.uk
Online or phone support for anyone under 19.

Hope Again

http://hopeagain.org.uk
A Cruse Bereavement Care web site to support young people who are living with loss.

Winston's Wish for Young People

http://foryoungpeople.winstonswish.org.uk/foryoungpeople
An interactive web site for young people to learn, ask questions and get support.

10 Five strategies to help children cope

1   *Help children develop coping strategies.*
   - Use the language of feelings: suggest labels to describe feelings, perhaps associate them with pictures and encourage children to use these to describe their own feelings. Many primary schools use 'feelings boards', whereby children place a picture or word to indicate how they feel today. These words clearly need to be age appropriate. 'Bubbly', 'fizzy', 'gloomy, 'happy', 'sad' might be more appropriate for younger children.
   - Provide safe places and activities where the more reserved and cautious children can open up but also can experience positive emotions like joy, excitement and wonder.
   - Provide them with ways to talk about their needs. For example, instead of getting impatient with another child, suggest ways they can say they want to talk or to be listened to or to be left alone.

2   *Demonstrate that everyone has feelings.*
   - Talk about how you feel, your own experiences of illness and loss. What makes you feel happy or sad, excited or worried.
   - Use situations or stories, perhaps from the media, history or literature, to help children understand different people's points of view or reactions.
   - Perhaps ask them to write down stories or accounts from different points of view, how they feel, how parents feel, how the teachers might feel.

3   *Ask self-reflective questions.*
   Be prepared to ask yourself and your colleagues a number of questions:
   - How well has the child/children come to terms with their feelings? What evidence do I have?
   - What have I done today (this week) to help the children become more aware of their feelings? Then, of course, what have I done, today (this week) to help the children deal with their feelings? What evidence do I have that this is effective?
   - Do I need to read more, try something different or use different techniques? Do I need to contact other professionals?
   - What do I know? What do I not know? As a teacher it is all too easy to see oneself as an expert on all things. However, even if we have had experience of something like cancer, we need to remember that there are many types, their aetiology and prognosis are often very different in children, and many people often suffer from multiple conditions and complications. As such, don't be too quick to jump in with an opinion or prediction. Admit when you need support.

4   *Work with parents.*
   - Suggest that parents use language at home to help explore and communicate feelings with the child.
   - Open channels for communication. Parents need to have a quick and effective way of communicating with the school and or class teacher. They need to be able to report any concerns they have and progress they feel is being made.

5   *Stay alert.*
   - Look for changes in behaviour, particularly children who appear isolated or withdrawn. Other symptoms of stress might include losing weight, increased tiredness and irritability.

- If working with older children, there is also a danger of self-harm to relieve internal anxiety.
- Older children may well have access to social media and mobile phones. Although this can be a source of support, it can also contribute to shared anxiety or spreading unfounded rumours. Where possible, try to monitor things like Facebook posts.
- Children are increasingly media savvy. They will 'google' things or make links to stories from soap operas or the news. This will often lead to over-sensationalising and an 'emotional contagion'. It is therefore worth asking them where they have obtained their information and exploring it yourself.

(based on Dowling, 2014)

Concluding comments

The emotional and behavioural impact of a life-limiting or life-threatening condition can be profound, not only for the child, but for siblings and the whole school community. Our research demonstrated that teachers have much anxiety about how to cope with this challenge. This chapter has provided information about the emotions that underpin behavioural changes, and practical suggestions for teachers to provide emotional support for the child, siblings and other children in the school.

10 Whole-school policies

In this chapter, we:

- Review the key principles of effective policy development
- Identify how to write an effective Supporting Children with Medical Conditions policy
- Consider the importance of effective consultation and collaboration
- Explore additional policies which need to link to the Supporting Children with Medical Conditions policy to effectively meet the needs of children with life-limiting or life-threatening conditions

Introduction

In our Teaching for Life research, teachers' descriptions about how they were made aware of the needs of pupils with life-limiting or life-threatening conditions highlighted a general absence of any frameworks or planned whole-school policies. As we have seen, generally it was left to parents to inform staff, and thereafter there was no consistency about who was responsible for keeping the health care needs of pupils updated. SENCOs were the most frequently cited (40% of responses).

The teachers identified that they wanted a policy which would include how and when a multi-professional team could work together to plan for an individual child with a life-limiting or life-threatening condition. They wanted the policy to provide guidance about how to find out who they could liaise with, who would lead the discussions and procedures for reviewing a child's needs, as they identified that they really struggled to fully understand those key issues and the key information that is needed:

> "I think you probably need a list of contact details, so in each Local Authority or something you've got somebody who is a specialist in students in primary school with cancer, students in secondary school with cancer or multiple sclerosis or something."

Teachers in the research naturally assumed that health care professionals would take the lead:

> "I'd be really surprised if it wasn't health led, this is a health issue, that's impacting on education, it's the health that's the most important thing here."

> "I'd see it that I had a responsibility to find out more, to inform members of school, but there must be someone who knows more than me."

"It wouldn't be our responsibility to support the whole family going through that process. We'd play an important role, but we wouldn't be leading on it."

However, as reported in Chapter 6, the teachers expressed real concerns about how hard this multi-agency team would be to achieve. One said,

"I've never yet been to any meeting where you have the professionals that you need at that meeting. You never ever get everyone you need at a meeting, and for someone with significant needs that would be really worrying that you're not going to have the medical people there that you need."

The teachers told us that they therefore wanted a policy which would:

- be a framework for a school to follow
- be shared and visible
- articulate with other school policies, systems and processes
- be discussed, to check that staff are confident about putting it into practice

The teachers wanted the school policy to provide information about:

- the sharing of sensitive/confidential information
- where to find out about appropriate professionals and local services who could work with them
- suggestions of where, when and how a multi-professional team could discuss and plan for the child
- who acts as the lead professional
- how and when a child's needs were normally to be reviewed
- format/structure of meetings
- decision making
- who keeps the child's health care plan
- who is responsible for administering health care such as administering medication
- implications arising from the school's attendance policy for children with ongoing medical conditions
- the responsibilities of individual staff/positions
- collective responsibilities of all staff
- pastoral responsibilities
- the key school policies which relate to medical conditions, e.g. bullying, inclusion and a whole-school approach to emotional health and well-being, which should include how staff can obtain emotional support
- staff training: the type and level, procedures for requesting training, e.g. a specific medical condition, training about health care planning or Education, Health and Care plans, loss and bereavement, training for a health care procedure

Those teachers who worked in schools which had a policy about having a child with a life-limiting or life-threatening condition felt, on the whole, reassured by it. *"At least there is a plan in place"* at a time of great emotional distress. For those with the experience of such a child in their school, they reported that it provided the assurances and strength that they needed to be able to cope. They had greater awareness of what they should be doing and the support that they could get.

Summary

Most teachers in the research identified that their school did not have a specific policy for responding to the needs of children with life-limiting or life-threatening conditions before having to deal with the situation. They felt strongly that this is an essential policy to have and to 'get right'. It needs to be visible and openly shared and reviewed to ensure that all of the processes and principles within it could easily fit with current practice.

Policy review

Whilst the governing body of the school remains legally responsible for fulfilling the school's statutory duties, in relation to meeting the needs of children with life-limiting or life-threatening conditions, the DfE (2015) guidance identifies that:

> In meeting the duty to make arrangements to support pupils with medical conditions, functions can be conferred on a governor, a headteacher, a committee or other member of staff as appropriate . . . Help and co-operation can also be enlisted from other appropriate persons.
>
> (DfE, 2015: 7)

> The arrangements should inform the school and others about what needs to be done in terms of implementation.
>
> (DfE, 2015: 7)

The planned arrangements should also make clear how the school and governing body will work with the Local Authority and health professionals to ensure that the child receives a full but appropriately flexible education and ways that they can be effectively and successfully reintegrated into school after periods of absence.

> The governing body should ensure that its arrangements give parents and pupils confidence in the school's ability to provide effective support for medical conditions in school. The arrangements should show an understanding of how medical conditions impact on a child's ability to learn, as well as increase confidence and promote self-care. They should ensure that staff are properly trained to provide the support that pupils need.
>
> (DfE, 2015: 7)

Developing a whole-school policy

Supporting Pupils at School with Medical Conditions (DfE, 2015) provides detailed guidance about how to develop a policy for supporting children with medical conditions. They explain:

> Governing bodies should ensure that all schools develop a policy for supporting pupils with medical conditions that is reviewed regularly and is readily accessible to parents and school staff . . . In developing their policy, schools may wish to seek advice from any relevant health-care professional.
>
> (DfE, 2015: 8)

In terms of what to include within the policy, the Department for Education (DfE) (2015) provides the following guidance:

'Governing bodies should ensure that the arrangements they set up include details on how the school's policy will be implemented effectively, including a named person who has overall responsibility for policy implementation. In respect of implementation, school policies should include:

- who is responsible for ensuring that sufficient staff are suitably trained;
- a commitment that all relevant staff will be made aware of the child's condition;
- cover arrangements in case of staff absence or staff turnover to ensure someone is always available;
- briefing for supply teachers;
- risk assessments for school visits, holidays, and other school activities outside the normal timetable; and
- monitoring of individual healthcare plans.'

(DfE, 2015: 8-9)

- 'Governing bodies should ensure that the school's policy sets out the procedures to be followed whenever a school is notified that a pupil has a medical condition.
- Procedures should also be in place to cover any transitional arrangements between schools, the process to be followed upon reintegration or when pupils' needs change, and arrangements for any staff training or support.
- For children starting at a new school, arrangements should be in place in time for the start of the relevant school term.
- In other cases, such as a new diagnosis or children moving to a new school mid-term, every effort should be made to ensure that arrangements are put in place within two weeks.'

(DfE, 2015: 9)

- 'Governing bodies should ensure that their arrangements are clear and unambiguous about the need to support actively pupils with medical conditions to participate in school trips and visits, or in sporting activities, and not prevent them from doing so.
- Schools should make arrangements for the inclusion of pupils in such activities with any adjustments as required unless evidence from a clinician such as a GP states that this is not possible.'

(DfE, 2015: 22)

- 'Governing bodies should ensure that the school's policy sets out how complaints concerning the support provided to pupils with medical conditions may be made and will be handled.'

(DfE, 2015: 24)

The role and responsibilities of the headteacher

Whilst the governing body has overall statutory responsibility for ensuring that all is in place to meet the medical conditions of any pupil at school, the DfE (2015) guidance also provides advice on the specific role and responsibilities of the headteacher:
   'Headteachers . . .

- should ensure that their school's policy is developed and effectively implemented with partners. This includes ensuring that all staff are aware of the policy for supporting pupils with medical conditions and understand their role in its implementation.
- should ensure that all staff who need to know are aware of the child's condition.
- should ensure that sufficient trained numbers of staff are available to implement the policy and deliver against all individual healthcare plans, including in contingency and emergency situations. This may involve recruiting a member of staff for this purpose.

- have overall responsibility for the development of individual healthcare plans.
- should also make sure that school staff are appropriately insured and are aware that they are insured to support pupils in this way.
- should contact the school nursing service in the case of any child who has a medical condition that may require support at school, but who has not yet been brought to the attention of the school nurse.'

(DfE, 2015: 13)

Practical considerations

Given that the numbers of children with life-limiting or life-threatening conditions are likely to increase and, as such, the exposure of not only teachers but all allied professionals to the practical, emotional and physical challenges of responding to their needs will also rise, there is a clear need to establish not only a supportive school culture but, importantly, detailed and effective policies that can support and underpin the embedded whole-school culture. As Jones and Pound (2008) note, policies therefore serve a dual purpose of underpinning practice and meeting legal requirements.

Understanding effective policy development

Reflect the school culture

For policies to be effective and meaningful, they should reflect the embedded culture of the school, with the policy then supporting the embedded culture of the school by clearly articulating the key principles and values and how they will be implemented in practice. Booth and Ainscow (2002) therefore illustrate the ways that policy, practice and culture are inextricably linked. An inclusive culture provides the foundation upon which inclusive policies and inclusive practices can be built (Booth & Ainscow, 2002; Ekins, 2017).

Consultation and collaboration

The best policies are developed in consultation with all stakeholders to ensure that different perspectives and expertise are effectively drawn together to inform the policy. Thus, not only should all stakeholders know of the existence of a policy and be able to implement it, they should also be involved in the writing and review of it. In short, the policy must be 'owned' by all stakeholders. In this way, schools can be assured that their policy will be both comprehensive and accessible to all.

Figure 10.1 Inclusive culture, policy and practice model (Booth & Ainscow, 2002)

Stages of developing a policy

The stages of developing a meaningful policy can be thought of as five interactive Ps:

- philosophy
- principles
- purposes
- procedures
- practice

(Jones & Pound, 2008: 70-71)

Management information systems

The policy should conform to the conventions of MIS (management information systems) and it should be laid out, signed off and stored in a standard format, conforming to the school's other policies.

- There should be a named person/position, for example SENCO, member of the senior management team, who is the responsible author. This does not necessarily mean they have written it, but they do have the responsibility for any editing.
- There must be careful and systematic version control to ensure that everyone is using and knows how to access the most up-to-date version.
- All policies should not only include a date of publication but a date of review. A standard convention is a review every three years as part of a revolving strategy of reviewing all school policies.

Writing an effective Supporting Children with Medical Conditions policy

The DfE (2015) provides guidance about writing a Supporting Children with Medical Conditions policy. This statutory school policy is focused on all children with medical conditions including asthma, diabetes, epilepsy, allergies and so forth, as well as the needs of children who have life-limiting or life-threatening conditions, even where a school does not currently have any children with those conditions.

Table 10.1 Stages of policy development

Stages of policy development	Characteristics	Testing questions	Ways to develop/test
Philosophy	Shared values and beliefs	Is there a consensus amongst staff?	Away days, standing agenda in team meetings
Principles	Develop out of the philosophy. Statements of intent	Are these written in such a way to be acceptable to all?	Give them to a working group for comments and feedback.
Purposes	The objectives: whom is it intended to impact?	What is the policy intended to achieve?	Are there tangible improvements?
Procedures	Clear guidance for practice	Are the procedures as set out practical? Do they complement existing policies? (e.g. attendance)	A member of senior leadership team, e.g. the SENCO, should be tasked with piloting any new procedures.
Practice	Change what people do and the way they react to each other	Has the policy altered the way people interact and react?	Policies could be linked to SMART targets. Their impact could be demonstrated in improvements or negatively, e.g. a reduction in staff turnover.

Consultation and collaboration

Effective consultation and collaboration prior to, during and after the development of the policy for subsequent monitoring and review may include:

- governors
- health care professionals
- parents
- psychologists and therapists
- pupils
- social care professionals
- staff
- teachers

Each stakeholder will have different perspectives to bring, and thoughtful communication to engage all parties will be essential to the process. Where the school already has children with life-limiting or life-threatening conditions, it will be important to find sensitive ways to ask both the child and their parents for their contribution to the policy development, and ongoing review and monitoring of the policy. The child and their parents will obviously have really valuable insights to offer, but staff must be mindful of the emotional overload on both the child and parents and therefore be prepared to wait until such a time when the child and/or parent is ready and able to engage in the process, if at all.

Where a school has not had experience of working with children with life-limiting or life-threatening conditions previously, it may also be helpful to approach colleagues at other schools, particularly colleagues from special schools, who may have had relevant experience. In this, it is important to recognise that 'we don't know what we don't know' and therefore actively seek ways to help the school identify what staff need to be aware of that they might not have thought about.

It will also be very helpful for the school to liaise directly with other professionals, most particularly health care professionals, but also social care professionals, psychologists and therapists. They can provide valuable professional expertise and perhaps different perspectives to ensure all aspects have been thought about and addressed in appropriate and, importantly, realistic ways.

Sections of the policy

The DfE (2015) provides clear guidance about what a policy designed to support children with medical conditions needs to include:

- roles and responsibilities
- initial procedures
- training
- sharing information
- cover arrangements
- school trips and visits
- risk assessments
- individual health care plans
- transitional arrangements

- working with others
- complaints procedure
- audit

Roles and responsibilities

The governing body has the statutory responsibility to have a policy in place and review it regularly. The headteacher's responsibilities are outlined earlier. There should be a named person with overall responsibility for the policy's implementation.

Initial procedures

Information about the procedure that will be followed when the school is first informed about a child's medical condition: who will be involved/informed; who will they liaise with; what information will they record (see Chapter 7).

Training

Information about staff training and staff support to enable staff to carry out their role of supporting pupils with medical conditions. It needs to include how training needs are assessed and how training is to be provided. This is an occasion where a relevant health care professional may be able to advise (see Chapters 3, 4, 6, 8 and 9).

Sharing information

Details about how information will be appropriately shared to ensure that relevant staff are made aware of the child's condition and know how to support them. This will include details about how the school liaises with parents (see Chapters 5 and 7).

Cover arrangements

This will include identifying who will take responsibility for meeting the child's medical needs if the named, trained person is not in school and how supply teachers will be provided with relevant information about the medical needs of the child if they are covering the class (see Chapters 7 and 8).

School trips and visits

Details about how any child with a medical condition will be supported to access school trips and visits (see Chapters 3 and 4).

Risk assessments

Details about how risk assessments will be developed and implemented (see Chapters 4 and 5).

Individual health care plans

The policy needs to identify who is responsible for the development of individual health care plans and how often these will be monitored and reviewed (see Chapter 4).

Transitional arrangements

This section will provide information about how to support children with medical needs when they change schools or need to reintegrate into the school after a period of absence or when their medical/health care needs change (see Chapters 4 and 9).

Working with others

The policy needs to explain how the school will work both with the Local Authority and with other professionals to support children with medical needs (see Chapter 6).

Complaints procedure
Details about the school's complaints procedure need to be provided.

Audit
Details of the version and date and who has responsibility for reviewing the policy. For example:

> This is:
>
> - Version 1.1
> - Dates: in effect from 1/3/17.
> - To be reviewed by 1/9/21.
> - Responsibility: Deputy Headteacher, in the absence of the Deputy Headteacher, the SENCO

Additional relevant policies

The Supporting Children with Medical Conditions policy will need to link to and with other key school policies such as the:

- Admissions Policy
- Attendance Policy
- Bullying Policy
- Inclusion Policy
- Safeguarding Policy

All will need to be regularly reviewed to ensure adherence to the statutory responsibilities of the school in respect to the child with a life-limiting or life-threatening condition.

Bereavement policy

Schools need to carefully consider and plan for a bereavement before it happens. A bereavement policy should ensure that the school can effectively support a bereaved child, a group of bereaved children, bereaved staff and the whole school community. When a bereavement happens, particularly the death of a child who has been part of the school, the shock and distress affect the whole community; even people who did not directly know the child will empathise and be upset. As explained in Chapter 5, when people feel strong emotions, their brain will not facilitate clear thinking. It is not the time to work out a bereavement policy.

Shipman et al. (2001 cited in Cranwell, 2007) carried out a study that showed 79% of the schools in their sample reported having children on roll who had experienced bereavement in the last 2 years, but less than 10% had a bereavement policy. A bereavement policy provides a clear structure and process to follow in the situation of a sudden bereavement. It should not merely be a description of process, for example authorised absence, but a combination of underpinning aims, emotional and practical support, with a recognition that the impact of a bereavement might be long term and unpredictable.

Many organisations will have a policy that relates to bereavement involving staff, normally in relation to time off to grieve, to make arrangements and for funerals. A school's bereavement policy needs to include support for a bereaved child, perhaps whose parent has died, but here, we focus on the death of a child.

Sections of the policy

A bereavement policy might usefully include the following sections and information.

Aims and objectives

The core aims should be the support of staff, children and those associated with the school before, during and after bereavement. As such this will involve the acknowledgement of impacts and the identification of available support from both within and external to the school.

Procedures

Although all cases are unique and need to be handled sensitively, there are likely to be some common practical steps:

- Contacting the child's family
  There should be a single point of contact, ideally the headteacher or perhaps the class teacher, depending on the prior relationship with the family. However, it must be acknowledged that the class teacher may also be in shock/mourning.

- Informing staff, children and parents
  The policy needs to clearly set out who will be responsible for informing staff, children and parents and what information is to be given out. Ideally, this needs to be carefully considered by members of the management team in consultation with teachers and parents. Given that in most cases, they will have notice of the child's deterioration, this can be agreed in advance. Timing is crucial since given social media, if delayed, children, parents and other staff are likely to learn of a death very quickly. When informing others, thought needs to be given to how much information is provided to whom, bearing in mind children are likely to ask questions. For example, when and where did they die? Of what? Who were they with? It is always best to be clear and honest and not to encourage speculation. Decisions also need to be made about information and communication, such as the family's wishes regarding contacting them and funeral or memorial arrangements (see Chapters 5, 7 and 9).

- Dealing with property
  Children may have personal property, drawings or art work on display or stored. Teachers are advised not to be too quick to remove this. It can be taken down as part of the normal cycle; family members or even friends may wish to keep it, even some time after a loss. In addition, family members or friends may wish to visit the school and see such things as artwork or workbooks.

- School records/informing the local authority/other stakeholders
  Depending on how the information is obtained, it is important that all those connected with the child are informed and that school records are updated. These will include registers, pupil progress records, club records and school mailing lists. The Local Authority may also need to know. It is important to systematically work through these lists and ensure they are updated, the necessary people are informed and mistakes do not happen like sending invitations or information to parents as though their child is still on roll.

- Support
  The policy should include the school's commitment to sources of support and advice for staff, pupils and parents.
  - Emotional support, such as counselling services, charities, support groups.

- Practical support resources staff could use with their classes to understand their feelings or commemorate the person (see Chapters 5, 6, 7, 9 and 11).

- Flexibility
  In some cases the news of a bereavement will be unexpected, whilst in others, there will be prior warning. The policy needs to have flexibility contained within it. It needs to recognise that there will be disruption to the normal school schedules, such as taught lessons, the inclusion of a memorial service and the impact of personal adjustment for everyone. This period, and the support needed, may be relatively short term or extend over weeks and months (see Chapter 11).

Practical resources

In this section, the following practical resources are provided:

1 An outline of a Supporting Children with Medical Conditions policy
2 An overview of additional relevant policies that complement a bereavement policy
3 Resources to support the development of bullying and anti-bullying policies

1 An outline of a Supporting Children with Medical Conditions policy

Section	Content
Rationale	Set out the aims and purposes of the policy
Objectives	Set out the specific objectives of the policy
Roles and responsibilities	Governing body's statutory responsibility – to have a policy in place and review it regularly Headteacher's responsibilities A named person with overall responsibility for the policy's implementation
Initial procedures	Information about the procedure that will be followed when the school first finds out about a child's medical condition (i.e. who will be involved/informed; who will they liaise with; what information will they record)
Training	Who will have specific training about the detailed medical needs The training available to all staff to ensure that they are informed about the condition
Sharing information	Details about how information will be appropriately shared to ensure that relevant staff are made aware of the child's condition and know how to support them Details about arrangements for liaising with parents
Cover arrangements	Who will take responsibility for meeting the child's medical needs if the named, trained person is not in school How supply teachers will be provided with relevant information about the medical needs of the child if they are covering the class
School trips and visits	Details about how any child with a medical condition will be supported to access school trips and visits
Risk assessments	Details about how risk assessments will be developed and implemented
Individual health care plans	Details about who is responsible for the development of individual health care plans and how often these will be monitored and reviewed
Transitional arrangements	Details about transitional arrangements between schools Information about transitional arrangements in place to support a child to reintegrate into the school or when medical needs change
Working with others	Information about how the school will work both with the Local Authority and with other professionals to support the needs of the child
Complaints procedure	Details about the complaints procedure to follow
Audit	Details of the version and date, and who has responsibility for reviewing the policy

2 An overview of additional relevant policies that complement a bereavement policy

Policy	Covers	Responsibilities	Statutory duty
Admissions policy	Process for admission Criteria for admissions Reasonable adjustments included in any selection process	**Administration staff & teachers** Ensures that the policies are adhered to equally and where reasonable adjustment issues are raised, they are passed on promptly to a budget holder **Headteacher/school managers** Ensures that the policy is enacted and reviewed. That where reasonable adjustment issues are raised they are acted upon promptly, *ideally* before the pupil arrives (including for selection)	Equality Act (2010) Reasonable adjustment
Attendance policy	Attendance expectations Processes for authorised absence Importance of being on time and processes for tracking 'lates' Reporting and analysis processes Reasonable adjustments and provisions for children who are unable to consistently attend school	**Class teacher** Keeps records Looks for anomalies or patterns Provides relevant background information Discusses issues with parent Arranges for academic support **Head teacher** Monitors overall attendance/absence rates/individual rates where concerns expressed Notes trends in absences Contacts families if concerns are not addressed Provides additional resources if necessary or makes referrals Liaises with other specialists where necessary **Administrative staff** Collates and records registration and attendance information Holds central contact information Ensures absence/late records are completed Maintains records, identifies patterns Sends out correspondence where necessary	Local authorities have a duty to know who in their area is being schooled and where.
Bullying policy	A clear statement of aims Who the policy applies to Indicators and signs of bullying A clear statement of escalating action A clear list and explanation of prevention and resolution strategies	**Parents/Children/Staff** Immediate and confidential reporting **Teacher** Collates observations of any behaviours to be reported **Head teacher** Ensures policy is publicised Reviews and monitors policy, including number and pattern of reported incidence	All UK state schools must have an anti-bullying policy by law.

Policy	Covers	Responsibilities	Statutory duty
	Information about support available both within the school and externally Appeals procedures	Enacts policy **Administrative staff** Ensures policy is available on request and accessible Passes on any reports, in line with policy	
Inclusion policy	Aims of the policy A statement about who the policy relates to (including but not limited to those with protected characteristics) The underpinning values of the school How these values are enacted in practice Routes for concerns/ complaints	**Parents/Children/Staff** Report any breaches of policy/concerns **Teachers & support staff** Ensure the policy is enacted in word and deed **Head teacher** Regularly reviews policy Ensures that the policy is enacted Ensures new staff are made aware of the policy and their responsibilities within it **Administrative staff** Ensures that the policy is available on request and that it is accessible	All children have a statutory right to education. The Equality Act (2010) protected characteristics are: age; disability; gender reassignment; marriage and civil partnership; pregnancy and maternity; race; religion or belief; sex; sexual orientation.
Safeguarding policy	The aims of the policy The other policies this relates to Behaviour and conduct responsibilities of all Procedure for reporting of hazards or potential hazards (note this may include concerns of neglect, abuse, radicalisation or bullying on or off site) Action to be taken on the identification of hazards Some explanation of potential hazards How to raise concerns or questions	**Head teacher** Ensures an up-to-date record is kept of Disclosure and Barring Service (DBS) clearance **Teachers & support staff** Ensure that they are familiar with policy Ensure that all equipment they use has had a recent safety check Ensure that they understand the operating procedures of any specialist equipment (e.g. wheelchairs) Ensure that they know emergency contacts/ procedures **Administrative staff** Ensures policy is available on request and accessible Ensures only those with evidence of DBS clearance are allowed access to the building. Those without should be accompanied. Ensures up-to-date records are kept of equipment safety checks Ensures they have a list of emergency contacts, including parents, and that this is readily accessible	Safeguarding Vulnerable Groups Act 2006 Children Act 2004 and *Working Together to Safeguard Children* (DfE, 2013) Children's Acts 1989 and 2004 The Children and Families Act 2014, S175 of the 2002 Education Act The Education (Independent School Standards) Regulations 2014

© 2017 Alison Ekins, Sally Robinson, Ian Durrant and Kathryn Summers

3 Resources to support the development of bullying and anti-bullying policies

Department for Education. (2014) *Preventing and Tackling Bullying*. Advice for headteachers, staff and governing bodies. October 2014.

Thompson, F. and Smith, P.K. (2010) *The Use and Effectiveness of Anti-Bullying Strategies in Schools. Department for Education*. Research Report DFE-RR098.

Specialist organisations

The Anti-Bullying Alliance (ABA): Founded in 2002 by NSPCC and National Children's Bureau, the Anti-Bullying Alliance (ABA) brings together over 100 organisations into one network to develop and share good practice across the whole range of bullying issues.

The ABA has also put together a fact sheet outlining the range of support that is available to schools and young people from the anti-bullying sector.

Kidscape: Charity established to prevent bullying and promote child protection providing advice for young people, professionals and parents about different types of bullying and how to tackle it. They also offer specialist training and support for school staff and assertiveness training for young people.

The Diana Award: Anti-Bullying Ambassadors programme to empower young people to take responsibility for changing the attitudes and behaviour of their peers towards bullying. It will achieve this by identifying, training and supporting school anti-bullying ambassadors.

The BIG Award: The Bullying Intervention Group (BIG) offer a national scheme and award for schools to tackle bullying effectively.

Restorative Justice Council: Includes best practice guidance for practitioners 2011.

(From DfE, 2014: *Preventing and Tackling Bullying*)

Concluding comments

Having clear and accessible policies which address all aspects of the school are essential. These provide the structure for practice and are informed by the embedded culture of the school. In addition to the standard school policies, it is now essential that schools have a Supporting Children with Medical Conditions policy, regardless of whether they currently have children with medical conditions enrolled in the school. It may also be very useful for a school to be proactive and consider the development of a bereavement policy so that they have thought through the issues that they may face and at least have the structure of something that can be implemented if such a sad occasion should arise. Having policies in place helps all staff to feel reassured that they have procedures to follow, and this is particularly important where the situation will understandably be so emotional and sensitive.

11 Whole-school culture

In this chapter, we:

- Examine the meaning and importance of the underpinning culture of the school context
- Examine our understandings of loss and bereavement
- Recognise ways to implement psychological support for staff
- Reflect on the signs and symptoms of stress, anxiety and depression
- Consider the importance of emotional resilience
- Reflect on the need for empathy and acknowledgement of the emotions of others
- Introduce some strategies to support an emotionally resilient whole-school culture

Introduction

Teachers in the Teaching for Life research described themselves as floundering at the centre of an emotional web as they tried to balance the needs of the child with the condition, their parents, other pupils and their parents, themselves and other staff, all within a school culture that could feel insecure and uncertain. They spoke about the challenge of trying to stay professional and simultaneously manage their own personal feelings:

> "It's not going to be easy, but it's how do we help them, obviously without breaking down ourselves."

> "There was absolutely no support, I was busking it and I felt very vulnerable. The teachers very upset, the parents very upset, obviously devastated. The other children were very upset and I was making it up as I went along and somehow, sort of got most of it right."

A key aspect of whole-school culture in this context was therefore having an embedded school culture which recognised and acknowledged emotion and the impact of emotion on all stakeholders, including, importantly, staff members themselves.

Effective whole-school cultures are proactive and embedded. So teachers in the research identified that at the moment of crisis (when a child with a life-limiting or life-threatening condition was diagnosed or indeed died) it was important that there was already in place a clearly presented and accessible policy which addressed as many as possible of the potential issues that they would come across and need to overcome in their interactions with the child, their parents, other staff and other pupils. This notion of a planned and clearly thought-out approach which fitted within the embedded whole-school culture was therefore essential. Key to this was having well-planned and proactive communication systems that had been carefully thought through ahead of any emotive situations occurring.

The teachers identified that they needed to work in a school that understood and positively responded to the emotional strains they might experience working with a child with a life-limiting or life-threatening condition. Having someone to talk to within the school setting, and for this to be an accepted and embedded aspect of the school culture, underpinning practice in the school as a whole, was therefore emphasised as particularly important. Teachers spoke about wanting someone to talk to about their worries and concerns or about matters that they would not want to ask the parents or other teachers. This could be someone unrelated to the situation, or it could be someone who had been through a very similar experience. Typically, they were motivated by not wanting to upset or add burdens to anyone, for example:

> "Am I worrying unnecessarily? This is my worry that I don't want to share with anybody in case I'm wrong. You don't want to upset people."

Staff identified that they needed 'reassurance' that they were doing the right thing, again something that, moving forward, would be seen to be embedded within a whole-school culture of practice rather than as something reactive and 'ad hoc'. Teachers therefore identified that fears about *what might happen* could be reduced by good sharing of information among staff and everyone having the *big picture*.

In addition to being able to foster appropriate communication systems with the parents of the child and with parents generally in the school context and also being able to talk to each other about the emotional strain, another central aspect of the embedded school culture teachers wanted was the ability to liaise directly with other professionals and experts, when they needed guidance and reassurance. Here reassurance emerged as key and this therefore needs to be seen as a central tenet of a supportive whole-school culture. It was, therefore, not just about the correct application of appropriate policies but about going beyond that to providing the responsive reassurance and emotional support that is needed. Teachers spoke about the illness trajectory, the 'ups and downs' of the child's journey through the illness and how the prognosis could be wrong. They articulated the difficulties of putting 'things in place', 'things constantly changing' and how worrying the uncertainty was. A person to talk to would be helpful:

> "It's having that conversation all the time isn't it. Really, really knowing that you can talk to somebody at any point and you have access or not at any point, and feeling confident that you're going to have that dialogue with people."

Our research showed that teachers will often turn to the parents for guidance but find that communication is extremely difficult. More than half of the teachers looked to the pupils themselves to help them understand the child's non-medical needs. This is within a culture that is very unclear about 'Should you talk about it?' and one that has significant anxieties about how to talk about it within the context of a school that has to meet many demands. Moving forward into a more positive and proactive whole-school culture, one that is built upon the notion of having shared agreed protocols about the open sharing of information (as appropriate and agreed with the parents and child), is therefore essential.

Summary

The importance of establishing a whole-school culture within which discussions and responses to the needs of children with life-limiting or life-threatening conditions can be developed and supported emerged as significant in the data from the teachers. Key themes to emerge included:

- the importance of a supportive whole-school culture which recognises and acknowledges emotion
- inter-professional working and collaboration being embedded within the whole-school culture
- supportive communication approaches

Policy review

The statutory guidance provided in *Supporting Pupils at School with Medical Conditions* (DfE, 2015) makes clear the responsibilities of the school and governing body in creating a whole-school culture: to include appropriate policies and practices which respond appropriately to the needs of children with medical conditions.

In particular, the following key issues in relation to establishing a whole-school culture are significant:

- 'The governing body should ensure that the school's policy clearly identifies the roles and responsibilities of all those involved in the arrangements they make to support pupils at school with medical conditions.'

(DfE, 2015: 12)

- The importance of a collaborative approach, in which key responsibilities are understood, shared and planned for is particularly emphasised:

'Supporting a child with a medical condition during school hours is not the sole responsibility of one person. A school's ability to provide effective support will depend to an appreciable extent on working co-operatively with other agencies. Partnership working between school staff, healthcare professionals (and, where appropriate, social care professionals), local authorities, and parents and pupils will be critical. An essential requirement for any policy therefore will be to identify collaborative working arrangements between all those involved, showing how they will work in partnership to ensure that the needs of pupils with medical conditions are met effectively.'

(DfE, 2015: 12)

Practical considerations

School culture

The culture of a school is ever changing, responding not only to emerging policy initiatives and political areas of focus but also to the needs of the school community itself (Ekins, 2017). Thinking about the underlying culture of the school setting is therefore essential to ensuring that the school as a whole can respond to all needs, including the needs of children with life-limiting or life-threatening conditions.

Reflective activity

- What are the key features of your school culture?
- Is there a clear sense of an embedded culture within your school context?
- How has this been created?
- Is it one that all members of the school community (staff, children, parents) agree with?
- Who or what determines your school culture?
- How does or can this embedded school culture then impact the development of appropriate practices to support children with life-limiting or life-threatening conditions?

As we have seen in Chapter 10, really understanding and developing a strong sense of the embedded culture of the school is essential, as this underpins everything in terms of policy and practice:

Inclusive Policy   **Inclusive Practice**

Inclusive Culture

Figure 11.1 Inclusive culture, policy and practice model (Booth & Ainscow, 2002)

In the current policy context, with a continuing (albeit shifting) focus on academisation (DfE, 2016), the focus on school culture is even more important. Thus, whilst on the one hand, schools seem to have more autonomy to respond to the needs of their local communities and develop their own ethos and policies, on the other hand, this greater 'freedom' could result in a lack of consistency and a feeling of isolation. A strong focus on the values and practices embedded in an effective school culture is therefore essential. As we have seen from the teachers' responses, this focus on the underpinning culture of the school will need to move beyond a simple focus on process and policy and instead also reflect and respond to the emotional needs of the school context.

When considering school culture today, it is important to recognise that this has become a much more complex and wide-ranging concept than previously. The recent impact of academisation and the need to work increasingly collaboratively with a range of services and professionals will therefore have impacted the development of effective school cultures. In order to ensure that this does not have a long-term impact on the ability of schools to support the needs of not only their pupils and families but also their staff, attention does need to be paid to the development of effective and supportive, emotionally resilient school cultures. Indeed, failure to take proper care of staff and those who access the organisation's services through the embedded school culture will simply result in disconnect, distress, absenteeism, burnout and high staff turnover and prove detrimental to the organisation's reputation, potentially resulting in challenges in recruitment of both staff and new pupils.

Agreed whole-school approaches, embedded in the over-arching culture of the school, to understanding and acknowledging loss and bereavement, providing and implementing psychological support for staff and building emotional resilience through supportive collaborative practices are therefore essential. Most importantly, these approaches will be most effective when they are embedded and seen to fit with the day-to-day culture of practice and relationships within the school setting.

Understanding and acknowledging loss and bereavement

Reflective activity

- What experiences of loss and bereavement have you or your school setting had already?
- What issues did those experiences raise for the type of support that you or the school setting more broadly needed?
- How effectively does your current school culture (including policies and practices) support staff and the wider school community through grief, loss and bereavement?
- What key values or principles embedded in your day-to-day school culture could be a support in times of grief, loss and/or bereavement?

As we have identified in Chapter 9, loss and bereavement are complex feelings, deeply impacting individuals in varying different ways and at different levels. Whilst on the surface an individual may apparently be coping well with a situation and appearing to 'stay strong' for the sake of others around them, that individual may be increasingly affected by their experience of loss and bereavement. Even where the individual staff member was not directly or closely linked to the child with the life-limiting or life-threatening condition themselves, the feelings that are exposed as a result of being in the school community may open up all sorts of feelings of grief and bereavement that have been buried for some time as a result of past personal experiences. Grief can also be directly linked to strong feelings of guilt, blame and lack of confidence. Sometimes individuals connected with the child with the life-limiting or life-threatening condition can end up blaming themselves for completely unconnected factors which they perceive have added to the difficulties for the child.

To be able to create a supportive whole-school culture, we first need to have a clear understanding of the grief process and to then use this awareness to implement effective strategies. In particular, the following key principles need to be recognised and acknowledged:

- That grief is a normal and natural response and process
- That its experience can be unique to each child and adult and a lifelong process
- That each person can heal in an emotionally safe and supportive environment

(from McGlauflin, 1998: 47)

One important aspect is to be open to the grief process, both as individuals and as a culture. Perhaps in Western cultures it is often believed that children should be protected from grief.

However, this well-meaning approach might end up isolating a child who is grieving alone (McGlauflin, 1998). As such, adults should foster an environment where grief can not only be discussed but can also be displayed. The notion of grief as cathartic and offering what has been called 'non-judgemental compassion' (McGlauflin, 1998: 47) has been accepted as part of the curriculum through SEAL and PHSE (personal health and social education) but could be extended to be part of the whole-school curriculum and school life, taking on opportunities to celebrate life and space to express grief.

Reflective activity

- How can this be achieved in a meaningful and sensitive rather than a superficial way?
- How can this be extended into daily school life rather than just being introduced at a time of crisis?
- What impact will this approach have?
- Do you already use PSHE and SEAL activities in your school setting?
- How are these used?
- Look again at the information that is presented in Chapter 9 relating to understanding and supporting the emotional and behavioural needs of children.
    - How could these be adapted and developed to meet the needs of adults in the school as well as children?
    - How could they be developed to provide a whole-school approach to issues around grief, loss and bereavement?

It must be remembered, however, that for adults, being open to grieve is for themselves a complex emotional undertaking. On the one hand, they open themselves to being responsible for the expression of others (McGlauflin, 1998: 47), but this openness can also reawaken their own experiences of loss as well as their personal and cultural assumptions. Teachers importantly need to be encouraged to break with their traditional identity of detached professionalism and be encouraged to share their own experiences of loss, perhaps of a friend or parent, with both colleagues and the children (McGlauflin, 1998: 47) where appropriate. There are many ways that openness to grief might be expressed in the classroom, including:

- allowing time to develop/extend conversations as they occur
- giving pupils (and staff) time to express their feelings
- changing lessons if pupils start to express their feelings
- inviting someone into a class to speak on an issue of concern or interest (this can range from medical to religious questions and may even involve questions about funerals and the treatment of remains)
- allowing time for private reflection including through the use of journals

(McGlauflin, 1998: 47).

Grief is a normal reaction to loss. McGlauflin (1998: 47–49) proposed 12 recommendations for counsellors, teachers and school staff to help integrate the grief process into the school.

Table 11.1 Recommendations for staff to help integrate the grief process into the school

1	Look at grieving as a valuable life skill.	Use books/stories with the themes of loss or historical events such as armistice days, which can provide 'teachable moments' to reinforce that grief is natural and learning to cope with it is part of life.
2	Learn to recognise opportunities.	Use opportunities in the life of school to encourage reflection. For example, anniversaries or holidays can be used as topics to create displays or 'memorial'/ memory boards. Accept and do not fear times when an absent person is mentioned. Indeed, use them to focus on the person's memories and feelings.
3	Respect the consciousness of grief.	Particularly in the immediate aftermath of loss, people can be overwhelmed or confused. As such, allow for the inappropriate or unexpected. This can include a loss of focus and concentration.
4	Honour every possible goodbye in the school.	Begin to celebrate goodbyes and transitions in schools: changes of class, moving years, graduating. As such, acknowledge the value of 'the last time you might see a person'.
5	Speak to a child/ children about a death or loss.	Be sure to speak to the child/adult as soon as they return to school after a loss. People are often afraid to do this and, as a result, do not mention it and carry on as usual.
6	Be as honest as possible.	Authors agree that adults should be as honest as possible about events, consequences and feelings. However, they are often reluctant to do this. Honesty begins with adults sharing with each other what they know and what they do not know or feel they should not disclose. Honesty respects each other and children and avoids miscommunication.
7	Speak from a place of compassion not pity.	Try to avoid appearing condescending. Ideally, react as equals (even between staff and pupils) who are seeking to understand a shared experience. Be mindful of language (avoid 'Poor Joey').
8	Do not be afraid to show emotion.	Giving and receiving emotions is a gift and shows genuineness. It also validates the feelings of each party, although many teachers may feel this is counter to their professional image.
9	Offer children (and adults) outlets for grief.	The teacher can do a great deal to provide outlets for the child, for example, writing a journal, allowing them to research pertinent topics (e.g. related to disease, funerals), creating a 'feeling area', a place they can go to be quiet and reflect. This could be in the form of a memorial garden or room, or simply a place to store and post memories. This could even be in a corner of a classroom. However, what should not be ignored is that the staff would also benefit from access to such places.
10	Continue with routines, discipline and high expectations.	For many, the school is the most stable part of their lives, especially after a loss. As such, although the school can make allowances for grief, they can set 'loving limits' (from Brodkin & Coleman, 1994; from McGlauflin, 1998: 48). However, routine remains important, and celebrating academic success can be a key marker of healing/returning to 'normal'.
11	Never forget about loss, even years later.	Loss and grief are carried through life, making us who we are. Anniversaries are a good opportunity to remember and celebrate a person and even talk about them with new classmates or staff. If memorials are left to deteriorate, this might cause distress to those who knew the person.
12	Support one another.	Supporting a child or each other is challenging. Staff need to support each other: look for signs of stress, anxiety and depression (see the foregoing) and endeavour to provide support, time and space.

Implementing psychological support for staff; dealing with stress, anxiety, depression – recognising signs in ourselves and others

Working in schools, we need to be aware of the emotional and psychological impact of responding to the needs of vulnerable children, including those with life-limiting or life-threatening conditions, on staff themselves. This awareness of and support for the psychological impact of the role therefore needs to be built into a supportive and proactive culture.

In particular, attention will need to be paid to the potential signs and symptoms of depression and anxiety.

Reflective activity

- What signs and symptoms of depression and anxiety are you already aware of?
- What support could you give or do you think would be helpful in supporting a colleague displaying any of those signs or symptoms?

The signs and symptoms of depression and anxiety may include:

- becoming anxious or agitated
- phobias
- social anxiety
- panic attacks
- stress or stress disorders
- reduced concentration and attention
- reduced self-esteem and self-confidence
- feelings of guilty and unworthiness
- a pessimistic view of the future
- thoughts of self-harm, even suicide
- disturbed sleep
- diminished aptitude

These signs and symptoms will vary from day to day and individual to individual. However, symptoms that are usually regarded as having special clinical significance include lack of interest in activities usually considered pleasurable, lack of emotional reactivity to pleasurable events, sleep and appetite disruption, or agitation. There are a number of types of anxiety. Generalised anxiety is characterised by excessive anxiety and worry (apprehensive expectation), difficulty in controlling work or anxiety associated with three or more of the following: restlessness, being easily fatigued, difficulty in concentrating, irritability, muscle tension and sleep disturbance.

Post-traumatic stress disorder (PTSD) has become more widely recognised in many areas over the last 30 years. Whilst this may initially not be considered relevant to discussions about staff supporting children with life-limiting or life-threatening conditions, for staff working in a school, coping with the day-to-day knowledge of a child's condition may result in a deep psychological impact similar to or including PTSD. Knowledge of a pupil's condition and potential deterioration is likely to extend over a considerable period, maybe even their entire school career; aspects of the curriculum may remind staff and pupils of issues related to death and loss, and schools often mark the passing of a pupil with some form of memorial visible to the school community. All of these factors, added to any personal issues that a staff member may already have been facing about death, bereavement or loss in their own life, may therefore impact how well a person is able to cope with the process and ongoing feelings of loss and bereavement. Symptoms of PTSD can include:

- recurrent, involuntary and distressing memories and dreams of the traumatic event(s)
- dissociative reactions, (e.g. flashbacks) in which the individual feels as those the events are recurring
- severe psychological distress and physical reactions when exposed to internal or external cues which resemble an aspect of the event
- persistent avoidance of stimuli associated with the traumatic event(s). This can include memories, thoughts and feelings as well as internal and external cues and could lead to avoidance of school altogether for staff or students.

Psychological distress in staff and pupils needs to be treated sensitively, by a trained professional. Treatments may include a range of different approaches, possibly incorporating:

- biological approaches, for example, medication to calm or raise mood
- behavioural approaches, for example, systematic desensitization
- CBT – cognitive behavioural therapy

With all situations, a balanced approach is needed – one which recognises that the underlying cause, not just the symptoms, needs to be positively addressed.

Understanding resilience

Reflective activity

- What do the terms 'emotional intelligence' and 'emotional resilience' mean to you?
- Think of an example of when you or a colleague or family member demonstrated the skills of 'emotional intelligence' or 'emotional resilience'.
- How do you think the two terms inter-relate?
- And which aspects of each concept are important to support the development of a whole-school culture to meet the needs of staff and stakeholders working together to support a child with a life-limiting or life-threatening condition?

In simple terms, emotional intelligence involves:

- knowing one's own feelings
- managing one's own emotions
- having a well-developed sense of empathy
- an ability to repair the emotional damage of oneself and others
- being able to emotionally interact

(adapted from Rodd, 2013: 68)

Emotional resilience relates to how well an individual is able to cope with and adapt to stressful situations or circumstances. Understanding resilience and the implications of this for the whole school community is important. It can be easy to assume that staff are impervious to the emotional burden. Each person has responsibility for professional self-care, but in addition, the organisation also has a responsibility to support its staff.

Just as with children, staff will react differently to loss and bereavement depending on their personal and cultural experiences. It is important to know which staff have been affected beforehand by bereavement. Teachers and other staff need to be cognizant of their own history of loss and separation. People who have had experience of loss and bereavement are not always the right people to support others who are or might be going through it. Not only is there the issue of potentially reliving the initial trauma (symptomatic of PTSD, as discussed) and as such distress, but there is a danger that the experience of others becomes framed in their own.

It is possible to develop or improve your emotional resilience by becoming more aware of the triggers of stress in your life, including acknowledging the impact of working with children with life-limiting or life-threatening conditions and supporting others through grief, loss and bereavement and by utilising simple strategies and effecting small changes in your own lifestyle to ensure that you become less stressed and able to cope and adapt to stressful situations.

Training to increase emotional resilience is not limited to staff. Children can also benefit from such training, and again CBT can be used as an effective programme to support the development of emotional resilience. Through CBT, participants can be supported to build resilience and promote realistic thinking and adaptive coping and encouraged to identify and challenge unrealistic beliefs and use evidence to make more effective appraisals. Participants can also be trained to use more effective coping mechanisms when faced with difficulties as well as practice behavioural techniques in relation to assertiveness, negotiation, decision making and relaxation.

As well as CBT, there has been a recent growth in the use of mindfulness techniques. Mindfulness is focused on 'paying attention with openness and curiosity to both internal experiences such as your thoughts, emotions and body sensations, and to external experiences going on around you, and accepting them in a non-judgemental way' (Dragon, 2015: 27). In short, it is about trying not only to pay attention to the whole of your perception but to be aware of the here and now, not to dwell too much in the past, where feelings of regret and sadness may lie, and not to fixate on the future with its inherent anxiety. So for example, when trying to sleep, practice focusing on your breathing, your body and its sensations (Dragon, 2015). As such, this has a great deal in common with meditation and systematic muscle relaxation, which have long been proposed as ways to reduce stress and anxiety. The key is 'to decrease emotional reaction and increase awareness and acceptance' (Dragon, 2015: 27), not to deny feelings but to accept that they are transient. This of course takes practice to do and time to engage in.

Reflective activity

- How could the school develop structured approaches to helping staff engage in programmes that will support and develop resilience and relaxation?
- How much awareness do you think there currently is in the value of these types of activities to support and enhance staff's emotional well-being?

Empathy and recognising the emotions of others

When considering the resilience or potential resilience of staff members, we need to be mindful that teaching itself is an emotive and affective practice, charged with positive and negative emotional experiences (Ekins, 2017). As such, not only are teacher's emotional states fluid, affected by the normal positive and negative experiences they encounter, but under conditions of extreme emotional pressure, normal 'hassles' or 'uplifts' can be become exaggerated and have a direct influence on their ability to function (Greenberg & Baron, 1997). Teachers therefore need to be aware of:

- the concept of emotional labour – when emotional display (or suppression) of emotion is part of the requirements of a job
- ways that emotional labour requires energy and can lead to fatigue, with this being magnified when having to deal with emotions of grief or loss, both actual and perceived for the future (i.e. once a teacher learns about a child's condition)
- the concept of empathy – that the display of emotions also requires empathy: understanding the inner world of another
- the term 'emotional contagion' – depicting how emotions can spread, in effect be 'caught' by others or at least shared
- ways the concept of empathy also consists of empathic concern, wanting to alleviate the distress of others
- how empathy involves understanding the source of our own thoughts and reactions

(Zaki, 2016)

- empathy fatigue, or 'burnout' – emotional and physical exhaustion, often experienced by those in the helping professions, whereby sufferers can no longer function. This can result in a depersonalisation and detachment from others in the workplace and an inability to function in a crisis situation or even in showing a callous and cynical approach to their welfare

(Warr, 1996)

Dealing with these complex issues is about achieving a balance, and it is about developing a whole-school culture that supports teachers to recognise, acknowledge and address all of these emotional issues.

Strategies

> **Reflective activity**
>
> - What strategies or approaches could the school implement to support the general well-being of the whole-school community?
> - How would you know if these were having a positive impact?
> - How could the ongoing, embedded strategies and approaches be developed/enhanced to support staff and the whole school community at times of crisis?

As noted, severe psychological distress in an individual should be addressed appropriately through a fully trained and qualified professional specialising in grief and bereavement. It is not advisable for individuals in school to try to provide in-depth emotional or psychological support for colleagues. However, some general strategies can be usefully applied and used to ensure that all staff within the school are able to work in a healthy culture of practice which recognises rather than tries to ignore the issues that all staff are facing.

PSHE (personal social health education) and circle times

PSHE lessons, including circle times, are well-known approaches to help children have a chance to talk about feelings. However, this is not just needed for children. Schools can provide the same sort of support for staff. Safe spaces and planned opportunities to talk are required. An identified individual that staff can talk to to share their worries and anxieties may also be helpful, although it is then also important to ensure that that person, often the headteacher or pastoral leader within the school, is also supported to be able to off-load any feelings of anxiety or grief that they are building up as a result of taking on board everyone else's concerns and anxieties. (See also discussions and practical resources in Chapter 9.)

Bereavement team

Many local authorities have a bereavement team, often based within the educational psychology service, so it would be helpful to contact them to look at getting support for all staff and pupils from such a service. If this is not available in your area, look at finding other qualified professionals (qualified psychologists or counsellors) who would be able to provide both whole-school/staff support as well as individual support and sessions. Here it may be helpful to contact the Health & Care Professions Council (http://www.hcpc-uk.org/), who will have lists of those qualified professionals who are registered with them.

Strategies to maintain emotional resilience

Table 11.2 Strategies to maintain emotional resilience

Tips		Activities
1	Build a community of support.	Resilient people have a strong network of support, be it friends or colleagues.
2	Manage your time effectively.	Try to plan your day, including time for breaks and reflection on your emotional reaction to events. This can include those that might 'take you by surprise' e.g. the content for meetings.
3	Develop achievable goals and take relevant action to achieve them.	Setting achievable goals helps you focus on the future rather than past disappointments. But do ensure they are realistic.
4	Become more aware of your emotional reactions.	Keep an emotional diary about your experiences and the associated thoughts and feelings. Use this to help identify common patterns as well as warning signs.
5	Prepare for mentor/ management/appraisal meetings.	Use these constructively to reflect on your emotional reactions and discuss these.
6	Prioritise work-life balance.	Set firm boundaries, set time to engage in relaxation and leisure activities that are not work related.
7	Build in time to relax.	Build in time to relax and monitor your own physical and emotional feelings and reactions. Include such things as weight, sleep patterns, feelings of pleasure/anxiety.
8	Learn from experience and be prepared to adapt your response.	Resilient people learn lessons from the past. Note times when you have coped successfully and consider applying these strategies in new situations.
9	Remain hopeful and optimistic.	Resilient people tend to remain optimistic. Relish challenges and opportunities. Seek opportunities for learning. This will make you feel more in control.
10	Be kind to yourself.	It is very easy in many professions to focus on what should have been done. Try to rationalise and use cognitive reframing techniques, for example, 'What is the worst that could happen? What advice could you give a colleague who is in a similar situation?'

(Adapted from Grant & Kineman, 2014, http://www.communitycare.co.uk/emotional-resilience-expert-guide, accessed 11/4/16)

Reflective activity

- Which of the activities listed would be helpful/possible to embed into your school context as a positive strategy to enhance the emotional resilience of all?
- How can this be achieved?

Reflective practice

Reflective practice (Brookfield, 1996; Schon, 1996) has become common in schools as a way to enhance professional development. Most staff in schools will be familiar with this as a concept and as a practice and can therefore use principles of reflective practice to support them through grief, loss, bereavement and dealing with emotional responses experienced as a result of working with children with life-limiting or life-threatening conditions. Reflection can be promoted in a number of ways:

- by providing time and space for individual reflection
- by developing individual or collective/collaborative activities such as journal writing
- by developing collaborative practical reflection activities – brainstorming, sharing of feelings/experiences
- by structured activities focused on deeper critical self- and collective-evaluation and review

Most importantly, everyone in the school community needs to be encouraged to examine (rather than deny) their feelings. Diverse feelings and emotional responses to grief, loss and bereavement also need to be positively acknowledged and understood within the context of different religious and cultural beliefs which may impact the individual and/or the community.

Planning team approaches

At times it may be helpful to form crisis action teams in the case of loss, death and bereavement. This action team can then coordinate a whole-school strategy for dealing with the issues, and this may be more supportive and effective than expecting a response and support to only be led/provided by one individual.

Effective communication skills

Our research highlighted the importance of well-developed communication skills as key to the development of an effective and supportive whole-school culture. This involves the ability to communicate one's own feelings and to listen to those of others (Rodd, 2013). Effective communication skills therefore involve meeting the needs of oneself and others.

Failure to appropriately attend to one's own feelings and needs can of course lead to stress and ultimately burnout as much as not attending to the needs of one's team. Part of this is placing appropriate boundaries around oneself and sustaining a normal routine. It must be remembered that the primary purpose of school is education both for the child with life-limiting or life-threatening conditions and their peers. It is perhaps too easy to lose sight of this central aim and thus turn inward, focusing on the child's condition and prognosis. See also Chapters 5, 6 and 7 for more about effective approaches to communication.

Table 11.3 Effective communication skills

Skills for meeting others' needs	Skills for meeting personal needs
Sending accurate and unambiguous messages	Appropriate self-assertion 'I' messages for 'owning' statements
Overcoming physical and psychological barriers	Conflict resolution
Listening and understanding	Delegation
Appropriate responding	Time management
Managing feelings	Stress management

(from Rodd, 2013: 69)

Practical resources

In this chapter, the following practical resources are provided:

1 Self-reflection tool: culture, policy and practice
2 Development planning: emotion/emotional resilience and communication
3 Mindfulness exercises
4 Cognitive behavioural therapy (CBT) techniques

1 Self-reflection tool: culture, policy and practice

Consider the model that follows and brainstorm collectively what key aspects of school culture, policy and practice are already in place in your school – specifically about meeting the needs of children and staff in relation to life-limiting or life-threatening conditions.

In a different colour, add ideas about what more could be done to develop each aspect of culture, policy and practice.

Policy   **Practice**

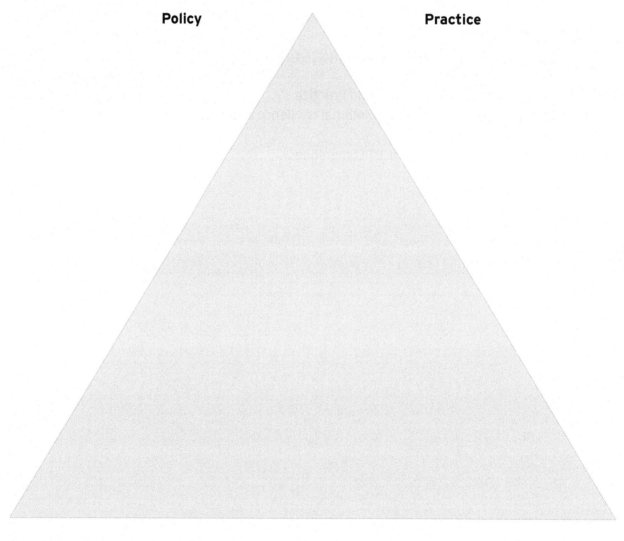

Culture

2 Development planning: emotion/emotional resilience and communication

What approaches do you already have in place, and what more do you need to develop to have effective systems to respond fully to emotion/the emotional resilience of the whole school community and effective communication systems?

	What do we already have in place?	What more could we do/develop?
Emotion/emotional resilience		
Communication systems		

© 2017 Alison Ekins, Sally Robinson, Ian Durrant and Kathryn Summers

3 Mindfulness exercises

These can be used by staff, children, parents and families. They are a way to relieve stress and anxiety and centre yourself. The aim is to focus on the moment rather than reliving the past or worrying about the future. It is also a way to see the everyday in a new way, to appreciate the beauty of objects, events and people and how fortunate we are. As such, they are techniques to deal with current anxiety and to build future resilience.

Living Well provides a number of mindfulness exercises which can be downloaded at https://www.livingwell.org.au/mindfulness-exercises-3 (accessed 4/11/16).

NHS Choices also provides information and tips about how to deal with stress and anxiety through mindfulness at http://www.nhs.uk/Conditions/stress-anxiety-depression/Pages/mindfulness.aspx (accessed 4/11/16).

Pocket Mindfulness at http://www.pocketmindfulness.com/6-mindfulness-exercises-you-can-try-today (accessed 4/11/16) provides six exercises that anyone can use:

1 **Mindful breathing**
   Stand, sit or lie down. Breathe slowly and then deeply in through your nose and out through your mouth. Let go of your thoughts by focusing on your breathing. Think about the air entering and leaving your body. This is the basis of meditation!

2 **Mindful observation**
   Pick an object in the natural environment and focus on it for a minute or two. Notice its structure and form. Allow yourself to appreciate its elements and connection with nature.

3 **Mindful awareness**
   Focus on an everyday object or action, for example, opening a door, reading a book. Take the time to connect with the object, its texture, construction, form. Try to appreciate how lucky you are to have these senses but also this rich variety of objects.

4 **Mindful listening**
   Select some music you have never heard before and listen to it with your eyes closed or in a darkened room. Try to focus on the journey it is taking you on. Let the music fill your mind to the exclusion of all else.

5 **Mindful immersion**
   When engaging in an everyday activity, like cooking or decorating – or, for children, drawing or tidying up – try not to focus on the end or outcome. Instead, think of the actions involved, the way dust catches the light or paint moves on paper. Try to see everyday tasks in a new and absorbing way.

6 **Mindful appreciation**
   When undertaking mindful immersion or indeed when engaging in one of the other exercises, consider three to five things that normally go unnoticed or unappreciated. For example, that there is always fresh bread in the shops, a colleague or teacher who always says good morning with a smile, a child who lends another a pencil. Try to find out more about it. Recognise it when you see it, thank the person or quietly be thankful for what you and others have.

4 Cognitive behavioural therapy (CBT) strategies

CBT is based on the notion that irrational thoughts can affect behaviours, and behaviours reinforce thoughts. So for example anxiety affects the body's flight-or-fight reaction, which in turn makes a person feel more anxious. Therefore, the aim of CBT is to break these links by primarily focusing on a person's intrusive thoughts. As such, it has much in common with the more modern concept of mindfulness and, like it, the techniques can be used with colleagues, children and their families.

NHS Choices provides a more detailed explanation of techniques and advice on how to find a therapist at http://www.nhs.uk/Conditions/Cognitive-behavioural-therapy/Pages/Introduction.aspx (accessed 4/11/16).

Everyday Health at http://www.everydayhealth.com/hs/major-depression-living-well/cognitive-behavioral-therapy-techniques (accessed 4/11/16) provides five CBT techniques one can use:

1 **Locate and name the problem and consider ways to address it.**
   Start by brainstorming or listing the problems/sources of anxiety as you see them. Once you have a list, consider ways they can be dealt with that are simple and practical. So for example, if you are anxious about medical treatments, look for YouTube clips, handle some equipment, visit a hospital, and you will see that they are not to be feared.
2 **Write self-statements to counteract negative thoughts.**
   This does not mean just writing the opposite of what you think but a rational response to how you are feeling. So when you feel sad, do not have a statement that simply says 'I feel happy'; better to have something like, 'Everyone is sad at times, but it does not last long and it will soon pass'.
3 **Find new opportunities to think positive thoughts.**
   It is all too easy at work to find the negative about the day – instead, train yourself to see the positive. Do people ask you to do things because they trust you or value your opinion? Does going to a meeting mean that you have a say in running the school?
4 **Finish each day by visualising or articulating its best parts.**
   In a journal or simply by recounting, think of what went well that day. This may be minor things like someone opening a door for you or praise or complements you received.
5 **Learn to accept disappointment as part of everyday life.**
   Accept what you can't control and focus on what choices you have. So for example, getting old and even death cannot be controlled. But use the time you have with someone to the fullest. If you have wasted yesterday, do not dwell on it and instead focus on today.

Other CBT techniques include:

- **Challenging irrational thoughts**
   These can be in yourself or others. So if someone has a phobia of needles or germs, get them to justify that: What are they actually scared of? What evidence do they really have? What is the worst that can happen? Is this really likely?

- **Set personal behavioural challenges**

  People often develop compulsive behaviours or routines because they irrationally believe these will prevent or cause something to happen. So for example, they do not go out in case they meet a stranger or think if they avoid talking about illness, it won't happen. CBT partly involves challenging these thoughts: 'Explain to me why you think that? What evidence do you have?' 'How could one thing lead to another?' But also actually enact the behaviour: talk about illness and nothing will happen. Say hello to a stranger, and you will see they will talk back.

- **Treatment of automatic thoughts**

  Much of anxiety comes from repeated and persistent thoughts. Indeed, obsessive compulsive disorder (OCD) is often the result of obsessive thoughts that we are compelled to do something about, which reinforces the thoughts (e.g. germ phobia and handwashing). CBT often tries to identify these thoughts and break the link through techniques such as distraction or systematic desensitization.

Concluding comments

Establishing a positive whole-school culture is an essential part of the process of developing a staff and school strong enough to be able to support a child and their family through a life-limiting or life-threatening condition. There is no simple blueprint for developing an effective and supportive whole-school culture. This, therefore, is an ongoing task – it is not something that can simply be developed to respond to the immediate, urgent needs of an individual. Rather, it is something that requires ongoing attention and development and the focus of all stakeholders within the school community.

Where a school culture is clearly understood and relates directly to key values and principles which explicitly acknowledge the importance of emotional resilience, positive working relationships and open communication, staff working within the school will find it easier to support themselves, each other and the children and families they work with through difficult times around grief, loss and bereavement. Alongside the practical application of policies and processes, there therefore needs to be an ongoing focus on how well the culture of the school is understood and how well it meets the needs of all those working within it.

12 Concluding comments

There have been multiple motivations for writing this book. The number and range of pupils with life-limiting or life-threatening conditions attending all forms of education has increased year on year. Far from being a source of fear and anxiety, in many ways this represents a story of hope, since it derives from improved survival rates at all ages as a result of advances in treatment and technology, which facilitate the inclusion of children and young people into the mainstream. However, it also represents a number of significant challenges. British schools have become more autonomous and structurally varied in recent years, a trend which is likely to continue. Similarly, the range and coordination of local services varies significantly in different regions. Many are fragmented, developing devolved and bespoke processes and departments to meet a variety of local needs in a climate of austerity. Some have turned to the third sector for support, whilst others have out-sourced functions entirely. As such, those working in schools are often faced with a bewildering array of organisations, specialists, terminology, policy changes and processes to navigate. This is whilst also dealing with their own workloads and statuary responsibilities as well as the emotional consequences for them and the school community when becoming part of a child's journey through a life-limiting or life-threatening condition.

Yet significant pieces of legislation, most notably the SEN and Disability Code of Practice (0-25) (DfE/DH, 2015) and the Children and Families Act (DfE, 2014), have enshrined a child-centred approach, supported by multi-agency cooperation and collaboration underpinned by processes such as the 'local offer'. This together with central government advice (chiefly the Departments of Education and Health and OFSTED; see Chapters 1 and 2), as well as more direct support offered by numerous charities, unions, public-sector agencies and allied professionals (see Chapters 3-9), mean that those working in schools as well as parents and carers should not feel isolated.

The structure of this book arose from the Teaching for Life research with teachers and schools. It researched the thoughts and experiences of those who had worked with children with life-limiting or life-threatening conditions and their families, as well as others who had not, who reflected on their initial response to how they would feel if they experienced that situation. Both of these groups of teachers were able to discuss their anxieties and fears about how they, their colleagues and their pupils did and might react to such experiences. They expressed concerns about how they would or could support the children and their families as well as other children and stakeholders within the school community. The teachers were unsure about how to come to terms with the emotional consequences of such experiences. What they asked for was sources of help and guidance, practical, emotional and strategic (Durrant et al., 2014).

This research made it clear that although there was a lot of good practice evident in schools, it needed to be shared. In addition, there was a need to collate policy, knowledge, resources and practical suggestions in one place. In doing this, there was a need for educationalists and health professionals to come together in order to ensure that the information supplied was accessible, primarily to those in schools who may lack specialist training and a medical/health-related vocabulary.

This book attempts to address what the teachers told us they needed to know, namely how to balance pedagogy and medical needs, and where to find information and support, as well as practical suggestions and resources, to support not only the child with a life-limiting or life-threatening condition but all those in the wider school community, including colleagues. As such, this book has been able to address many of the recommendations in the research report.

Key recommendations from the Teaching for Life report: what teachers wanted

- Local and national information about the range of potentially useful health and education practitioners and the types of knowledge and skills that they have, as well as how best to access them

    (see Chapters 3, 4, 5 & 6)

- A directory of local/accessible services that can support a child and their family including health care, psychological, voluntary-sector and local authority services. Ideally such a list needs to be live, monitored and continually updated, since the names and remits of such services constantly change and evolve.

    (see Chapters 6 and 9 and the Additional Resources at the end of the book)

- Information and guidance on developing a whole-school approach towards emotional health and well-being which includes the school's approach towards dealing with illness, death, bereavement and related issues such as bullying and stress and ways to link this with key policies

    (see Chapters 9, 10 & 11)

- Educational support to enhance teachers' emotional literacy skills with particular attention to illness, death and bereavement, which needs not only to be part of all teachers' and educators' initial induction but part of their ongoing professional development

    (see Chapters 9, 10 & 11)

- Psychological support for school staff, such as helpline/mentoring/counselling service over and above what is currently offered by teaching unions and professional associations and charities recognition that provision for the emotional needs and resilience of teachers needs to be given parity with other aspects of their pedagogic development

    (see Chapters 9, 10 & 11)

- Information to enable teachers who have not had experience of working with children with a life-limiting or life-threatening condition to develop their understanding and, where necessary, talk with those who have and access external sources of support

    (see Chapters 3, 4, 5, 6, 7, 8 & 9)

- Support and training for senior and middle managers to help clarify their roles, responsibilities and resources, share best practice, train and support staff and take a lead in developing a whole-school culture

    (see Chapter 11)

As much as this book represents a necessary addition to a school's resources, there is still much work to be done in providing the support and guidance needed and we would therefore put forward the following recommendations for further work that could be undertaken:

Wider recommendations

- To examine the use of the Common Assessment Framework (CAF) and the new Education, Health and Care Plans as a means through which children with life-limiting or life-threatening conditions and their families could be better supported; to understand how the two processes articulate with one another and to communicate these findings and how this varies regionally

- Given that not only the range but, in some cases, the quality of organisations/services and individual professionals varies, it is a challenge for schools to know not only who to contact but how effective they are. As such, it would be useful to see the development of a live directory of professionals and services which not only provides local contact details but also a mechanism for service users to evaluate and thus recommend to others those whose support has been of particular value and those whom they would not wish to recommend.

- Strategies are needed to improve the quality and speed of accessing medical information and support for teachers. For example, a helpline/dedicated response team for teachers manned by children's nurses and other professionals would not only help alleviate a great deal of anxiety but enable quicker and more bespoke information and support to be provided.

- The former Labour government and coalition governments as well as the current Conservative government have championed virtual schools and virtual school heads across the country. However, these have predominantly been tasked with providing education for looked after children (LACs) or those who have been excluded. Given the reduction in hospital and special schools, these virtual schools would appear to provide the ideal means of ensuring that children with life-limiting or life-threatening conditions, who are often absent from school for extended periods, continue to receive the education they deserve. This would have the additional benefit of ensuring they have not fallen behind in terms of learning development on return to school and would provide a way for them to keep in contact with their peers (including other children with a life-limiting or life-threatening condition). To facilitate this, a mechanism needs to be developed to give children, parents and teachers access to these virtual schools on a flexible and extended basis. In addition, the increasing opportunities that technology provides to not only educate but maintain social relationships should be further researched and then integrated into practice.

What we must never forget is that children with life-limiting or life-threatening conditions are people first and foremost – with hopes, aspirations, fears and joys. In our policy- and target-driven, audit culture it is sometimes too easy to see ill children as their condition, something to be identified and then subjected to a process, rather than unique and whole individuals with much to give and teach us.

As authors of this book, we intend it as an accessible but technically accurate and informative handbook whilst acknowledging that it is only part of a more extensive toolkit that is needed to support those currently experiencing or who may soon experience working with children with life-limiting or life-threatening conditions and their families. We believe this is a much-needed first step in the development of a broad suite of resources.

Dr Alison Ekins
Dr Sally Robinson
Ian Durrant
Kathryn Summers

Additional resources

1 Glossary of terms

Allied health professionals	Registered health care professionals who are not nurses, doctors or pharmacists.
Cancer	Malignant tumours, including leukaemia and brain tumours.
Care plan/support plan	A record of the care that is to be provided by health services or social services to support an individual.
CBT	Cognitive behavioural therapy.
Cerebral palsy	Cerebral palsy is a motor disease as a result of non-progressive brain damage in early life.
Clinical commissioning groups (CCGs)	Local NHS organisations that are responsible for planning and purchasing health care services for their local population.
Complementary therapists	Complementary therapists and alternative medicines are treatments which fall outside mainstream health care.
Comprehensive Health Assessment Tool	A way of assessing health needs of young people who are in the youth justice system.
Continuing care package	The combination of health care services required to meet the individual needs of children and young people over a period of time because of a disability, an accident or an illness.
Cystic fibrosis	An inherited condition caused by a genetic mutation. Children with cystic fibrosis have smaller airways and are predisposed to frequent viral infection and increased amounts of thick respiratory secretions, contributing to infection.
Decision support tool	A questionnaire/checklist which makes up part of the assessment process for both continuing care packages and Education, Health and Care (EHC) plans.
Designated medical officer/clinical officer	The health professional who ensures that the local NHS meets its statutory responsibilities for children with special educational needs and disabilities. They are the point of contact for local authorities, schools and colleges seeking health advice.
Disability	'A physical or mental impairment which has a substantial and long term adverse effect on that person's ability to carry out normal day to day activities' (Equality Act, 2010).
Doctors	Doctors practice medicine, the science-based practice of diagnosis, treatment (medicines or surgery) and prevention of diseases.
Duchenne muscular dystrophy	Duchenne muscular dystrophy (DMD) affects 1 in 3,500 male infants and is characterised by progressive loss of function due to muscle fibre degeneration. The condition is variable, but most boys lose the ability to walk at between 8 and 10 years of age. Progressive respiratory insufficiency begins early in the second decade of life.
Early support programme	Health care, education and social care support for parents and carers of disabled children.
Education, Health and Care Plan (EHCP)	A record of the education, health care and social care support required by a child or young person who has undergone statutory assessment for special educational needs or a disability.
Emotional intelligence	Involves knowing and managing your feelings and emotions; having a well-developed sense of empathy and being able to emotionally interact (Rodd, 2013).

Emotional resilience	How well an individual is able to cope with and adapt to stressful situations or circumstances.
End-of-life care	Support given to people, by health care or social care professionals and others, who are in the last years or months of their life.
Health and social care	Health care and social care services. It tends not to include public health services.
Health and Wellbeing Board	Representatives from the NHS, social care and public health use an assessment of the local population's health needs (the JSNA) to produce a plan to provide services to meet local priorities.
Health care	This includes services that seek to prevent, treat, cure, rehabilitate and care.
Health care plan/individual health care plan	A record of the health care required by an individual to meet desired outcomes. It records specific tasks and services that seek to prevent, treat, cure, rehabilitate and care.
Health care professional	Health care professionals work with the ill or disabled population. They offer clinical care and the observation and treatment of patients and comprise clinicians such as paediatricians, community child nursing services, doctors, physiotherapists and occupational therapists.
Healthwatch England	An independent 'watchdog' that gathers and represents the views of the public in respect of health and social services.
Healthy Child Programme	The government's guidance for preventative health care that spans pregnancy to 19 years. It guides the work of health visitors and school nurses.
Independent supporter	An independent, trained person who supports families through the Education Health and Care (EHC) assessment process.
Integrated care	Person-/child-centred joined-up health care and social care.
Integrated personal budget	Money provided by the local authority and the NHS to enable an individual to buy a package of educational, social and health care services.
Integrated Personal Commissioning (IPC)	A grand plan for England which enables the joining up of health care funds, social care funds and education funds to provide personal health budgets for individuals who have significant needs.
Joint Strategic Needs Assessment (JSNA)	The collection of evidence about the health of the local population.
Key worker	A point of contact for children and families who can help them to ensure the support they receive is coordinated.
Lead professional	Where a child requires support from a group of practitioners, the lead professional acts as the single point of contact for the child and family, enables them to navigate the system, ensures appropriate interventions are planned, delivered and reviewed and coordinates the other practitioners.
Leukaemia	Cancer of the white blood cells.
Life-limiting conditions	Conditions from which there is no reasonable hope of cure and from which children will die.
Life-threatening conditions	Conditions for which curative treatments may be possible but can fail.
Local Offer	The Local Authority's information about the education, health and social care services in and beyond their locality.
Medical regime	The sequence of medical treatments delivered over a period of time, e.g. surgery followed by chemotherapy, followed by radiotherapy.

NHS England	The National Health Service in England, whose chief executive reports to the Department of Health. Its aim is to improve health through health care services. NHS Scotland, NHS Wales and NHS Northern Ireland report to their respective governments.
NHS trusts	NHS trusts are public-sector bodies that provide community, hospital, mental health and ambulance services for NHS England and NHS Wales.
Nominated children and young people's health assessor	A health practitioner who is skilled in the health assessment of children.
Nurses	Nurses organise, plan and provide health care, often complementing medicine and augmented by attention to physical, psychological and social care needs.
Palliative care	Care from the point of diagnosis through life, death and beyond. Its focus is on maximising the quality of life for the child and family and includes managing symptoms; providing psychological, social and spiritual support; organising short breaks; and delivering care through death and bereavement.
Palliative care team	A team of health care and social care professionals who come together to support families when a child's condition cannot be cured. It can include nurses, doctors, therapists and providers of social and spiritual care.
Personal budget	Money provided by the Local Authority to enable an individual to buy social care and educational services. It may include the personal health budget.
Personal health budget	Money provided by the NHS to enable an individual to buy health care services.
Personalised care and support plan	The agreed record of the services which an individual will buy with their budget/personal health budget.
Personalised care and support planning	The discussions about what services an individual needs and how to best spend their estimated personal budget/personal health budget.
PSHE	Personal, social and health education.
Psychologists and therapists	Psychologists and therapists use psychological theories to underpin their work.
Public health	This includes communication, education and policy development and includes services that seek to prevent ill health and promote good health.
Public health workforce	The public health workforce works with the whole, including the healthy, population.
Responsible commissioner	The organisation that has a statutory duty to secure care for an individual.
SEAL	Social emotional aspects of learning.
SEN	Special Educational Needs: SEN with Support or SEN with an Education, Health and Care Plan. Identified under four broad categories of need: • Cognition and learning • Communication and interaction • Social, emotional and mental health • Physical/sensory (DfE/DH, 2015)
SENCO	Special educational needs coordinator. This is a statutory role within all maintained schools, including academies.
SEND	SEN and disability.
Social care	Social care is the provision of protection, personal care, social support or social work services to individuals who are at risk.
Social care workforce	This comprises social workers and social carers.

Specialist nurses	Nurses or midwives who have taken additional, often postgraduate education to provide a high level of expertise in health care or public health.
Specialised services	Expert health services for less common conditions. They require a clinical team with very specific training and equipment.
Sustainability and Transformation Plans	Plans for health services and Local Authority services to meet priority needs of a place and the population that lives within it. Key aims include addressing 7-day services, better prevention of illness and improving cancer outcomes. Plans need to articulate with those set out by local Health and Wellbeing Boards.
Universal health services	Health care and public health services which are available to all the population, spanning hospital and community/primary care, disease prevention and health promotion.
Vanguards/vanguard sites/NHS vanguards	New integrated modules of health care and social care. They are places where professionals are working to improve the joining up of primary care (general practice), hospitals and other community health services and social care.

2 Useful contacts and sources of information

Information about medical conditions

Contact a Family (2012) Contact a family for families with disabled children http://www.cafamily.org.uk/. Accessed 25 October 2016

NHS Choices – your health your choices http://www.nhs.uk/pages/home.aspx. Accessed 25 October 2016

Leukaemia Care – www.leukaemiacare.rog.uk 24-hour dedicated helpline

CLIC Sargent.org.uk

Chemo to the Rescue www.chemo-to-the-rescue.com

Cystic Fibrosis Trust www.cftrust.org.uk

Muscular Dystrophy Campaign www.muscular-dystrophy.org

Organisations that can support teachers and schools with bereavement

Childhood Bereavement Network

www.childhoodbereavementnetwork.org.uk

The network has local free services to support bereaved children. Families can refer themselves directly to these; teachers can receive information and support from them.

Child Bereavement UK

http://childbereavementuk.org

Child Bereavement UK offers:

- Training for schools
- Schools information pack
- An e-learning resource for schools
- Films created by young people for teachers, parents and friends

Their web site includes a Schools section and includes:

- Supporting a bereaved pupil
- A death affects the whole school
- Terminally ill children at school
- School policy
- Special educational needs
- Lesson plans and ideas
- Resources

Cruse Bereavement Care: Help for Schools

http://www.cruse.org.uk/schools

Cruse Bereavement Care's Schools pages include how to deal with:

- Impact of bereavement
- Changes in behaviour
- Death of a pupil
- Returning to school

- Violent deaths
- Staff death
- Dealing with crisis
- School bereavement policy

They also produce a Schools Pack which can be purchased.

Grief Encounter

www.griefencounter.org.uk
Grief Encounter provides support for bereaved children, young people and families. They also provide Good Grief bespoke training workshops for professionals.

Winston's Wish

www.winstonswish.org.uk
Winston's Wish provides support for bereaved children and families and training for professionals including teachers.

Young Minds in Schools

www.youngminds.org.uk/training_services/training_and_consultancy/for_schools
The Young Minds charity provides a range of courses to support emotional well-being in schools and for teachers.

Support for children who have suffered a loss

Childline

www.childline.org.uk
Online or phone support for anyone under 19.

Hope Again

http://hopeagain.org.uk
A Cruse Bereavement Care web site to support young people who are living with loss

Winston's Wish for Young People

http://foryoungpeople.winstonswish.org.uk/foryoungpeople
An interactive web site for young people to learn, ask questions and get support.

Unions

Unions can provide a range of personal support and legal advice. Do note, however, that other than advice they provide on their web site, to access legal advice or other forms of representation for most unions, you will have to be a paid-up member.

Health service

Unison
Unison is a large public-sector union with many members particularly in the health and allied services.

In relation to bullying and harassment:
Telephone: 0800 0 857 857
Or visit the following page of their web site:
http://www.unison.org.uk/knowledge/discrimination/bullying-and-harassment/overview/

Teaching and lecturing

Unions
ASCL: Association of School and College Leaders
130 Regent Road
Leicester
LE1 7PG
T: 0116 2991122
F: 0116 2991123

The Association of Teachers and Lectures
http://www.atl.org.uk/about/contact.asp
General enquiries
info@ascl.org.uk

NASUWT
http://www.nasuwt.org.uk
Rose Hill
Rednal
Birmingham
B45 8RS
Tel: 0121 453 6150
Fax: 0121 457 6208
Email: nasuwt@mail.nasuwt.org.uk

The National Association of Head Teachers (NAHT)
NAHT Headquarters
1 Heath Square
Boltro Road
Haywards Heath
West Sussex
RH16 1BL
info@naht.org.uk
0300 30 30 333

National Union of Teachers: NUT
https://www.teachers.org.uk
Telephone 020 3006 6266
Email: nutadviceline@nut.org.uk

University and College Union
http://www.ucu.org.uk
UCU head office
hq@ucu.org.uk
Tel:020 7756 2500
Fax:020 7756 2501

Professional bodies

British Association of Teachers of the Deaf (BATOD)
www.batod.org.uk

College of Teaching
www.collegeofteaching.org

General Teaching Council for England
www.gtce.org.uk

General Teaching Council for Northern Ireland
www.gtcni.org.uk

General Teaching Council for Scotland
www.gtcs.org.uk

General Teaching Council for Wales
www.gtcw.org.uk

Support networks

Education Support Partnership
https://www.educationsupportpartnership.org.uk
Telephone: +44 20 7697 2750
Fax: 0845 873 5680
Email: enquiries@edsupport.org.uk

Samaritans
08457 90 90 90 (UK) 1850 60 90 90 (Republic of Ireland).

SupportLine
http://www.supportline.org.uk/about/index.php
Telephone: 01708 765200

References

Adams, J. (2010) *Explaining to Young Children that Someone Has Died.* Child Bereavement UK. Available at www.childbereavementuk.org/files/5614/0117/9770/Explaining_to_young_children_that_someone_has_died.pdf. Accessed 15th October 2016.

Association for Children's Palliative Care (2009) *A Guide to the Development of Children's Palliative Care Services.* London: ACT (renamed Together for Short Lives). Available at www.togetherforshortlives.org.uk/professionals/resources/2430_a_guide_to_the_development_of_childrens_palliative_care_services. Accessed 23rd October 2016.

Association for Children's Palliative Care (2010) *A Family Companion to the ACT Care Pathway for Children with Life-limiting or life-threatening Conditions ACT Valuing Short Lives* (2nd edn.). Bristol: ACT England.

Black, D. (1998) Coping with loss: Bereavement in childhood. *British Medical Journal* 316: 931.

Booth, T. and Ainscow, M. (2002) *Index for Inclusion.* Bristol: CSIE.

Bowlby, J. (1998) *Attachment and Loss Volume 3: Loss.* London: Random House.

British and Irish Legal Information Institute (1985) *Gallick versus West Norfolk and Welsbach Area Health Authority.* London: United Kingdom House of Lords Decisions.

Brookfield, S. (1996) Breaking the code: Engaging practitioners in critical analysis of adult educational literature. In Edwards, R., Hanson, A. and Raggatt, P. (Eds.), *Adult Learners, Education and Training: Boundaries of Adult Learning.* London: Routledge, pp. 57–81.

Chambers, P. (Ed.) (2008) *Pupils with Cancer. A Guide for Teachers.* London: Specialist Schools and Academies Trust.

Children's Cancer and Leukaemia Group (2014) *Children and Young People with Cancer: A Parent's Guide: Children's Cancer and Leukaemia Group.* Available at www.cclg.org.uk. Accessed 24th October 2016.

Children's Cancer and Leukaemia Group (2015) Available at www.cclg.org.uk/Types-of-childhood-cancer. Accessed 19th October 2016.

CLIC Sargent (2012) *No Child with Cancer Left Out: The Impact of Cancer on Children's Primary School Education.* London: CLIC Sargent.

Coyne, I., Timmins, F. and Neill, F. (2010) *Clinical Skills for Children's Nursing.* Oxford: Oxford University Press.

Cranwell, B. (2007) Adult decisions affecting bereaved children. *Bereavement Care* 26(2), 30–33.

Cunningham, S. and Best, C. (2013) Guidelines for routine gastrostomy tube replacement in children. *Nursing Children and Young People* 25(10), 22–25.

Cystic Fibrosis Trust (2013) *Starting School, the School Pack Fact Sheets 2016.* Available at www.cysticfibrosis.org.uk/life-with-cystic-fibrosis/starting-school. Accessed 20th October 2016.

Data Protection Act 1998, c.29. Available at www.legislation.gov.uk/ukpga/1998/29/contents. Accessed 23rd October 2016.

Department for Education (2011) *Teacher's Standards.* London: Department for Education. Available at www.gov.uk/government/publications/teachers-standards. Accessed 15th October 2016.

Department for Education (2014) *Children and Families Act 2014.* London: HMSO. Available at www.legislation.gov.uk/ukpga/2014/6/contents/enacted. Accessed 22nd October 2016.

Department for Education (2014) *Early Years Foundation Stage.* London: HMSO.

Department for Education (2014) *Preventing and Tackling Bullying.* London: HMSO.

Department for Education (2014) *Supporting Pupils at School with Medical Conditions. Statutory Guidance for Governing Bodies of Maintained Schools and Proprietors of Academies in England*. London: Department for Education/Department of Health.

Department for Education (2015) *Supporting Pupils at School with Medical Conditions. Statutory Guidance for Governing Bodies of Maintained Schools and Proprietors of Academies in England*. London: Department for Education/Department of Health.

Department for Education (2016) *Children's Social Care Reform: A Vision for Change*. London: Department for Education.

Department for Education (2016) *Policy: Academies and Free Schools*. London: HMSO.

Department for Education/Department of Health (2015) *Special Educational Needs and Disability Code of Practice: 0 to 25 Years*. London: Department for Education/Department of Health.

Department of Health (2016) *National Framework for Children and Young People's Continuing Care*. London: Department of Health.

Department of Health (2016) *Our Commitment to You for End of Life Care: The Government Response to the Review of Choice in End of Life Care*. London: Department of Health.

Dowling, N. (2014) *Young Children's Personal, Social and Emotional Development* (4th edn.). London: SAGE.

Dragon, N. (2015) Mindfulness in practice. *Wellbeing* 23(3), 27.

Durrant, I., Robinson, S., Summers, C., Ekins, A. and Jones, H. (2014) *Teaching for Life*. Full Report. ISBN 978-1-909067-48-6.

Dyregov, A. (1991) *Grief in Children: A Handbook for Adults*. London: Jessica Kingsley.

Ekins, A. (2015) *The Changing Face of Special Educational Needs* (2nd edn.). Abingdon: Routledge.

Ekins, A. (2017) *Reconsidering Inclusion: Sustaining and Building Inclusive Practices in Schools*. London: Routledge.

Ekins, A. and Grimes, P. (2009) *Inclusion: Developing an Effective Whole School Approach*. London: McGraw Hill.

Fraser, L. K., Miller, M., Aldridge, J., McKinney, P. A., Parslow, R. C. in collaboration with Hain, R. (2011) *Life-limiting or life-threatening Conditions in Children and Young People in the United Kingdom: National and Regional Prevalence in Relation to Socioeconomic Status and Ethnicity. Final Report for Together for Short Lives*. Leeds: University of Leeds.

Gatta, G., Capocaccia, R., Stiller, C., Kaatsch, P., Berrino, F., Terenziani, M. and EUROCARE Working Group (2005) Childhood cancer survival trends in Europe: A EUROCARE Working Group study. *Journal of Clinical Oncology* 23(16), 3742-3751.

Geldard, K., and Geldard, D. (2002) *Counselling Children: A Practical Introduction* (2nd edn.). London: Sage.

Glasper, E. A., McEwing, G. and Richardson, J. (2015) *Children's and Young People's Nursing at a Glance*. Chichester: Wiley.

Gov.UK (2016) *School Attendance and Absence*. Available at www.gov.uk/school-attendance-absence/overview. Accessed 1st November 2016.

Grant, L. and Kineman, G. (2014) *Emotional Resilience Expert Guide*. Available at www.communitycare.co.uk/emotional-resilience-expert-guide/. Accessed 11th April 2016.

Great Ormond Street (2016) *Septicaemia-Great Ormond Street Hospital for Children-NHS Foundation Trust*. Available at www.gosh.nhs.uk/medical-information-0/search-medical-conditions/septicaemia. Accessed 19th October 2016.

Greenberg, J. and Baron, R. (1997) *Behaviour in Organisations* (6th edn.). Upper Saddle River, NJ: Prentice Hall.

Health and Safety Executive (2014) Risk Assessment. A brief guide to controlling risks in the workplace. London: HSE.

H. M. Government (2004) *Every Child Matters: Change for Children*. London: Department for Education and Skills. Available at www.infed.org/archives/gov_uk/every_child_matters.htm. Accessed 23rd October 2016.

H.M. Government (2015) *Information Sharing: Advice for Practitioners Providing Safeguarding Services to Children, Young People, Parents and Carers*. London: H.M. Government.

Hoffman, M. L. (1989) Moral development. In Bornstein, M. H. and Lamb, M. F. (Eds.), *Developmental Psychology: An Advanced Textbook* (2nd edn.), Hillsdale, NJ: Lawrence Erlbaum Associates, pp. 497–548.

Hough, M. (1998) *Counselling Skills and Theory*. London: Hodder & Stoughton.

Jacobs, M. (1985) *Swift to Hear: Facilitating Skills in Listening and Responding*. London: SPCK.

Jones, C. and Pound, L. (2008) *Leadership and Management in the Early Years from Principles to Practice*. Maidenhead: Open University Press.

Knighting, K., Rowa-Dewar, N., Malcolm, C., Kearney, N. and Gibson, F. (2010) Children's understanding of cancer and views on health-related behaviour: A 'draw and write' study. *Child: Care, Health and Development* 3(2), 289–299.

Macmillan (2013) *Brain Tumours in Children*. Available at www.macmillan.org.uk/cancerinformation/cancertypes/childrenscancers/typesofchildrenscancers/braintumours.aspx. Accessed 20th October 2016.

Macqueen, S., Bruce, E. and Gibson, F. (2012) *The Great Ormond Street Hospital Manual of Children's Nursing Practices*. Chichester: Wiley Blackwell.

Massey, A. (2013) *Provision Mapping: Improving Outcomes in Primary Schools*. London: Routledge.

McGlauflin, H. (1998) Helping children grieve at school. *Professional School Counselling* 1(5), 46–49.

Muscular Dystrophy UK (2015) *Fighting Muscle-wasting Conditions*. Available at www.musculardystrophyuk.org/about-muscle-wasting conditions/information-factsheets for schools and teachers and schools. Accessed 20th October 2016.

National Patient Safety Agency (2008) *Clean Hands Save Lives: Patient Safety Alert*. London: NPSA. Available at www.npsa.nhs.uk/resources.

NHS (2016) *NHS Choices. Consent to Treatment – Children and Young People*. Available at www.nhs.uk/Conditions/Consent-to-treatment/Pages/Children-under-16.aspx. Accessed 15th October 2016.

NHS Choices (2016) *Air Embolism-NHS Choices*. Available at http://www.nhs.uk/Conditions/Air-embolism/Pages/Introduction.aspx. Accessed 19th October 2016.

NHS England/Local Government Association (2016) *Integrated Personal Commissioning. Emerging Framework*. London: NHS England.

Nursing and Midwifery Council (2008) *Standards for Medicines Management*. London: Nursing and Midwifery Council.

Nursing and Midwifery Council (2010) *Standards for Medicines Management*. London: Nursing and Midwifery Council.

OFSTED (2015) *School Inspection Handbook*. Available at www.gov.uk/government/publications/school-inspection-handbook-from-september-2015. Accessed 7th July 2016.

Paul, P. S., Perrow, R. and Webster, A. M. (2014) Brain tumours in children: Reducing time to diagnosis. *Emergency Nurse* 22(1), 32–36.

Peate, I. and Gromley-Fleming, E. (2015) *Fundamentals of Children's Anatomy and Physiology: A Textbook for Nursing and Healthcare Students*. Chichester: Wiley Blackwell.

Piko, B. F. and Bak, J. (2006) Children's perceptions of health and illness: Images and lay concepts in preadolescence. *Health Education Research* 21(5), 643–653.

Plain English Campaign. Available at www.plainenglish.co.uk/files/howto.pdf. Accessed 18th October 2016.

Pyle, K. (2013) *NFER Teacher Voice: NFER Teacher Voice Omnibus. March 2013 Survey*. London: CLIC Sargent.

Robinson, S. and Summers, K. (2012) An evaluation of the educational support for teachers who teach children with life-limiting illness in schools. *Pastoral Care in Education* 30(3), 191–207.

Rodd, J. (2013) *Leadership in Early Childhood: The Pathway to Professionalism* (4th edn.). Maidenhead: McGraw Hill.

Royal College of Nursing (RCN) (2012) *Essential Practice for Infection Prevention and Control: Guidance for Nursing Staff*. London: RCN.

Royal College of Nursing (RCN) (2014) *An RCN Toolkit for School Nurses: Developing Your Practice to Support Children and Young People in Educational Settings*. London: Royal College of Nursing.

Schon, D. (1996) From technical rationality to reflection-in-action. In Edwards, R., Hanson, A. and Raggatt, P. (Eds.), *Adult Learners, Education and Training: Boundaries of Adult Learning*. Routledge: London, pp. 8–31.

Selwood, K. (2013). Children with cancer: quality of information for returning to school. *Nursing Children and Young People* 25(5).

Shipman, C., Kraus, F. and Monroe, B. (2001). Responding to the needs of schools in supporting bereaved children. *Bereavement Care* 20(1), 6-7.

Simmonds, N. J. (2013) Ageing in cystic fibrosis and long term survival. *Paediatric Respiratory Reviews* 14(1), 6-9.

Stephenson, T., Wallace, H. and Thomson, A. (2002) *Clinical Paediatrics for Postgraduate Examinations* (3rd edn.). London: Churchill Livingstone.

Sunderland, M. (2003) *Helping children with low self-esteem*. Brackley: Speechmark Publishing.

Sunderland, M. (2003a) *The Day the Sea Went Out and Never Came Back (Helping Children with Feelings)*. London: Speechmark.

Sunderland, M. (2003b) *Helping Children with Loss: A Guidebook*. Brackley: Speechmark Publishing.

Sunderland, M. (2003c) *Helping Children Who Bottle Up Their Feelings*. Brackley: Speechmark Publishing.

Together for Short Lives (2013) *A Core Care Pathway for Children with Life-Limiting and Threatening Conditions*. Third edition. Available at www.togetherforshortlives.org.uk/assets/0000/4121/TfSL_A_Core_Care_Pathway__ONLINE_.pdf. Accessed 8th August 2016.

Waller, T. and Davis, G. (2014) *An Introduction to Early Childhood* (3rd edn.). London: SAGE.

Warr, P. (1996) *Psychology at Work* (4th edn.). London: Penguin Books.

West Midlands Children and Young People's Palliative Care Toolkit (2012) Available at www.togetherforshortlives.org.uk/professionals/externalresources/2918. Accessed 25th July 2016.

Zaki, J. (2016) *How to Avoid Empathy Burnout. Caregivers Can Benefit by Understanding a Patient's Pain without Feeling It Themselves*. Issue 35: Boundaries – Nautilus. Available at http://nautil.us/issue/35/boundaries/how-to-avoid-empathy-burnout. Accessed 11th April 2016.

Index